M●NEY BY

Design

MONEY BY

Design

Unshakable and Time Tested
Principles for Financial Success

JOHN LOUIS MURATORI

MONEY BY DESIGN™

ISBN 978-0-9704753-9-8

Printed in the United States of America.

All rights reserved under International Copyright Law.
© Copyright 2010 by John Louis Muratori. ALL RIGHTS RESERVED.
Published by: GateKeeper Publishing, LLC • Cheshire, CT 06410

www.gatekeeperpublishing.com

Cover & Interior Design: April McMillan

Library of Congress Cataloging-in-Publication Data

Muratori, John Louis

Money By Design: Unshakable and Time Tested Principles for Financial Success

ISBN 978-0-9704753-9-8 (Trade paper)

1. Personal Finance • Economics • Money Management

DEDICATIONS

This book is dedicated to those *pastors and ministers who have labored faithfully and consistently* throughout the years without seeing a financial harvest. May a lack of finances never again be a hindrance to the work of the Lord.

In addition, this work is dedicated to *every believer who has faithfully and consistently given to the Kingdom of God*. Your unwavering commitment to the furtherance of the Gospel has not gone unnoticed. May a season of harvest in your life begin now.

Finally, it is for you, *the emerging generation*, including my sons John and Joshua, that I have labored for two years to write this book. May you be equipped with these biblical principles as you rise from obscurity to capture our culture for the Kingdom of God.

ACKNOWLEDGEMENTS

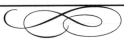

To my beautiful wife, Carmela:

There are not enough words to express my love and appreciation for you and your faithfulness to me during our life's incredible journey. Thank you for yielding our precious time together over the last two years to complete this grueling and exhaustive project.

To my two sons . . .

John: Your passion for life and musical gifts are an inspiration to everyone around you. Keep laughing and enjoying the process of life — your future is limitless.

Joshua: Your creativity and entrepreneurial spirit are an inspiration to me. I've watched as you turned your hobbies into business ventures at the age of twelve. I'm amazed at how you can light up a room.

To GateKeeper Publishing:

Thank you for your cutting edge approach to publishing. Your commitment to this project has gone above my expectations. Special thanks to VP of Operations Sam DeFrancesco for your friendship and project oversight. Along with April McMillan for your skill in the graphic design layout in what turned out to be a beautifully designed cover.

Most importantly, my deepest thankfulness to my Lord and Savior, Jesus Christ, for saving my soul and allowing me to serve You. You have given me something that money, wealth, and riches could never purchase — Your unfailing love, precious peace, and guarantee of eternal life with You.

WHAT OTHERS ARE SAYING

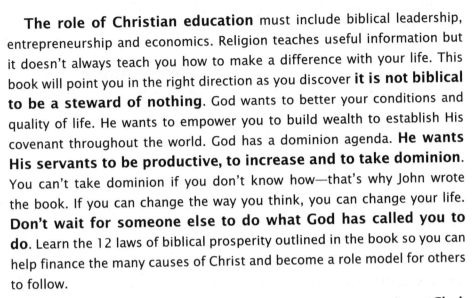

The role of Christian education must include biblical leadership, entrepreneurship and economics. Religion teaches useful information but it doesn't always teach you how to make a difference with your life. This book will point you in the right direction as you discover **it is not biblical to be a steward of nothing**. God wants to better your conditions and quality of life. He wants to empower you to build wealth to establish His covenant throughout the world. God has a dominion agenda. **He wants His servants to be productive, to increase and to take dominion**. You can't take dominion if you don't know how—that's why John wrote the book. If you can change the way you think, you can change your life. **Don't wait for someone else to do what God has called you to do**. Learn the 12 laws of biblical prosperity outlined in the book so you can help finance the many causes of Christ and become a role model for others to follow.

— **Jonas Clark**
Publisher, The Voice magazine

John shares his real life struggles to overcome a poverty mentality, which he defines as "a fear of not getting." I, too, grew up with the same poverty mentality and **this book broke mightily into my heart and mind**, challenging me to transform my ungodly attitudes toward money and to enjoy God's blessings in the area of finances.

I believe you will be powerfully moved by this book. **No "name it, claim it" here, and no poverty either**. What we have is a broad and well-defined highway upon which we can walk that will usher into our lives biblical financial prosperity. Congratulations, John, on **a life-changing book**. I am going to read it twice!

— **Dr. Mark Virkler**
President, Christian Leadership University

I have known John for many years, and his combination of teaching, vision and organizational strategy helps business leaders find the keys to success regardless of their industry or territory. While many people are looking for the quick way to success, **John is able to identify better methods to create wealth, build successful, healthy businesses and reach higher levels of success**.

— **Ed Turose**
Sr. National Account Executive,
Coca-Cola North America, Minute Maid Business Unit

I am a financial planner, and also majored in finance in College. I have read financial books from the smartest and wealthiest people in the world, yet **have never come across a MASTER PIECE like this before**. The research is extremely thorough. I can fully vouch for this text as **a complete manual for modern economics**, wealth creation, and stewardship principles. **The principles in this book transcend generations, gender, and social background**. If you are a parent or grandparent this is a gift that could absolutely open the financial eyes of your child. This is the type of read that only comes around once in a great while.

— **Shawn Everett**
Financial Planner
President, Wealth Managers, LLC

THANK YOU for allowing the Lord to use you in this way! This has been an answer to the cry of my heart. I have had wrong conceptions about finances all of my life, and just in the past 6 months the Lord has begun dealing with me in great depth to deliver me from wrong teachings from my childhood. I've always believed in the Lord's blessings, His provision for more than just our needs, etc, but I've had trouble applying that to my life and having **a system to combine Scripture with good business tactics that are ethical and supernaturally inspired**. THANK YOU!!

— **Rosemarie Eisenhauer**
CRA Charleston, SC

I was quite impressed with the depth of substance, research, and prayer, and a genuine effort to really break down this topic through practical, applicable, contextual, and **biblical principles that are universal**. We know that God's patterns and principles always work, and I really appreciate John's ability to weave these together for anyone who is seeking Kingdom purposes. **This book is a must-read not only for individuals but also for leaders of businesses and organizations**. It will challenge their thinking and renew their minds with the right attitude and principles that **will guarantee success with a purpose.**

— **Doug Stringer**
*Founder and President, Somebody Cares America
and Turning Point Ministries International*

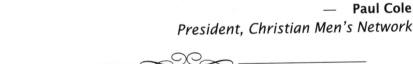

John Muratori is a bold man. Boldness is the mark of confidence; confidence, the mark of vigorous faith—and that faith has instilled in a John a **depth of wisdom that is proving to be a dynamic blessing** to the Kingdom of God in the earth. Listen to John Muratori ....**a voice of positive Godly wisdom within the contemporary cacophony of negative chaos.**

— **Paul Cole**
President, Christian Men's Network

I would highly recommend John Muratori's book to every Christian. It is insightful, motivating, and instructional. **This book will bless and equip every believer in prospering for the Glory of God**. It was excellent reading and had many great insights. One insight I especially enjoyed was the chronicle and birth of modern capitalism.

— **Pastor Duane Vander Klok**
*Sr. Pastor, Resurrection Life Church
Founding President, Resurrection Life Church International
Host, television program, "Walking By Faith"*

In my opinion, this book is **a milestone in the history of writing on biblical principles as they apply to finance and true wealth.** It is so well written, I couldn't put it down. Frankly, I don't have much use for the "name it and claim it" overly simplistic writing that is out there. Muratori, combines a deep understanding of the Bible with a real passion for the subject. The truth jumps off the page. The **concepts are so solid, that I began to apply them immediately.** One section, that deals with the beginnings of capitalism, banking and investing is worth the price of the book all by itself. It's **something I have not seen anywhere else.** Anyone who reads and studies this book, will understand how the system works so that they can put it to work in their own lives. Secrets the elite have known are laid bare in this truly inspired book. Wall Street insiders will be shocked at how this book lays out the truth about money, debt, investing, personal and family prosperity, generosity, compassionate uses of resources and a whole lot more. Christians and non-Christians alike will gain tremendous insights by reading this book.

— **Nick G.**
Writer and businessman

As a Bio-Medical Science major, Business and Finances has never been something of particular interest for me, yet the inevitable arrival of my future in the employment realm is soon approaching. This book has gone against any prior misconception I had on a business book because it is **a "how to guide" for living,** from establishing the importance of the basic facets of life such as work ethics, power of creativity, and the importance of seeking knowledge in every aspect of your life, that we may at times ignore. **I highly recommend this book from the college student to the well-established entrepreneur this book has something that reaches everyone.**

— **Jocelyn Mercado**
Graduate Student

This book came at the right time for me. As a father and husband, I was looking for the tools to take my family to the next level of wealth. I can say with total confidence that this is **a financial blueprint that could help anyone—not just the church.** A must read for anyone tired of pie and sky financial books. This is real life reading with real life strategies.

— **Gwynmar Fraser**
Program Supervisor
Dept. of Mental Health and Addiction Services

John Muratori is a secret agent for Jesus Christ. He came to us clothed as Clark Kent and changed into his superman garb right before our very eyes. He delivered **a powerful word with razor sharp prophetic accuracy** that was both serious yet sprinkled with timely humor. **His understanding of marketplace positioning was both revelatory and life changing.** I highly recommend this man of God who carries **an uncompromising, refreshing impartation** for the body of Christ.

— **Pastor Eric Warren**
Ambassadors for Christ Fellowship, Columbus, Ohio

Lessons in life this valuable don't come around every day. Every word has been a blessing to me. I thought your book would be a "how-to" in the secular sense, sort of an improved version of a Robert Allen or a Robert Kiyosaki book. Boy, was I ever mistaken. **This one has the Hand of God all over it. Thanks for setting the record straight!**

— **Roger W.**

This book has blown away the poverty mentality from my life. I have always believed that as Christians it is my duty to have a poverty mentality and live simply. After reading the book and finding the history about the Jewish people how they were trained by their Rabbis to be leaders in the gates it is no wonder the "lie" that Christians should sit as couch potatoes and insulate ourselves from the world has affected our thinking. As a result the church no longer sits in the gates of the city as leaders. **This has empowered me to get out of the gutter** and get my five kids in leadership positions in the community with myself and my wife as well. Thank you Muratori. Thank You Jesus.

— **Martin R.**

My husband and I have known for some time that **we are called to create wealth for the Kingdom of God**. Thank you, John, for making our vision clearer and stronger!

— **Susan F.**

Very good, scripturally based guide to financial management for Christians. I felt he came close to **the "true" prosperity doctrine, rather than the hyped ones on television**.

— **Wesley W.**

TABLE OF CONTENTS

Section 1: Rich Church, Poor Church

Section 2: Money By Design

Section 3:
12 Twelve Biblical Laws of Wealth Creation

Section One

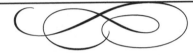

RICH CHURCH

Por Church

CHAPTER ONE

Meeting Mr. Poverty

I had a rude awakening at age nine, when I realized my family's true economic status. Until then, I never really noticed the things we had, much less those we lacked. I assumed everybody lived the way we did. Entering middle school accelerated this newfound realization. The next three years were miserable for me.

My father worked two and sometimes three jobs to pay the bills while I was growing up. He worked a quarter century at the same factory, a workplace with few environmental controls or precautions. These poor working conditions eventually took a toll on my father, and he died at fifty-eight from a heart attack. I was eighteen and experienced another rude awakening when I realized my father never reached his goals.

"Dad, why do you work so hard and take so little time off?" I asked him frequently as a child.

"I'm going to work really hard now while I have the energy so when I get older we can relax and enjoy life," he always answered.

He worked so hard, he died trying to relax. Dad never got to enjoy the fruit of his labor. Sadly, if my father lived long enough to retire and grow old, he would not have had enough money to live comfortably or even modestly. Social Security and a tiny pension should not be the only fruit of a lifetime of hard work.

My father came to America from Italy as a young boy, and settled in an Italian community similar to his homeland. His dad worked with his hands, spending long hours to support the family, and passed down an unspoken philosophy of money that went something like this:

> "Get a good job, like in a factory. Don't hop from job to job, or you will have to start over at the bottom. Strive to buy a house, and then strive to pay it off. Keep most of your money in a safe place, like under your mattress or in a shoebox in your closet. Don't trust the bank or government, and do not risk your hard-earned money anywhere you might lose it."

This same philosophy was passed down to me through our family lifestyle. Some things in life are not taught, but caught. How we lived and what I experienced as a child rooted within me certain financial beliefs, principles, and perspectives. If we aren't willing to have such cherished, deeply embedded views challenged, our financial circumstances will never change.

> When the risk of change and moving into the unknown outweighs the dissatisfaction and disgust with the present, then change has its best chance of happening.

Because I am the third generation from an immigrant family, I did not experience life as they did. I was born and raised in America, and my ethnicity was less intrusive. By the time I reached the sixth grade, I had different goals and desires from my parents. However, their philosophy stayed with me, and though my aspirations were different, I still believed I could attain my dreams through hard work.

Going to school with brand-less sneakers, hand-me-down clothes, and peanut butter and jelly sandwiches for lunch was getting difficult. Every day I was ridiculed by kids jeering, "Jeepers, creepers, where'd you get those sneakers?" I can't count the number of fights I got into while in elementary school. I remember walking home from school in tears wishing things were different and thinking "Something's got to change."

This crisis birthed in me a passion for more. If my circumstances were going to change, I had to make it happen. But I was twelve years old and had no knowledge about wealth or how to build it. As I look back, I realize every influence around me reinforced a poverty mentality.

There are more powers trying to hold you back than trying to make you successful. I don't blame my parents for the lack we had growing up. In fact, I commend them for making every effort to give us the necessities. My father was caught in a system that set and controlled the rules of the game. This same system runs through every aspect of our society and culture, influencing government, education, and religious institutions. It is particularly evident in the judicial branch. At the core of this system is "financial profiling." Families are placed into one of the following demographic categories: upper, middle, or lower class. Today, the middle class has been expanded to include two additional categories: upper middle class and lower middle class. These classifications dictate where and how you get educated, your neighborhood, and your job opportunities. Do not be fooled — the system is real. Most complain that the system is unfair, but true achievers spend less time whining and more time forging the steps to success.

> There are more powers trying to hold you back than trying to make you successful.

I grew up a devout Roman Catholic, going to church every week. I served as an altar boy and even considered going into the priesthood. My experiences during those years taught me that God had nothing to say about finances, except that we were to give some of our money to the church. I never heard a message about building wealth, financial advancement, prosperity, or any other subject remotely close. I later learned that priests take a vow of poverty. How could the priest lead people where he had never gone or had no intention of going? When we went to church, we felt good about ourselves. However, my dad was never empowered by the church to succeed in life. He heard messages that reinforced the poor church mentality.

I'm not criticizing the Catholic Church, considering the same problem pervades denominational and non-denominational churches as well. This book was written out of concern for what I have seen over the last twenty years of ministry, along with serving as a consultant to numerous pastors and other church leaders. It's shocking to discover how many pastors are in financial ruin. They struggle to make ends meet or live in trailer parks, because after years of ministry, such a lifestyle is all they can afford. Others travel from church to church, not because they want to, but because they need the offerings to survive.

If this is what the landscape of church leadership looks like, then it is no wonder the majority of Christians are not reaching their financial potential.

I grew up hearing "poor church" messages that cloaked poverty as humility and mistook hardship for piety. These teachings glorified "lack" and "want" to the point that the church viewed money as evil. This mind-set has caused churches to view the rich as the enemy. The message has been: "Since it is harder for a rich man to enter the Kingdom of Heaven than it is for a camel to go through the eye of the needle — run, run, run far away from riches — otherwise, it will be harder to get to Heaven!" The "poor church" message has scared Christians from building wealth, and the majority of believers are living below their financial potential. Struggling from paycheck to paycheck, they are enslaved to debt and unable to serve God to their maximum because of financial pressures.

The Church possesses the greatest book ever written on stewardship, riches, wealth, and finance — the Bible. It's time the Church gets liberated from the "poor church" message and mentality.

CHAPTER TWO

Financial Dilemma

I gave my life to Jesus at the age of nineteen. When I was twenty-two I planted my first church. At that time, I owned a clothing store with my sister that I opened in the evenings for Bible studies. That group grew so fast we had to move to a larger facility. We eventually became a flourishing young church with a passion to see a city changed.

During this time, I began building relationships with other pastors and church leaders. Once, in a pastors' meeting, I asked a question that prompted laughter. I realized it was going to take a good deal of money to change a city, so I asked, "How do you make money in church?" Since I was new to these types of gatherings, I didn't know what subjects were discussed. I figured that with so many leaders present, we could come up with numerous strategies on how to build wealth and change our cities.

If I looked to man for my prosperity, then from man my prosperity would have to come.

In the marketplace, I attended creative roundtable meetings frequently. At seventeen, I was in charge of sales for a telemarketing team at a newspaper company. I met with my team at the start of each week to discuss the winning strategies of the previous month, plus any new creative ideas to boost our numbers.

I was excited to attend my first pastoral roundtable, but that excitement turned quickly to frustration. After the laughs subsided, one pastor said, "You do not make money young man; you raise money. You have to get before your church and challenge them to give more. Teach your church to give." "Amen," the others responded.

They went on to share with me fifty ways to handle an offering. I learned how to take an offering, receive an offering, and pull an offering. I have heard these methods echoed throughout the last twenty years.

Thus, everything I've learned from the church and in formal training about wealth building can be summed up in two familiar words: "tithes" and "offerings." That was the extent of the wealth knowledge I learned.

Like the philosophies my father handed down to me, these pastors passed on what was given to them. This is arguably the top reason why people are turned off by church. Try to invite someone to church and one of the first things he or she may say is, "The church is only after your money," demonstrating that even non-believers have discernment — sometimes more than Christians. How many more Dateline and Primetime specials exposing crooked televangelists selling miracles do we need before we wake up and stop supporting them?

As a young pastor, that ministers' meeting left me empty and discouraged. I drove back to my office musing over what had transpired. The meeting provoked me to do something I have never done again in my entire ministry — I looked at the individualized giving statements of our church members. Three things happened almost immediately.

First, I discovered almost ninety-eight percent of the people were giving more than a tithe. Were they to get second and third jobs just to give more? I saw my father as if he were a member of the church. What if he were sitting there with his family, trying to make ends meet. What type of message would assist him? I knew he would need a message of empowerment, not condemnation. The church I served was already giving sacrificially.

Second, as I reviewed our church giving records, I felt the conviction of the Holy Spirit fall upon me. I looked at the names and amounts given, but I didn't want to be persuaded by, or show favor based on how much or how little a person gave. James noticed favoritism and partiality toward the "well-to-do" in the early church and warned:

> Suppose a man comes into your meeting wearing a gold ring and fine clothes, and a poor man in shabby clothes also comes in. If you show *special attention* to the man wearing fine clothes and say, "Here's a good seat for you," but say to the poor man, "You stand there," or "Sit on the floor by my feet," Have you not discriminated among yourselves and become judges with evil thoughts?
>
> —James 2:2-4 (NIV) Emphasis added

The reference to fine clothing signifies financial status. The common man had the same cloak for work and church. He was not in a position to own expensive garments used only for special events. James condemned giving undue recognition and influence simply because a person was affluent.

Over the years, I have seen pastors make the colossal mistake of promoting big givers to places of influence, only to become puppets. Their church's need for finances impaired their judgment, causing them to make decisions that were influenced by money, not the Holy Spirit.

Third, while examining members' contribution records, the Holy Spirit showed me I was looking in the wrong place for money and resources. If I looked to man for my prosperity, then from man my prosperity would have to come. That meant I would be empowering some person or group of people to be my sustenance. I didn't feel this was a rebuke from the Lord. On the contrary, I felt the Holy Spirit leading and igniting a desire in me to establish and trust God for my approval, acceptance, and provision. If I looked to God for my prosperity, then God would sustain me in any circumstance that life would deal me.

I noticed throughout Scripture that some people were under an "open heaven," a place where there was always provision, whatever the need. In every case, it was individuals who looked to God and not man for their prosperity and advancement. David said:

> Some trust in chariots and some in horses, but we trust in the name of the LORD our God.
>
> —Psalm 20:7

> Preserve me, O God: for in thee do I put my trust.
>
> —Psalm 16:1

> The LORD is my rock, and my fortress, and my deliverer; my God, my strength, in whom I will trust; my buckler, and the horn of my salvation, and my high tower.
>
> —Psalm 18:2

In the New Testament, Jesus lays a proper foundation about the providential care of God through His instructions to His disciples.

> Therefore, take no thought, saying, what shall we eat? Or, what shall we drink? Or, wherewithal shall we be clothed? For after all these things do the Gentiles (unbelievers) seek: for your heavenly Father knowest that ye have need of all these things. But seek ye first the kingdom of God, and his righteousness; and all these things shall be added unto you.
>
> —Matthew 6:31-33

Too many people spend more time praying about the necessities of life than seeking the Kingdom. If we would seek, build, establish, and expand the Kingdom of God, then God would cause our prosperity and influence to expand also.

From that early period onward, I began seeing things in Scripture I had never noticed. It was as if a veil had been removed from my eyes. I was not only noticing, but also comprehending Scriptures pertaining to finances, wealth, stewardship and other related themes that I had previously neither seen nor understood.

The Apostle Paul, writing to the church at Ephesus, challenged its people to break through and establish new mind-sets concerning the riches of

God's glory. The Ephesian believers were living like spiritual paupers. Their prayer to God was, "Help us, Lord, to survive and get by," while at their disposal was the fullness and prosperity of God. Paul specifically prayed:

> That the God of our Lord Jesus Christ, the Father of glory, may give unto you the spirit of wisdom and revelation in the knowledge of Him: The eyes of your understanding being enlightened; that ye may know what is the hope of His calling, and what ***the riches of the glory of His inheritance in the saints***, ...
>
> —Ephesians 1:17-18 Emphasis added

Over the years, I have met with leaders from around the country. I've sat in leadership summits and closed-door meetings discussing the church's state of affairs. With over two decades of ministry, I can say with certainty that the "poor church" message has blinded the minds of churches. Like Paul, I pray that the eyes of your understanding will be opened to the principles, concepts, and strategies hidden within the Bible for creating and sustaining wealth.

Contrasting Views

There are two prevailing philosophies to change your financial situation. The first, which I call the decrease philosophy, which happens to be the most popular, emphasizes decreasing expenses and eliminating debt.

This form of budgeting and financial management is focused solely on debt reduction.

You cut up your credit cards, reduce your exposure, pull everything in and establish a bunker mentality until your circumstances change. In this scenario, all debt is viewed as bad.

In effect, you limit your risk while simultaneously limiting your experience of life. One of the dangers of this type of thinking is that while reducing risk it also eliminates faith.

If we would seek, build, and expand the Kingdom of God, then God would cause our prosperity and influence to increase.

For any individual, church or organization this will prove to be detrimental. The decrease philosophy recommends decreasing until you are debt free. You must absolutely eliminate all debt and limit all expenses.

While the Decrease Philosophy attempts to eliminate all debt and expenses, it also creates guilt and a joyless existence.

Churches usually run programs that emphasize a decrease philosophy because of the promise that people who budget better — will give more. Instead, the opposite happens. Their offerings suffer because the congregation is focused on "spending less" and transfers that thinking to their giving.

This is in contradiction to what the Bible tells us.

> There is that scattereth, and yet increaseth; and there is that withholdeth more than is meet, but it tendeth to poverty. The liberal soul shall be made fat: and he that watereth shall be watered also himself.
>
> —Proverbs 11:24-25

> I have seen a grievous evil under the sun: wealth hoarded to the harm of its owner,
>
> —Ecclesiastes 5:13

On the other hand, the increase philosophy focuses on a different form of budgeting. This philosophy positions you for growth, expansion and productivity. It encourages faith with the ability to use creativity to generate wealth. For example, where the decrease philosophy recommends eliminating all credit. The increase philosophy uses credit to its advantage.

An example of this is found in our organization, which uses low-interest credit cards to pay for as much of our monthly expenses as possible. The credit card company doesn't charge interest if the balance is paid in full at the end of the month, which we always do. Using this type of leverage produces increase through creative bill paying. We receive hundreds of thousands of airline miles giving us free travel for major portions of our yearly itinerary, along with free upgrades to first and business class. We also receive cash back and free gasoline with other cards.

Wisdom looks to utilize portions of both philosophies. I'm suggesting debt reduction or downsizing as a means to position one self to shift resources to places where increase or alternative income streams can be produced.

An increase philosophy challenges you to activate your faith, while a decrease philosophy eliminates faith and encourages you to depend on yourself. Decrease looks at circumstances and is motivated by fears such as economic uncertainty, risk or even death to name a few.

Which philosophy has governed your financial planning? What changes can you make to develop more of an increase mentality? There are only two ways to change your financial position, lower your expenses or increase your income. Why not do both?

This book encourages you to have faith that God is going to give you a strategy to get out of debt and direct your steps towards opportunities for increase on your journey to financial freedom. The model is in line with biblical truth.

> The just shall live by faith.
>
> —Hebrews 10:38

> But without faith it is impossible to please him: for he that cometh to God must believe that he is, and that he is a rewarder of them that diligently seek him.
>
> —Hebrews 11:6

As you learn the tools and principles explained in the remaining chapters, also ask God for an outlet for financial creativity and wealth creation. Seek a strategy for increase and multiplication. God never dealt with addition and subtraction, only multiplication. Use His principles and He will multiply your resources. They are built on a foundation of Biblical stewardship, which empowers the reader to manage debt and apply the principles of wealth creation, exercising faith in a God who is able to supply above and beyond what you can ask or think.

> Now to Him who is able to do exceedingly abundantly above all that we ask or think, according to the power that works in us...
>
> —Ephesians 3:20

CHAPTER THREE

Anthill University

As a young boy, I had a passion and desire for "more." This desire sparked an entrepreneurial spirit within me. My early ventures gave me an initial understanding about how money works. Later, when I entered ministry, I thought I was going to increase my financial knowledge. Instead, mentors and instructors suggested those business and financial experiences weren't applicable to being a pastor, but that to be a successful minister I needed to learn theology, hermeneutics, apologetics, Greek, and Hebrew. So, learn I did. I gained the tools necessary to search and study the Scriptures for myself. This wealth of wisdom was necessary to ensure that my study time yielded good doctrine. Again, all I was taught about money during that time could be summed up in two words: "tithes" and "offerings."

The more I studied the Scriptures, the more I noticed God prospered His faithful followers. This rich message needs to be preached in the church. As I searched the Scriptures, discovering principles about biblical finance, I started to recognize some of the same concepts I learned when I was younger.

Principles can be taught and illustrated in many different ways, and our life's experiences can yield transferable wisdom. For instance, God once asked Solomon this question:

> "Ask for whatever you want me to give you."
>
> —2 Chronicles 1:7

When I first read this verse, I was very young in the Lord. I remember thinking, "I'd like God to ask me that question." What would you request? A mansion, riches, good looks, or perhaps the perfect mate? I now look back and thank God He didn't pose that question to me as an immature believer because I didn't have the wisdom or experience to answer it appropriately. Solomon already possessed much wisdom, as was evident in his response to God. Could it be that God asked Solomon a question that he was wise enough to answer?

> Give me wisdom and knowledge, that I may lead this people; for who is able to govern this great people of yours?
>
> —2 Chronicles 1:10

Perhaps the exchange was like that experienced by a contestant on a game show. The "host" asks, "Solomon, with the right answer to this question, you will get what's behind door number one." Solomon thinks for a second and says, "My answer is, give me wisdom and knowledge to lead these people." At that moment, balloons are released from the ceiling and the band plays while the announcer excitedly reveals Solomon's prize.

> Wisdom and knowledge is granted unto thee; and I will give thee riches and wealth and honor, such as none of the kings have had that have been before thee; neither shall there any after thee have the like.
>
> —2 Chronicles 1:12

I once pondered, "Did this wisdom come upon him instantly? Did Solomon walk out of that encounter with wisdom that was immeasurable?"

I've arrived at the conclusion that the wisdom came cumulatively. God opened Solomon's capacity to understand and comprehend complex things. As you read through the life of Solomon, you can witness his ability, or gift of wisdom, in action. His wisdom increased throughout his whole life. Ecclesiastes is a dissertation on life written by Solomon in his later years, in which he tells of how he searched for wisdom like a pearl of great price.

> And I gave my heart to seek and search out by wisdom concerning all things that are done under heaven:
>
> —Ecclesiastes 1:13

This, too, is how wisdom is acquired in our lives. We must set our hearts upon it.

The Pursuit of Wisdom v. The Pursuit of Riches

Everything in life, no matter how insignificant, can teach us something and increase our wisdom. As Solomon walked through life, he stumbled upon wisdom in some of the most unusual places. One day, for example, he came upon an anthill and learned amazing things about work and prosperity.

> Go to the ant, thou sluggard (lazy, indolent); consider her ways and be wise: which having no guide, overseer or ruler, provideth her meat in the summer, and gathereth her food in the harvest. How long wilt thou sleep, O sluggard? When wilt thou arise out of thy sleep? Yet a little sleep, a little slumber, a little folding of the hands to sleep: So shall thy poverty come as one that travelleth, and thy want as an armed man.
>
> —Proverbs 6:6-11

King Solomon was confronted with many of the social issues nations wrestle with today — including welfare. History shows that empires, kingdoms, and nations that were ineffective in addressing social welfare problems became crippled and sometimes extinct. America is also in danger of being bankrupted in part by its welfare entitlement programs. King Solomon found wisdom and direction in a "working class" colony of ants. God inscribed His principles in nature, and, like Solomon, we can

> Prosperity
> should be
> understood
> as the fruit of
> productivity.

learn much by studying how the Creator has designed the world to work.

These aren't words that will win a popularity contest. Recent presidents who have tried to reform welfare have found their efforts stifled and choked by special interest groups, lobbyists and the media. There are now second and third generation welfare dependents, waiting month after month for the mailman to bring a check. Even their young children learn what time of the month to ask for new things. This does nothing but reinforce a poverty mentality. Government assistance was designed to help needy people until they could get back on their feet. It should never be construed as a reward for laziness, rebellion, or irresponsibility.

King Solomon noticed these ants had no guides (captains), overseers (teachers, instructors), or rulers (government officials). What they did have was enough sense and work ethic to provide food and housing for themselves. Maybe he gave this proverb as a state of the Kingdom address — challenging people not to become a burden to the nation. Solomon warns that the enemy to prosperity is procrastination and slothfulness, which lead to poverty. Prosperity should be understood as the fruit of productivity.

One of the very first things I learned about becoming financially independent was to stay away from "get rich quick" schemes. If it's too good to be true, then it's probably too good to be true. So many Christians are looking for a check in the mail, overnight riches, or winning the lottery, that they fail to be productive with what they have. They need to learn and apply wealth-building financial principles, and then they would benefit from the fruits of their labor. Solomon gave this same advice in Proverbs.

> He that *plows* his land shall have plenty of bread, but he that pursues after vanity (riches) shall have plenty of poverty. A *hasty* person tries to get *rich quick*, but it only leads to poverty.
>
> —Proverbs 28:19, 22 Emphasis added

Unfortunately, the Church has been deceived with "get rich, name it, and claim it" messages for years. I am appalled at preachers claiming to have a "money anointing" who have their churches shout "the money cometh" while they look up toward Heaven and pull their arms back like slot machines. Are they expecting to hit it big in the Heavenly Casino?

Some well-known televangelists claim authority to cancel out debt. People run to the altars throwing money and their bills at the preacher's feet in hope that their debt will be wiped out. What are these people thinking? Do they actually believe when they get home the bank is going to call and inform them they don't need to pay their mortgages or credit card debts anymore? To top it off, after the broadcast, these same preachers with debt canceling "money anointing" beg viewers for much needed ministry donations. Why don't they just cancel out their debt and pray over their ministry bank account declaring increase?

> As long as Christians are chasing after riches, they will never have the time and wisdom to build wealth.

This is just another disguise of the "poor church" message. Wisdom says these people need to stop dancing around their checkbooks, pick up their bills from the altar, and make their payments on time before their credit scores are lowered and the banks look at them as a risk. The enemy of our soul wants the church broke and impoverished.

Wisdom plays a major role in creating, sustaining and distributing wealth. As long as Christians are *chasing after riches*, they will never have the time nor develop the wisdom to *build wealth*.

Chapter Four

Financial Power Principles

Building wealth is an exciting and rewarding journey. My journey began with dissatisfaction over my circumstances. I looked to educational institutions, thinking I was going to learn skills for handling money wisely. Frustration started simmering during my middle school years because I had yet to learn anything about making money. Finally, one day I stayed late at school hoping to get some answers.

"Excuse me," I said to a teacher, "may I ask you a question?"

"Sure, what's on your mind?" she responded.

"Can you tell me how to make money?" I asked.

She gave me a strange look and replied, "Well, John, you have to study really hard, get good grades, and then one day you'll get a good job and make a lot of money." "That's it?" I thought. "What now?"

My conversation with my teacher and the fact that I hadn't learned anything useful for making money started to really bother me. I felt a tug to give in to a reality where nothing was going to change. The drive and desire for "more" was beginning to settle into a willingness for something far less. Have you ever felt like this in your life? I didn't know whether I was giving up or giving in. Either way, the wind was out of my sails.

It concerns me that American children aren't being equipped with a solid work ethic.

Many days passed, and I still couldn't shake the feeling of resignation. Then one day, while walking into the house from school, I noticed the newspaper on the porch had a white flyer sticking out of the fold. Curiosity got the best of me, and I pulled the flyer out to see what it said. I couldn't believe it. The newspaper company was looking for additional paperboys for numerous routes in my neighborhood. It read:

"Newspaper routes available — Make Money — call fast for best routes."

I ran in the house and asked my mom if I could call. "Sure," she said.

That was the start of my entrepreneurial ventures. I took the largest paper route in my neighborhood. We lived in a housing project where each building had ten condo-type units. The entire complex consisted of one hundred buildings, covering a one-mile radius, and was so big it had three separate parks, each with baseball diamonds and playgrounds. Other kids in the area took the remaining newspaper routes. The papers were dropped in one spot where we all met to take our bundles and start delivering. I had the largest and longest route, with almost ninety apartments. Because of this, my friends would be back playing long before I was done. Nevertheless, I was committed to the opportunity to make money.

I delivered newspapers in the rain, snow, and heat of the summer. While my parents might not have had an abundance of wealth-building principles to hand down to me, they did pass on what they had — a dedicated work ethic. My father learned the principle from his father and passed it on to me. Ever since I can remember, I have worked hard.

When I was growing up, my mother had a chore list for every day of the week. Saturdays were big workdays, when we cleaned the entire house. My mother went a little overboard with the cleaning. I wasn't allowed to play until all the tasks were finished. When I complained she said, "Life isn't about fun and games." She never told me what life was about, but according to her, it wasn't about fun and games. I had one of two choices, I could bellyache and complain, or I could move fast and get it done. I chose to get up, move fast, and get the job done. My father and mother taught me that since I was a part of the family, I had to share in the responsibilities. Developing work habits was at the core of what they taught me.

Such time-tested golden principles have become almost extinct today. We are raising a generation of lazy and unthankful children. This is due in part to a group of psychologists writing volumes on how we shouldn't put too much responsibility, discipline, or hard work on our children because it may scar them for life. The result is a generation of irresponsible, undisciplined, and indolent kids.

It concerns me that American children aren't being equipped with a solid work ethic from childhood. How will they compete in the changing markets of today's economy?

A while back, I attended an owners' meeting for the fastest-growing "sub" sandwich franchise in America. The proprietors were given a list of common problems plaguing owners. Topping the list was being forced to hire and rely on high school kids to work evening shifts. There was a lengthy list of allegations, such as — teens were unreliable, difficult to train, undisciplined, unaccustomed to work, and gave away free food to all their friends. Owners were told, "If you're going to hire from this pool of workers, you must have adult supervision (babysitters) on duty, or your profits will eventually walk out the door."

Over the years, I've developed extensive mentoring in every company and ministry I oversee. Through "reward programs" and many other incentives, we are instilling a solid work ethic in our employees and interns so they may enjoy the fruit of their labors.

Taking Advantage of Opportunities

At age twelve, I had the great opportunity to begin working and making money. The newspaper company would pay me a nickel for every paper delivered. This gave me $4.50 per day, which equaled $31.50 per week, plus tips, for delivering newspapers to ninety apartments. In addition, the paper company relied on the paperboy to collect the money from the customer at the end of each week. I learned how to construct a spreadsheet to keep an accurate running record for every customer. I could easily find out who had paid and who had an open balance. I created a simple formula to calculate the cost-to-profit ratio. I knew the dollar amount to be paid to the newspaper company, so I would first subtract that number from the gross collected every week. The remainder represented my profits, a mixture of earned money worked into the subscription price, plus tips. Finally, I had to manage the route. I had to contact the newspaper company about any changes to the subscriptions, such as cancellations.

MY PAPER ROUTE

90 papers x 25¢ (retail price) = $22.50 x 7 days = $157.50 gross

90 papers x 20¢ = $18.00 x 7 days = $126.00 newspaper company's profit

90 papers x 5¢ = $4.50 x 7 days = $31.50 + tips = my profit!

I can't emphasize enough how valuable these tools were for understanding and building wealth. At that young age, I managed hundreds of dollars every month. Today, I use the same tools to handle hundreds of thousands of dollars. I perform financial analysis for clients on investment properties, business ventures, mergers, startups, and acquisitions with the same tools I mastered delivering newspapers. Of course, I've increased my understanding of complex financial formulas, but at the end of the day, the basic tools are the same.

For example, one day a friend called, asking me to review the numbers on a potential investment property he was considering. In a matter of minutes, this simple calculation showed the income potential for that investment.

Profit and Loss of a Three-Family Investment Property

Income		Expenses	
Unit 1	$750	Mortgage	$1,260
Unit 2	$900	Taxes	$250
Unit 3	$1,000	Insurance	$50
		Maint.	$60
Total	$2,650		$1,620

$2,650 - $1,620 = $1,030 Monthly Profit

$1,030 x 12 = $12,360 Yearly Profit

I've spent years counseling both young and old who have gotten themselves into financial difficulty, and the story is usually the same. They lack understanding of about how money works and the skills needed to manage finances. The majority of people who come to my office believe their financial problems are due to a lack of money. In most cases, more money means more problems. They got into trouble because they couldn't handle the money they already had. Without understanding financial principles, no amount of money will solve the problem.

The Power Principles of a Kid

I was twelve, in seventh grade, and making almost fifty dollars a week. I was finally making money. In addition, my desire for "more" was reignited. I was able to purchase new sneakers and clothes, and still had money left in my pocket.

Over the next three years, I learned lessons about money that school wasn't teaching, and my father didn't hand down to me. In fact, it was those early days that prepared me for the business world. Slowly but surely, the other paperboys got tired of their routes and asked me if I wanted to buy them. After I purchased the first route, I put together a standing offer to purchase any other paper route. I offered one week's profit as a purchase price for any route in the neighborhood. Soon, I had the largest route of any paperboy in the city.

Power Principles

I used what I call the "power of acquisitions" to increase my newspaper business. Understanding and using this principle would help shape my future. Putting it to work at such a young age also removed the negative emotions commonly associated with it. The power of acquisitions can be applied towards purchasing existing businesses, properties, and investments. When used successfully, it can be instrumental in accelerating and compounding wealth.

There were a few other lessons I learned at that time. The next was to take care of every customer. I call this the "power of value." This coupled with the "power of gratitude" was responsible for bringing multiplication to what I already possessed. I dropped off my papers with a smile. When I collected the money, I always greeted my customers with a joyful hello and thanked them for their payment. The more smiles and value I placed on my customers, the bigger the tips became! My profitability increased through having a thankful spirit. I always went the extra mile. If I noticed a crooked welcome mat, I straightened it before dropping the paper on the doorstep. These two power principles can ignite prosperity in every aspect of your life. Apply them to your existing work environment and your relationships, and watch what happens.

When Jesus was faced with the need to feed thousands of men, women and children with only a few fish and loaves, He took what He had, raised it to Heaven and gave thanks. Could it be that Jesus understood the "power of gratitude" and demonstrated that, when used properly, it produces tremendous multiplication? Paul also understood the power of gratitude and encouraged believers to apply it to every area of their lives.

> In every thing give thanks; for this is the will of God in Christ Jesus concerning you.
>
> —1 Thessalonians 5:18

It's sad, but I see these principles lacking in the next generation of workers. One night I walked into a coffee shop with my younger son, Joshua. We were the only people in the store except for the two young workers behind the counter. A girl was on the phone arguing with her boyfriend, and a boy was walking in and out of the back room as if I wasn't there. I waited about five minutes until even my son's patience was gone. At this point most people might have waited longer or walked out. I felt for the owner, who left his livelihood and future prosperity in the hands of two kids who apparently couldn't care less about what sacrifices he made to start his business.

I leaned over the counter and said to the girl on the phone, "Excuse me, you need to hang up that phone immediately and take care of the owner's customers. If you want to talk on the phone do it on your time. Your paycheck is a direct result of every customer who comes in that door."

> Where there is a void, there is an opportunity.

By that time, the young man came out from the back. I asked him, "What is your job description, walking in and out of the back room?" I ordered my donuts and coffee and asked for a business card, making sure the number and name of the owner were on the card. The following day I contacted the owner and informed him of my experience in his store the night before. He was stunned. He apologized numerous times during our conversation. He told me the story of what it took to open the coffee shop, and I felt his hurt and frustration. Unfortunately, this story is all too common.

Here is a principle that I have found to be true in business. "Where there's a void, there's an opportunity." This is a common sales principle — find a need and fill it, and where there is no need, create one. If you will apply these principles, you can get a job almost anywhere. The more you value your owner's business, the more he will value you. When your market value increases, it will amount to increases in your paycheck.

CHAPTER FIVE

Leader–Shift

A great deal has been written about *leadership*. However, if the ship is going in the wrong direction a shift is needed. For example, Moses' leadership was stalled in the wilderness. Those forty years became a time of maintaining the status quo. However, the appointment of Joshua represented a complete shift to advancing Israel into the *Promised Land*. Joshua signified a Leader-shift as he assumed the responsibility of total transition for the Jews.

Before Israel can possess the land, they must first cross the Jordan. The Jordan becomes the catalyst of this transition — the place of decision and point of no return.

From this moment forward they will transition more than just their geographical location.

They must transition from:

- Dependency to responsibility
- Wanderers to warriors
- Faithlessness to faithfulness
- Detour to destiny
- Welfare to worker

Even the provisional care of God transitions,

> And the **manna ceased** on the morrow after they had eaten of the old corn of the land; neither had the children of Israel manna any more; but they did eat of the fruit of the land of Canaan that year.
>
> —Joshua 5:12 Emphasis added

Other transitional leaders in the Bible include Abraham, Debra, David, Nehemiah and Jesus. Some contemporary examples would be Martin Luther, Charles Grey, George Washington, Abraham Lincoln, Winston Churchill, and Nelson Mandela. During their leadership the masses they led followed — sometimes reluctantly or suspiciously. Charting the difficult course through transition, they brought about great advancement.

Some however, were not so successful. I would have to put Noah at the top of this list. The people of that day resisted his leader-shift and avoided necessary transition. He gave a clear message that no one heeded. While history looks back at their warnings as prophesies for our current day — their lives were rattled with rejection, ridicule and some were even put to death.

The true mark of a leader is to be able to transform people.

———⦿———

Today, we are also living in a time of transition. The economic crisis of 2008-2009 has triggered a global economic transition. Finance undergirds society, as we know it. Uncertain economies create unstable societies. There are changes coming in the worlds of business, politics, religion, banking and international economies. Most will be extremely painful.

As you will learn, timing is critical in every aspect of life — especially when it comes to money. Positioning yourself ahead of the curve and educating yourself with unshakable principals will ensure your financial security.

Like the children of Israel, each one of us will take a similar journey as we become wealth builders. Let's chart a careful course.

Questions that Spark Movement

Questions are the triggers that start the movement toward change. It's when we question the status quo and limits set by society we begin to ignite a small spark that, if fostered, could change the world — or at least our world. All breakthrough, promotion and success begin with a question. *Why can't I have this or that? Why can't we do business differently? What's stopping me from starting a business, getting a degree, receiving a promotion or raise?*

Perhaps the most frequently asked question is, *"Why do good people struggle and seem to never get ahead, while dishonest people seem to get everything they want?* This question has been around forever and has frustrated even the wisest as far back as Solomon. In his day it was asked this way, *"Why do the wicked prosper?"*

As you read the Bible, you will find this question several times. For example, the book of Jeremiah. Not many positive things occurred during the ministry of Jeremiah the prophet — no big crusades, mass conversions, or stately dinner invitations, not even modest recognition. Jeremiah was ostracized, beaten, imprisoned, and scorned by his own countrymen. Even his writings, which include an entire book called "Lamentations," were not accepted until years after his death. Yet Jeremiah was a great prophet who was called to minister to backslidden, exiled Israel.

Many who stand for truth in a fallen culture can identify with Jeremiah. We sometimes find ourselves ridiculed, slighted, and disliked. We learn that a stance against injustices comes with a price. In my ministry, there have been times when I saw little fruit, yet my personal relationship with the Lord flourished. During those seasons, I took great solace in Jeremiah. Sometimes doing the "right thing" costs you comforts and pleasures. This is when the question "Why do the wicked prosper?" appears in the corridors of our minds. It is exactly what happened to Jeremiah. He questioned God about his plight and why difficulty and trouble seem to elude the wicked.

> Righteous art thou, O LORD, when I plead with thee: yet
> let me talk with thee of thy judgments: Wherefore doth the
> way of the wicked prosper? Wherefore are all they happy that
> deal very treacherously (deceitfully)?
>
> —Jeremiah 12:1 Emphasis added

Jeremiah knows God is righteous, but he needs more understanding regarding God's judicial verdicts (judgments) concerning the wicked. Jeremiah notices the wicked are happy and are experiencing a good and prosperous life. No good and pleasant thing is held back from them. Yet, they are deceitful and only mention God with their lips. Jeremiah wants to know, "How can they be blessed? This does not make sense!"

> Thou hast planted them, yea, they have taken root; they
> grow, yea, they bring forth fruit: thou art **near** in their mouth,
> and **far** from their reins.
>
> —Jeremiah 12:2 Emphasis added

Jeremiah sees the wicked as being planted, rooted, and fruitful. The fruit he is referring to is that of prosperity. These people are so prosperous they are in need of nothing and nobody.

There is no doubt Jeremiah is quoting from the first chapter of Psalms, where it is noted that this fruit should be the blessing of the righteous and not the wicked.

> Blessed is the man that walketh not in the counsel of the
> ungodly, nor standeth in the way of sinners, nor sitteth in
> the seat of the scornful! But his delight is in the law of the
> LORD, and in His law doth he meditate day and night. And
> he [referring to the man that delights in the Lord] shall be
> like a tree planted by the rivers of water that bringeth forth
> **his fruit** in his season; his leaf also shall not wither; and
> whatsoever he doeth shall prosper. **The ungodly are not so**: but
> are like the chaff, which the wind driveth away. Therefore, the
> ungodly shall not stand in the judgment, nor sinners in the
> congregation of the righteous. For the LORD knows the way
> of the righteous, but the way of the ungodly shall perish.
>
> —Psalm 1:3-6 Emphasis added

Jeremiah goes to God for answers, and asks, "Why then are the wicked prospering and not under your judgments?" The prosperity of the wicked is afflicting his soul, ministry, and relationship with God.

Jeremiah is not the only one asking this question. The writer of Psalm 73, likewise, is asking that very question.

> But as for me, my feet were almost gone; my steps had well nigh slipped. For I was envious at the foolish, when I saw the **prosperity of the wicked**.
>
> —Psalm 73:2-3 Emphasis added

You must grasp the depth of what the writer is expressing. This is a poetic way of saying he almost walked away from God! His foundation (principles, values, and standards) was almost removed, and his steps (ministry, mission, and purpose) almost slipped. I know many pastors and church leaders who have slipped away from the ministry and forsook their call because they could not come to grips with this question.

Have you, like them, ever become envious of the prosperity of the wicked? Maybe it happened to you while changing television channels or peering at the magazines while standing in line at the grocery store. Have you marveled at how Hollywood's little darlings are so rich and prosperous yet so immoral, ungodly and blasphemous? From the sporting world to the music scene, we see the same things: drug abuse, infidelity, rape, cultism, and the propagation of immorality.

> Behold, these are the ungodly, who **prosper** in the world; they increase in riches.
>
> —Psalm 73:12 Emphasis added

The psalmist noted that they prospered in the world (easy, carefree living), and their riches were multiplying.

These are just a few of the many individuals in the Bible who were troubled with the question, "Why do the wicked prosper?" I, too, have pondered this question for many years.

When I started teaching financial seminars, it was the number one question asked in the open sessions. This led me to search the Scriptures for answers to this age-old question.

In Psalm 94 David is so perturbed he repeats the question twice in the same verse. "How long shall the wicked prosper?"

> LORD, how long shall the wicked, how long shall the wicked triumph?
>
> —Psalm 94:3

David experienced years of difficulty and affliction. His troubles were multiplied when Samuel the Prophet anointed him as God's man for the position of king over Israel. The soulish King Saul attempts to kill him numerous times. Young David is forced to flee for his life. He finds himself a fugitive — a king without a country and in need of refuge. This circumstance leads David to Achish, king of Gath — the hometown of Goliath, the giant David killed with a sling.

> And David arose and *fled* that day for *fear* of Saul, and went to Achish the king of Gath. But the servants of Achish said unto him, Is not this David the king of the land? Did they not sing one to another of him in dances, saying, Saul hath slain his thousands, and David his ten thousands? And David laid up these words in his heart, and was so afraid of Achish the king of Gath. And he changed his behavior before them, and feigned himself mad in their hands, and scrabbled (scratched) on the doors of the gate, and let his spittle fall down upon his beard. Then Achish said unto his servants, lo, ye see the man is mad: wherefore then have ye brought him to me? Have I need of mad men, that ye have brought this fellow to play the mad man in my presence? Shall this fellow come into my house?
>
> —1 Samuel 21:10-15 Emphasis added

David stands before an ungodly king and pretends to be a madman, a lunatic with spit drooling down his beard. What a feeling of disgrace, dishonor, shame, and humiliation this must have been for David. This is where David introduces a "new style" of music I call the "The Jew's Blues" into his Psalms. David discovered and played the "blues" long before the city of New Orleans.

> I am worn out from groaning; all night long I flood my bed with *weeping* and drench my couch with tears. Mine eye is consumed because of *grief*; It waxeth old (sunken, worn out) because of all mine enemies.
>
> —Psalm 6:6-7 Emphasis added

If that weren't enough, he now has to flee for his life and hide in the cave of Adullam.

> David therefore departed thence, and *escaped to the cave Adullam*: and when his brethren and his father's entire house heard it, they went down thither to him. And every one that was in *distress*, and every one that was in *debt*, and every one that was *discontented*, gathered themselves unto him; and he became a captain over them. And there were with him about four hundred men.
>
> —1 Samuel 22:1-2 Emphasis added

While hiding in a cave, David attracts a motley crew of society's outcasts — emotionally and mentally distressed individuals. They included those stricken with anger, bitterness, and rejection, and so in debt that they had lost everything, becoming bankrupt. It is interesting that debt is mentioned in the list of issues plaguing this group. How do we know they were bankrupt? Because David would have asked them, "What kind of resources, money, and possessions do we have amongst us?" After hearing the answers, "None, nada, nothing, zilch, zip, zero," this could have been the point at which David cried out, "Lord, how long shall the wicked prosper and how long will my enemies prevail?"

Leadership Mandate

David could have walked away. Instead, he learned what it meant to be a true leader. In my opinion, the true mark of a leader is the ability to transform people spiritually, civically, and financially. Life had so buffeted these individuals that they had become discomforted and despondent. It became David's challenge to transform them.

This is David's final transformation as a leader. This challenge will prepare him for the throne of Israel. Through a mutual commitment to mentorship, these four hundred dejected individuals became the famed *"Mighty Men"* of David. The greatest warriors in the Bible. The success of David was tied to the success of those he led. What a lesson to be learned and practiced today.

Early in my ministry, I prayed God would send millionaires to my church. Then God spoke to me, "I've already sent them." As I looked at the landscape of my congregation I wondered, "Where are they?" After much prayer and soul-searching, I realized it was my responsibility to give our members the principles and strategies to create wealth and become people of means.

Similarly, the true test of pastors and leaders today is to transform the people in their sphere of influence into wealth-builders for kingdom purposes.

Part of my ministry is devoted to putting these principles into the hands of a new generation of entrepreneurs. Today our ministry is marked with the fruit of average people becoming wealth generators, using the tools and principles outlined in this book.

Unfortunately, much teaching in today's church is nothing more than a contemporary version of the poor church message, which will neither equip, nor empower those who hear it.

Section Two

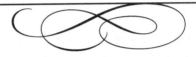

MONEY BY
Design

CHAPTER SIX

Kingdom Worldview

The Prosperity Plumb Line

A plumb line is a tool used by contractors to ensure the structure they're building is straight — perpendicular to the surface on which the structure rests. Without it, walls would be crooked and would not join evenly with other parts of the structure, like floors, roofs, and other walls.

Establishing a plumb line for prosperity will ensure that you always have a measuring tool to consistently build *precise, straight,* and *strong.* You will come across many crooked practices and principles that can be tempting when you desire to build wealth. However, none will produce fruit of lasting value.

> There is a way which **seemeth** right unto a man, but **the end thereof** are the ways of death (destruction).
>
> —Proverbs 14:12 Emphasis added

One of my close friends is a contractor and says *plumbing* is essential in building any size of structure, whether a shed or skyscraper. He states that consistently checking the plumb line affects the structure's overall *integrity*. It is worth noting a few other things he pointed out:

⁂ A structure out of plumb is subject to cracks, leaks, and deterioration.

⁂ If the building is out of plumb at its foundation, it will be magnified throughout the entire structure.

⁂ An out of plumb building will have *stability* issues which will increase in severity over time.

⁂ The likelihood of an out of plumb building suffering irreparable damage or collapse is almost certain.

> The key that unlocks the Bible is not the human spirit, but the Holy Spirit.

I have witnessed many of these same flaws in people who have built wealth incorrectly or who lacked wisdom and understanding concerning money matters.

With that in mind, I consider this chapter to be the "plumb line" as we create and build wealth. We must not lose sight of the prophetic destiny and eternal purposes of wealth in the hands of the believer. This chapter is the foundation of what sets this book apart from every other book on finance.

Mysteries Uncovered

There are certain spiritual truths Jesus did not share openly. He taught them through parables, stories, types, and shadows because the truths were too important to leave in open sight. He hid them in places we have to discover, seek, and search after. Jesus left specific instructions for those who are searching:

> Ask, and it shall be given you; seek, and ye shall find; knock, and it shall be opened unto you.
>
> —Matthew 7:7

The Bible is filled with mysteries and *hidden treasures* of wisdom and knowledge. *Why the wicked prosper* is one of the *greatest* of those mysteries.

> But we speak the wisdom of God in a mystery, even the hidden wisdom, which God ordained before the world unto our glory:
>
> —1 Corinthians 2:7

The Bible is foolproof. The foolish read it but cannot comprehend, because it must be spiritually discerned. This is why so many secular teachers, professors, scientists, psychologists, and others can read, study and teach the Bible, but are not changed or spiritually enlightened by it. The key that unlocks the Bible is not the human spirit but the Holy Spirit.

> But the natural, (non-spiritual) man does not accept or welcome or admit into his heart the gifts and teachings and revelations of the Spirit of God, for they are folly (meaningless nonsense) to him; and he is incapable of knowing them (of progressively recognizing, understanding, and becoming better acquainted with them) because they are spiritually discerned and estimated and appreciated.
>
> —1 Corinthians 2:14 (AMP)

The disciples walked with Jesus for three and a half years, yet did not understand the meanings or applications of much of what He taught. Once, they asked Him privately:

> Why speakest thou unto them in parables? He answered and said unto them, because *it is given unto you to know the mysteries of the kingdom of heaven*, but to them it is not given.

> For whosoever hath, to him shall be given, and he shall have more abundance; but whosoever hath not, from him shall be taken away even that he hath. Therefore speak I to them in parables; because they seeing see not, and hearing they hear not, neither do they understand.
>
> —Matthew 13:10-13 Emphasis added

By this time, the disciples had listened to numerous parables, stories, and teachings that they did not understand. They must have thought, "If it was given to us, then why don't we understand?" The reality is, until now, they had not sought answers. Jesus was instructing that access was made available to them to know the secrets to the mysteries of the Kingdom of Heaven. So then, like present-day treasure hunters, we can look through the archives of history and the written record of Scripture, and with the help of the Holy Spirit find the treasures of the Kingdom of Heaven.

Jesus taught the disciples four important truths concerning the Kingdom of Heaven through His teachings.

First, heaven is a legitimate kingdom, with a *King, government, culture, and judicial laws that are enforced.* These kingdom references are seen throughout the entire Bible. The disciples, who were under the rule of Rome, understood the word *kingdom.* Also, as Jews, *they operated under* a theocratic form of government when relating to God. When it comes to God, there's no politicking or lobbying, much less concern about public opinion polls. You cannot vote God out of office.

The Jews were equipped both spiritually and socially to understand the framework of the Kingdom of God. On the other hand, our *Western* mind-set is based on a system of government called a *"democracy."* This mind-set creates many hindrances to understanding and interpreting the Scriptures. With only a few monarchies remaining in the modern world, very few Americans would understand how to approach the Emperor of Japan or the Queen of England — much less the King of Kings and Lord of Lords. The Psalmist warns:

> For the LORD most high is terrible; He is a great King over all the earth. He shall subdue the people under us, and the nations under our feet.
>
> —Psalm 47:2-3

Second, to access the "*Kingdom of God*" here on Earth, we must possess the keys that unlock its mysteries, treasures and benefits. Understanding and interpreting Scripture requires more than just reading the Bible. It involves acquiring necessary keys or tools for biblical interpretation. Without those keys, readers will have difficulty penetrating the surface.

Third, God has bestowed upon Jesus the title of King.

> And He hath on His vesture and on His thigh a name written, **KING OF KINGS, AND LORD OF LORDS**.
>
> —Revelation 19:16 Emphasis added

Along with the title, God has given Him all authority in the Kingdom. Jesus refers to this power in the Great Commission and the Apostles remind believers that Christ uncovered and defeated all powers.

> And Jesus came and spake unto them, saying, All power is given unto Me in heaven and in earth.
>
> —Matthew 28:18

> And having spoiled principalities and powers, He made a shew of them openly, triumphing over them in it.
>
> —Colossians 2:15

Fourth, whoever uncovers these mysteries will be given abundant increase. These were the building blocks I lacked and did not learn during my introductory years of ministry. This study of the Kingdom of God yielded powerful principles not taught in school, much less the Church. They became the basis of my understanding of "*kingdom economics.*" *This is what the Church has failed to teach its members.* While I had a good handle on economics, I had limited insight about the Kingdom of Heaven. Living in America, I had only read about kingdoms, empires, and monarchies. I overlooked many of those references in Scripture.

With God, there's no politicking or lobbying.

———⟡———

For example, "kingdom" is mentioned over one hundred and sixty times in the New Testament alone! That is more than the words "fruit," "prayer," "joy," and "sin." Jesus was very purposeful in laying a proper foundation concerning kingdoms from the start of His ministry.

Jesus possessed a world view based upon the "*Word of God*" and the coming Kingdom. Today, only a small portion of the Church expresses its faith through a biblical worldview. A recent survey by pollster George Barna finds only 9 percent of born-again Christians hold a biblical world view. Barna found that only 4 percent of the general population have a biblical world view and suggests many of the nation's moral and spiritual challenges are directly attributed to this fact.

> Only 9%
>
> of born-again
>
> Christians
>
> hold a biblical
>
> worldview.
>
> —⦅∽≪⦆—

Only 7 percent of Protestants overall maintained a biblical world view according to the study. Of adults who attend mainline Protestant churches, only 2 percent shared those values. Among Catholics, less than one-half of 1 percent had a biblical worldview. The denominations that produced the highest proportions of adults with a biblical worldview were non-denominational Protestant churches (13 percent), Pentecostal churches (10 percent) and Baptist churches (8 percent). Among the most prevalent alternative worldviews was postmodernism, which seemed to be the dominant perspective among the two youngest generations.[1]

By and large, a biblical worldview is not taught within most churches in the twenty-first century. The Kingdom of God has been replaced with the kingdom of self in most Christian circles. Today, the most popular preachers and desired messages are self-help and motivational. Jesus instructed His disciples to be Kingdom motivated and to crucify self in order to access power and help from Heaven. He taught that in every aspect of life His followers are to have a Kingdom mind-set.

When believers submit to the will of God, they allow the Kingdom of Heaven to invade the earth through them.

Culture Wars

This conflict of opposing kingdoms and cultures was first seen in the Garden of Eden. It was a secular world view that influenced Adam and

Eve to disobey God and choose their own way. A biblical worldview would have led them to denounce the serpent's opposing philosophy and adhere to the law of God. The culture of the garden was held together by the law of God. It sustained life, provision, fertility, and prosperity as long as it was followed. Adam was free to eat of every tree in the garden except the tree of the knowledge of good and evil. God offered unlimited prosperity, blessing, fruit, and productivity to Adam and Eve. Yet ,the serpent was able to convince them to fixate on the one thing they were commanded not to eat, and he convinced them that God was withholding some good thing from them. Moreover, if they would eat of the tree of the knowledge of good and evil, they would be as God.

satan introduces an alternative world-view to Adam and Eve through which they will be able to have all of the benefits and provisions of the garden without having to adhere to the King's rule. *They wanted to stay in the Kingdom, but not submit to the King.* This alternative lifestyle has been offered throughout the ages. The garden became the birthplace of *secularism* and *humanism,* unleashing the kingdom and culture of evil on mankind.

By rejecting the social control and government of God, Adam and Eve adopted a secular philosophy. Today, when believers live their lives with no Kingdom influence they are embracing a secular mind-set. This will inevitably produce a *"secular Christian"* — one who attends church, but is uninfluenced by a biblical worldview in their day-to-day decisions, personal relationships, or marketplace activities.

Kids who are raised in secular, Christian homes will not see the benefit of using the Bible as a manual for life, and consequently, they will gravitate toward worldly philosophies, because our culture is saturated with secularism.

When I grew up, I had very few choices when flipping through the channels. I had no home computer, let alone Internet. There were no iPods or e-mail. Our chat room was the dinner table. Today, kids have the Internet, hundreds of channels of TV and radio, instant messaging, cell phones, periodicals, newsletters, and MTV, to name just a few of the sources of secular brainwashing. They are oversaturated and seduced by our secular culture. This saturation is causing thousands of these same kids to leave the faith every year.

First Things First

Jesus taught His disciples *"first things first"* principles. While many are willing to do anything necessary to gain the whole world, Jesus warned: *make sure you don't lose your soul in the process* (Mark 8:36). How then, can a believer acquire wealth and riches yet stay in the will of God? I submit to you, that by putting the Kingdom of God first, you will allow the windows of heaven to open over your life.

Making ends meet and finding ways to prosper are not new concepts. Questions about prosperity came to Jesus on a regular basis. His answer was always the same — do not be like the Gentiles *(unbelievers, those outside the faith)* who only seek power, riches, and prestige. Rather, Jesus said:

> Seek ye first the kingdom of God and His righteousness; and all these things shall be added unto you.
>
> —Matthew 6:33

They wanted to stay in the Kingdom, but not submit to the King.

Don't make the mistake of thinking that because Jesus lived two thousand years ago, people were any less concerned or interested in advancement, position, power, prosperity, wealth, land, homes, and cattle. They were looking to better themselves and increase their influence as much as we are today. Jesus consistently directed them to put the Kingdom first.

There have been times in my ministry where the needs have been so great they have overwhelmed my relationship with God, caused immense pressure, and created incalculable stress. In every instance, the Holy Spirit always prompted me to position the Kingdom first for those things to be worked out. Once I put *first things first*, God always gave me creative ideas, divine strategies, and new concepts to meet every need. When my desire was only for God's outstretched hand, it always came closed. Yet, when I desired the heart of God, His hand always appeared outstretched.

Because the poor church message is so prevalent in the Church today, many believers are looking to other streams of knowledge instead of the Bible. We must guard ourselves from secular ideologies about prosperity, wealth, and riches. Certain practices of generating revenue are counter-productive to the believer, including income gained from unrighteous activities or unlawful business deals which are forbidden.

There are many books written by wealthy individuals who bait you with the lure of their riches, power, and prestige. However, the spirit behind their books is not the Holy Spirit. The last thing the Church needs is to be is an "*apprentice*" to a secular mind-set with no understanding of kingdom principles or ways of accessing the blessings of heaven.

If you will develop a kingdom worldview as the plumb line of your life, you will build wealth and prosperity that will become a legacy for generations to come.

> A good man leaveth an inheritance to his children's children.
>
> —Proverbs 13:22 Emphasis added

CHAPTER SEVEN

Why Do The Wicked Prosper?

We've examined the foundation for wealth building and established that a *Biblical Worldview* is the plumb line for financial success. Now let's probe more deeply the age-old question, *"Why do the wicked prosper?"*

The basis for the answer is in the account of the temptation of Christ. The Scriptures record that after Jesus was baptized by John, He was led into the wilderness by the Holy Spirit to be tempted by the devil. At the time, Jesus was in His fortieth day of fasting and was extremely hungry. Opportunistically, satan comes to tempt Jesus three times. It is the third temptation that is particularly significant. It reads:

> Again, the devil taketh him up into an exceeding high mountain, and **sheweth Him all the kingdoms of the world,**

and the glory of them; And saith unto him, all these things will I give thee, if thou wilt fall down and worship me. Then saith Jesus unto him, get thee hence, satan: for it is written, thou shalt worship the Lord thy God, and Him only shalt thou serve.

—Matthew 4:8-10 Emphasis added

Notice what satan specifically offers to Jesus — all the *kingdoms* of the world. He is clearly declaring they are under his authority and control. Included in his offer was the *"glory"* of these kingdoms, which was their *prosperity and financial riches.*

I cannot emphasize enough the importance of this exchange. Many have tried to imply that satan was speaking metaphorically and actually never controlled these kingdoms. Some say he just offered them to Jesus to see what He would do. That makes no sense at all and is nothing more than denial. If this information were not legitimate, it could not have been classified as a temptation.

> A battle rages between the kingdoms of light and darkness.
>
> ———⁂———

Webster's defines temptation as: *The act of tempting or state of being tempted, especially to evil: Enticement, something tempting: the cause or occasion of temptation.* This is the only place in the entire Bible where satan exposes himself by revealing his prized possessions — the *"kingdoms"* of this world and their *wealth (glory).* The adversary likes to do his dirty work in deception, deceit, cunning craftiness, and trickery. He baits and sets traps in places we are unaware. He attempts to do his business while concealed in secret and dark places. Our enemy is not offended or dismayed that countless people do not believe in his existence — in fact, his success depends upon it. Let us not be like so many who have overlooked this exposé on the prince of darkness.

If the world kingdoms were not under satan's control, Jesus would have declared him a liar, reminding the devil that His Father owns the cattle on a thousand hills (Psalm 50:10). However, this was not Jesus' response, since He knew it would not have been applicable or a legitimate defense against the temptation.

Originally, God gave dominion over creation to Adam. However, Adam's sin allowed the devil to usurp that authority. This transference of dominion is acknowledged throughout the Bible and is especially echoed within the writings of the Apostles.

> In whom the god of this world hath blinded the minds of them which believe not, lest the light of the glorious gospel of Christ, who is the image of God, should shine unto them.
>
> —2 Corinthians 4:4

> Wherein in time past ye walked according to the course of this world, according to the prince of the power of the air, the spirit that now worketh in the children of disobedience.
>
> —Ephesians 2:2

We see the battle raging between kingdoms of light and darkness throughout the entire earthly ministry of Jesus. It is essential to notice that Jesus only began to reveal the *"Kingdom of Heaven"* message after His victory over temptation in the wilderness.

> From that time (*temptation*) Jesus began to preach, and to say, Repent: for the kingdom of heaven is at hand.
>
> —Matthew 4:17 Emphasis added

This message is the greatest threat to satan's kingdom. Adam failed his time of testing, and that turned the Garden into a wilderness. However, Jesus was led by the Holy Spirit into the wilderness to take back His garden. Why did Jesus preach the Kingdom of Heaven and not just the good news of salvation? Something very important was taking place in the Lord's encounter with the tempter. Jesus was revealing that the Kingdom of Heaven will confront this dark kingdom of evil. The whole of Scripture reveals that the Kingdom of Heaven will reside upon the Church. The Church will move and operate with the power and authority of the Kingdom of Heaven. Jesus stated,

> ...and upon this rock **I will build my church; and *the gates of hell shall not prevail against it.*** And I will give unto thee the keys of the kingdom of heaven: and whatsoever thou shalt bind on earth shall be bound in heaven: and whatsoever thou shalt loose on earth shall be loosed in heaven.
>
> —Matthew 16:18-19 Emphasis added

The Church is the only power the gates of hell cannot prevail against.

The Church is the only power the gates of hell cannot prevail against. This is the reason Jesus and His Church are under constant attack in our society. It is why prayer has been banned at school events and outlawed from public schools, along with the Ten Commandments. The truth is, there are satanic spiritual forces attempting to limit or even banish Jesus from every aspect of our society and culture. The only way satan can prevail against the Church is by eliminating and outlawing the Gospel message from a society. Children, indoctrinated with humanism and secularism, are taught that their ancestors are apes, and then we are shocked when they behave like animals. Our youth are banned from reading the Ten Commandments that teach moral laws like, *"Thou shalt not murder,"* and then we are horrified at school massacres like Columbine and Virginia Tech.

More than any other New Testament writer, the Apostle Paul had tremendous insight into the mission, purpose, and power of the Kingdom of Heaven. He draws a direct connection between the Church and the Kingdom of God. He reminds believers that Christ is the supreme power of the universe.

> Which He wrought in Christ, when He raised him from the dead, and set Him at His own right hand in the heavenly places, *far above all principality, and power, and might, and dominion, and every name that is named, not only in this world, but also in that which is to come*: And hath put all things under His feet, and gave Him to be the head over all things to the church, which is His body, the fullness of Him that filleth all in all.
>
> —Ephesians 1:20-23 Emphasis added

The Church is also seated together with Christ.

> And hath raised us up together, and made us sit ***together in heavenly places*** in Christ Jesus:
>
> —Ephesians 2:6 Emphasis added

The devil would rather give up the kingdoms of this world to stop the coming Kingdom of Heaven on the earth. Jesus clearly preached, *"The kingdom of heaven is at hand."* He was preparing to usher in a new world power greater than the Roman Empire. While Israel was a thorn in satan's side, it was minuscule compared to the coming impact of the Kingdom of Heaven.

The tempter offers Jesus temporal riches and earthly power with the intent of preventing the arrival and advancement of the Kingdom of God. The devil failed in this attempt to snare Jesus, yet the offer is still on the table for anyone willing to take the bait and compromise with the enemy. The adversary still offers power, prestige, and temporal satisfaction to entice and blind unsuspecting individuals.

In my travels, I have witnessed people sacrifice their values, character, marriages, and families for the lure of happiness only to find they've fallen into a trap and an inferior life.

Whether people believe it or not, there is a battle waging between good and evil. It is seen throughout the pages of Scripture, from the Garden of Eden to the building of the tower of Babel, to the wicked imaginations of mankind causing the Flood, from which only Noah and his family were spared. The battle is remarkably demonstrated when Moses confronts Pharaoh and his sorcerers, Jannes and Jambres, in seeking freedom for the Jews. With a strong arm, God sent ten plagues upon Egypt, showing Him to be the supreme and only true God. Like a cosmic chess match, this battle between the Kingdom of Heaven and the kingdom of hell rages on.

Thus, with a Kingdom mind-set, let's look at three reasons *"Why the wicked prosper."*

Three Reasons Why the Wicked Prosper

1. The "Golden Rule"

The number one reason the wicked prosper is the *"Golden Rule"* — *"He who has the gold makes the rules."* The enemy of righteousness knows that it takes *resources* and *money* to further his agenda. In the account of the temptation, satan declared he controlled the wealth and prosperity of nations. At first glance, you might not think this is important. However, history concurs that nations with the greatest wealth have had the greatest militaries, the longest reigns, and exert the most power over the world.

He who has the gold makes the rules.

You don't need to be a prophet to predict whether our country will increase in lawlessness or righteousness. Instead, you only have to look at who has the *greatest purse*. This is among the reasons we must become better stewards of the resources under our control. The wealth the enemy has amassed for the funding and propagation of wickedness is staggering. Just take a glimpse into the war chest satan has at his disposal:

The international *"illicit drug business"* generates as much as $400 billion in trade annually according to the United Nations International Drug Control Program. It has become the nation of Colombia's number one export — surpassing its international export of coffee. According to a report prepared for ONDCP by ABT Associates in 2000, between 1989 and 1998, American users spent $77 billion annually on cocaine and another $22 billion annually yearly on heroin.

It is no wonder that four out of five families in America have been directly impacted by drugs. You don't have to look any further than your extended family to see the ravages of drug addiction. From the inner city to the upper levels of society, the crippling effect of drugs is unmistakable. The very fabric of the American family is being attacked by the insidious power of drugs. It is a present-day epidemic. The drug industry has steadily grown through solicitation and propagation. Today drug users are younger than ever before. Our government's response to this — the multi-million dollar campaign, "Just Say No!"

The *"porn industry"* yields over $200 billion per year. There are porn shops in almost every city in America. Technology has become pornography's greatest ally. Now, users no longer have to leave their homes and risk being seen. In the privacy of their own homes, they can access an entire world of filth, including graphic sexual images, abominations with children and every perversion known to man.

The Internet has become the most dangerous place for our children to wander unattended. It is often beyond the jurisdiction of local law enforcement agencies. Instead, it falls to the FBI, who complains it is not big enough and lacks the funds to counteract the proliferation of pornography. The FBI sometimes equates policing the Internet to *"looking for a needle in a haystack."* This assault is also affecting the Church. Statistics show that online pornography falls into the top three issues plaguing Christian men young and old.

> The wicked prosper to support the ongoing expansion of immorality.

Gambling is another huge revenue generator for the kingdom of darkness. Records indicate that Americans place legal bets of over $300 billion a year. That's equivalent to 5% of the Gross National Product, or one-third more than the total amount spent on elementary and secondary education in America. This amount is nearly four times that given to religious institutions. More than three-fourths of that money was spent in casinos, but state lotteries are growing in popularity and are promoted lavishly through TV and radio campaigns using enticements like *"You can't win if you don't play."* Individuals with big homes and fancy cars lure people to take their chance on the *"good life."* Today, many parents buy scratch off tickets for their kids, not comprehending that they are introducing them to the gambling industry, which will exploit these children throughout their lives.

Nothing is mentioned about fortunes lost, marriages destroyed, and lives left in disarray due to a demoralizing addiction to gambling. Not to mention the problem of increased crime that casinos bring to a city.

The great spiritual money machine of deception — psychics and eastern cult practices draw another $150 Billion per year. This revival of spiritism, coupled with the dilution of Christianity, has opened the door for millions of people to be deceived.

What I have cited is not even the tip of the iceberg. Lawlessness is generating trillions of dollars for the ongoing propagation and proliferation of wickedness. The wicked prosper to support the ongoing expansion of immorality and profanity. This is one of the greatest conspiracies in the history of man. Jesus put it this way:

> He that is not with me is against me; and he that gathereth not with me scattereth abroad.
>
> —Matthew 12:30

The things noted above are happening as the Church wrestles with the issue of prosperity. *"Does God take pleasure in the prosperity of His servants?"* The answer is an unequivocal **Yes!** There is a battle taking place for the very soul of our nation, and God seeks to transfer wealth and prosperity to His children to confront these evil forces. As I travel the nation speaking on the topic of wealth creation and distribution, I am seeing more and more young "Christian millionaires" arising out of obscurity by the hand of God.

> The quickest way to transform a city— BUY IT!

I believe the key that unlocks the door to untold riches is understanding *"Why the Wicked Prosper."* King Solomon understood the power and influence of money and said, *"Money answereth all things"* (Ecclesiastes 10:19).

The quickest way to transform a city is too, **"Buy It!"** The Bible teaches that dominion is always connected to the possession of land. Something happens in the spirit realm when land is deeded to an individual. The first thing God told Abraham after He blessed him was:

> Arise; walk through the land in the length of it and in the breadth of it; for I will give it unto thee.
>
> —Genesis 13:17 Emphasis added

During the leadership tenures of Moses, Joshua, David, and other rulers of Israel, land was the commodity of victory and national security. Moses said,

For if ye shall diligently keep all these commandments which I command you, to do them, to love the LORD your God, to walk in all His ways, and to cleave unto Him; Then will the LORD drive out all these nations from before you, and ye shall possess greater nations and mightier than yourselves. ***Every place whereon the soles of your feet shall tread shall be yours: from the wilderness and Lebanon, from the river, the river Euphrates, even unto the uttermost sea shall your coast be.*** There shall no man be able to stand before you: for the LORD your God shall lay the fear of you and the dread of you upon all the land that ye shall tread upon, as he hath said unto you. Behold, I set before you this day a blessing and a curse;

—Deuteronomy 11:22-25 Emphasis added

It is critical that believers see this truth. God wants you to be homeowners and to place your stake in the ground and possess the land.

Most people have no idea of the long-term effect of how and where they spend their money. When I say people are funding wickedness, I'm not suggesting they are knowingly making a contribution into wicked exploits. However, if they followed the flow of their cash, they would see that in many cases their money has ended up in the hands of enterprises with evil intentions. We simply must become better stewards by researching where we spend our money. It is my prayer that this chapter is an eye-opening experience for you.

> Most people have no idea of the long-term effect of how and where they spend their money.

Paul warns us of the deceptive ability satan has to blind unsuspecting individuals from the truth.

In whom the god of this world hath blinded the minds of them which believe not, lest the light of the glorious gospel of Christ, who is the image of God, should shine unto them.

—2 Corinthians 4:4

The Tale of Two Men

On my journey to create wealth, I have learned that money is power. In the hands of good people, it has the potential to influence the world for good. However, in the hands of the corrupt, it has equal potential to spawn corruption.

Consider a tale of two men. The first, Hugh Hefner, is viewed by many as a cultural icon. He is extremely wealthy and uses that wealth to propagate magazines, web sites, videos and pornographic literature contributing to the demise of healthy cultures. By opening the door to "packaged lust," he became the pioneer of the porn industry. How many little boys had their eyes opened to the world of porn through the graphic sexual images in the pages of an old *Playboy* magazine? Statistics indicate a direct correlation between sex offenders and the use of pornography. Money generated by Hefner's enterprises ends up perpetuating corruption in societies around the world.

The second is Bill Gates, founder of Microsoft and one of the richest men in the world. Gates has come to the realization that the wealth he has amassed gives him the power to positively affect the world around him. Though he does not profess to be a Christian, he is using his financial resources to make a significant change in the lives of children suffering with AIDS. He recognizes what King Solomon said thousands of years ago, *money influences everything*. (Ecclesiastes 10:19)

In both cases, money became a vehicle for change. One is changing the world for the better; the other is making it much worse. The book of Proverbs informs us:

> Whoso causeth the righteous to go astray in an evil way, he shall fall himself into his own pit: but the upright shall have good things in possession.
>
> —Proverbs 28:10

There is a satanic agenda to demoralize humanity and corrupt every good thing. The hand of satan can be seen throughout history. He is the father of wickedness and is behind every evil device designed to fund the destruction of mankind.

In the twenty-first century, satan is having an easier time than ever corrupting good morals and righteous standards. He is profiting greatly from each and every human failure. However, the Bible speaks of a future day of reckoning for those who propagate and benefit from wicked endeavors.

> Rest in the LORD, and wait patiently for him: fret not thyself because of him who prospereth in his way, because of the man who **bringeth wicked devices to pass**.
>
> —Psalm 37:7 Emphasis added

2. The Church Is Too Intimidated to Wield the Power of Wealth

The Church in the twenty-first century needs to have answers for this life as well as answers for eternal life. If it fails to educate its people on prosperity and stewardship, it will allow an open door for false and secular teachings.

I recently had an uncanny experience while on my way to a national wealth-building conference as the keynote speaker. I decided to pick up a magazine at the airport newsstand to read on the long trip. I could not believe my eyes when I saw the September 2006 issue of *Time* magazine, which had as its cover story *"Does God Want You to be Rich?"* The issue displayed a picture of a Rolls Royce on the cover with a cross as the hood ornament. Please note that Time is one of the most liberal magazines in the country. The article quoted Bible verses and declared that Christians should follow the instructions of Jesus and "lay not up for themselves treasures on earth."

Notice the topic of concern, "Wealthy Christians." We see no articles in *Time* about the attack on family values or the redefining of the family unit and long-term effect it will have on our civilization. We see no articles on the blatant Hollywood attack on the deity of Christ or on the mockery of Jesus in cartoons, art or other materials on state college campuses. Yet, *Time* is concerned about Christians who believe God wants them to be rich. Understand what I am saying. I have worked with government agencies for many years. Right now, our government is making strategic moves to track and infiltrate terrorist cells. Yet, in leftist circles, there is a belief that there is *nothing* more dangerous to their way of life than believers with wealth. *Time, The Washington Post,* and other liberal media outlets are more terrified by wealthy Christians than Islamic Extremists. This exact belief was expressed by Rosie O'Donnell on ABC's "The View."

There is a satanic agenda to demoralize humanity and corrupt every good thing.

Time is peddling and propagating that old *"poor church"* message. They understand that *money is power*, and along with other secular progressives are attempting to ensure that Christians remain silent and powerless.

Who appointed *Time* magazine as the doctrinal police of the Church? Notice how the gate of media is used to weaken and strip believers of their God-given promises and God-ordained position.

It takes money to reach the lost, preach the Gospel, print resources, and support missions. The Church must have financial power to provide answers to the social calamities of our day. **How can we transform communities and impact cultures without resources?**

3. There Is a Shortage of Churches Engaging the Enemy

Years ago, when I began teaching these financial principles, it was *not* in congregational settings. Rather, it was in closed meetings and summits with pastors and national leaders from all over the United States and in various parts of the world. After hearing the principles I shared taught by many of those leaders within their messages, newsletters, and written materials, I decided, with the encouragement of my spiritual mentors, to write this book.

I have wrestled with being *pigeonholed* as a *prosperity teacher*. I believe this is why God orchestrated my second book **"Seven Women Shall Take Hold of One Man,"** to be published first.

I wrote *"Seven Women"* out of concern and travail over the Church and our nation. Our plight has become a wake-up call, an alarm for the twenty-first century Church in need of reformation, restoration, and revival. The book's title comes from a prophecy given by the Prophet Isaiah, who vividly describes the present-day condition of the Church and our current culture. He also shares God's plan of provision, protection, and revival. In that book, I ask a question I have wrestled with for many years: *"Where will the Church be in five to ten years, and what will our communities look like?"*

That question still runs through every financial seminar, business meeting and conference I teach. The fact is, a war is waging in our culture, which started in the Garden of Eden. Adam's failure to subdue the garden allowed humanism and secularism to be birthed in the earth. However, this is the greatest hour of the Church. It must engage and impact our present culture.

The Battle Between Good and Evil

The Bible is an accurate legal record of the affairs of Heaven and Earth. It gives eyewitness accounts of the battle between good and evil, Heaven and Hell. This battle has been raging throughout history. At times, evil has prevailed, yet, not by strength, wisdom, or consensus, but by default. The great statesman, Edmund Burke, challenged the people of his day to fight against the rise of evil and said, *"All that is necessary for the triumph of evil is that good men do nothing."*[1]

I have watched everyone come out of the "closet" except the Church. I am a Christian and not ashamed of it! Wickedness is prospering because the righteous are allowing it. This is one of those times in history that evil is triumphant because good men sit back and do nothing. This is not mere opinion. Statistics prove the majority of Americans favor Judeo-Christian values, prayer in school, bans on abortion, protection of family values and oppose gay marriage. How, then, can these values be stripped from the majority? It is because the Church is MIA (Missing In Action) in this battle.

Powerless at the Gates

Sad to say, but much of the Church and Christians generally have failed to advance the Kingdom of God. In this absence of light, the kingdom of Satan has pressed forward, redefining the family unit, and advancing the homosexual agenda. Since prayer has been removed from public schools, they have become one of the four most dangerous places for America's youth. God has been kicked out of the courtrooms and locked out of the Supreme Court.

How, then, can the Church begin to change the tide and engage the culture? The answer is found in the Book of Genesis, where God gives Abraham a multi-generational promise. It reads:

> That in blessing I will bless thee, and in multiplying I will multiply thy seed as the stars of the heaven, and as the sand which is upon the seashore; **and thy seed shall possess the gate of his enemies;** And in thy seed shall all the nations of the earth be blessed; because thou hast obeyed my voice.
>
> —Genesis 22:17-18 Emphasis added

This blessing secures the ongoing proliferation of the righteous seed and the power for each of its emerging generations to capture the "gates of his enemies." God declared that the cultural compass of a nation, city, or community lies at the gates. What then, are these gates referring to? They are the seats, or places of authority that have the greatest influence or shape the philosophies, ideologies, and beliefs within a people — *"The Mind Molders!"* I am not speaking of low-level authorities, rather those who impact the mass population. History records that these gates are so strategic that during wars they are targeted first by militaries. Possessing the enemy's gates ensured victory.

There are seven strategic gates that shape the culture of every nation. I plan to pen a comprehensive book on these seven gates some time in the future. Since this topic is so exhaustive, I must limit the content in this book.

Mountains & Gates

God instructed Abraham about possessing gates, not mountains.

At first glance you might not think this is important, but if not interpreted correctly you will miss the significant differences of these symbols. Historically, mountains always symbolized places of enlightenment, discourse, and revelation. Greek philosophers such as Socrates, Plato, and Aristotle, established mountaintop enlightenment centers for the purpose promoting Greece's rigorous systems of logical deduction and education. Jesus gave His famous sermon "The Olivet Discourse" from the Mount of Olives.

When God communicated His commandments to the people of Israel, He brought Moses to the mountaintop to receive them. Many religious and spiritual pilgrimages entail the scaling of mountaintops for clarity and revelation.

Jesus regularly communed with God on the mountain, but did his ministry in the gates. He confronted religious and political leaders in the places that held the greatest opportunity to influence others and produce social change.

> All the gifts that we receive in our times of intimacy with God are given with the intent that we might possess and rule in the gates.

All the gifts, anointing, revelations, dreams, visions, prophecies that we receive in our times of intimacy with God are given with the intent that we might possess and rule in the gates.

The weight of scripture is specific about possessing the gates. Sadly, in recent years the church has failed to use their mountaintop experiences to then take dominion in the gates of societal influence.

Instead, the church has tried to transform our cities with our speech and messages, instead of using the authority and wisdom of God to produce change in the gates. God is revealing to Israel that they would not always have a dominant mountain voice in the centuries to come. It was important for Abraham not to mistake his communion with God for dominion in society. Dominion, survival, prosperity, and success are achieved by possessing the gates of a society.

Today, this principle is still practiced by Jews worldwide. History records that for over three thousand years the Jewish people have positioned themselves to occupy the gates of societies wherever they have sojourned.

A Vivid Picture

Jesus paints a vivid picture of the end-time Church by referencing the story of Lot. He says that as the days of Lot were, so shall it be at the Second Coming of Christ. Possibly our day!

> *Likewise also as it was in the days of Lot;* they did eat, they drank, they bought, they sold, they planted, they builded; But the same day that Lot went out of Sodom it rained fire and brimstone from heaven, and destroyed them all. Even thus shall it be in the day when the **Son of Man is revealed.** In that day, he which shall be upon the housetop, and his stuff in the house, let him not come down to take it away: and he that is in the field, let him likewise not return back. Remember Lot's wife.
>
> —Luke 17:28 Emphasis added

A careful look at the story in Genesis will show that Lot stood in the gate of Sodom, which was the seat of authority.

> And there came two angels to Sodom at even; and **Lot sat in the gate of Sodom:** and Lot seeing them rose up to meet them; and he bowed himself with his face toward the ground; (Jesus stated that the days of Lot would be similar to that of the last days.)
>
> —Genesis 19:1 Emphasis added

Although Lot ruled in the gate, he became so secularized that his leadership was powerless and ineffective. His failure in the gates eventually led to the demise of his own family. Many lessons can be learned from the story of Lot.

To advance the Kingdom of God, the Church must recapture the gates of influence within our society. The Church must use the power of God and all of the Kingdom's resources to occupy every gate of influence.

As Martin Luther King Jr. said,

> *"To ignore evil is to become an accomplice to it."*

The Gates in Bible Times

In Scripture, gates symbolize the cultural compass of a nation, city or community. Gates are the positions of authority that shape the worldview, philosophies, ideologies, and beliefs of the people in a given society. The challenge now is for the Church is to reclaim those seats that have slipped through our fingers. Gates are woven all throughout the Bible. Here are six examples:

1. **In the Scripture, gates symbolize that place where important people, such as nobility, elders, and town fathers, *people spent their leisure, conducted business, and executed justice.***

   Now the two angels came to Sodom in the evening as Lot was **sitting in the gate of Sodom.** When Lot saw them, he rose to meet them and bowed down with his face to the ground.

   —Gen 19:1 Emphasis added NASB

2. **The Bible depicts the gates as the place for a culture's worship. What is worshipped by the masses in the gates of contemporary culture?**

   The priest of Zeus, whose temple was just outside the city, brought oxen and garlands to the **gates**, and wanted to offer sacrifice with the crowds.

   —Acts 14:13 NASB Emphasis added

3. **The gates, as symbolized in Scripture, comprise the place where the values of a culture are propagated.**

   And all the people gathered as one man at the square which was in front of the **Water Gate,** and they asked Ezra the scribe to bring the book of the law of Moses which the LORD had given to Israel. Then Ezra the priest brought the law before the assembly of men, women and all who could listen with understanding, on the first day of the seventh month. He read from it before the square which was in front of the Water Gate from early morning until midday, in the presence of men and women, those who could understand; and all the people were attentive to the book of the law.

—Nehemiah 8:1-3 NASB Emphasis added

4. Gates represented the judicial practices of a nation.

If a man have a stubborn and rebellious son, which will not obey the voice of his father, or the voice of his mother, and that, when they have chastened him, will not hearken unto them: Then shall his father and his mother lay hold on him, and bring him out unto the **elders of his city, and unto the gate of his place.**

—Deuteronomy 21:18-19 NASB

5. Gates are places where the masses can be reached.

Wisdom crieth without; she uttereth her voice in the streets: She crieth in the chief place of concourse, in the **openings of the gates:** in the city she uttereth her words...

—Proverbs 1: 20-21 Emphasis added

6. Gates are where kings sometimes placed their thrones.

And the king of Israel and Jehoshaphat the king of Judah sat each on his throne, having put on their robes, in a void place **in the entrance of the gate** of Samaria; and all the prophets prophesied before them.

—1 Kings 22:10 Emphasis added

Those who occupy the gates of a nation determine the national and cultural consensus regarding belief and worldview of the society during their period of ascendancy. There are four specific groups who occupy the seven strategic gates in contemporary western nations and are regarded as the *Establishment.* They are:

1. The Entertainment Establishment

2. The Information Establishment (News outlets including publications, media, Internet)

3. The Academic Establishment

4. The Political Establishment

The Seven Gates of Societal Influence

1. The Gate of Counsel

The "gate of counsel" provides direction, emotional health and spiritual healing for such things as dating, marriage, parenting, conflict, forgiveness, spirituality, religion, business, mentorship, physical health, and psychological wholeness. Counsel has been taken from the safety of privacy and confidentiality and has become a spectacle on national television. Shows like "Jerry Springer" have polluted the airways. Under the banner of "Reality TV," anything goes. Today, less people are turning to the Church for counsel and direction. Rather, they have become dependent upon programs like Oprah and Dr. Phil. In fact, many churches no longer provide counseling for their congregations for fear of being sued.

There was a time the Church possessed this gate, and politicians, corporate executives, business owners, and community residents turned to the Church for counsel and direction for the affairs of life. The Bible teaches that the health and security of a nation and its people rely on godly counsel.

> *Counsel* is mine, and sound wisdom: I am understanding;
> I have strength.
>
> —Proverbs 8:14 Emphasis added

> Where no *counsel* is, the people fall: but in the multitude of counselors, there is safety.
>
> —Proverbs 11:14 Emphasis added

The New International Version states it more clearly.

> For lack of guidance a nation falls, but many advisers make victory sure.
>
> —Proverbs 11:14 (NIV)

2. The Gate of Judicial And Moral Law

Apparently, God has been banned from the courtroom. We live in a culture quickly abandoning absolutes and replacing them with the leftist philosophy of moral relativism, which has made great inroads into the judicial system. Today our courts are implementing what I call, **"judicial evolution,"** the belief that law should evolve with the current trends of a society. This philosophy has become a riptide supported by liberal judges.

"Judicial Evolution" has crept into Church leadership.

Instead of restraining such behavior, the courts through their rulings are encouraging such conduct. So then, if moral decay intensifies within a society, the courts must set rulings that restrain such behavior. The courts were designed to set social boundaries to withstand cultural immorality.

Without question, our entire legal system was built upon Judeo-Christian principles. The founding fathers looked to the Bible as a guide for creating and establishing the laws of the land. The use of the Bible in American jurisprudence should not be underestimated. In structuring a society to secure the greatest liberty and promote the greatest happiness, the Bible was viewed not only as relevant, but also as authoritative guidance. The overwhelming evidence of this truth would warrant its own book.

The "gate of law" once was under the direction of God. If the Church does not implement a strategy to recapture this gate, it may end up losing its right to assemble and to preach the uncompromising Word of God.

> When the righteous are in **authority,** the people rejoice:
> but when the **wicked beareth rule,** the people mourn.
>
> —Proverbs 29:2 Emphasis added

This "judicial evolution" has also crept into Church leadership. There's a growing number of national leaders who have publicly stated that they will not preach on sin or its effects. They do not believe it is their responsibility to teach people about right and wrong. This is a dangerous shift. Every minister has a responsibility to God first, and then to the people to instruct about right and wrong, good and evil. Failing to do so may cause the "gate of moral law" within the Church to be captured by public opinion and "evolving" views. The prophet Ezekiel warned the leadership of his day, saying:

> And they shall teach my people the difference between the holy and profane, and cause them to discern between the unclean and the clean.
>
> —Ezekiel 44:23

3. The Gate of Social Services

God places a church in a community to evangelize and serve its residents. Jesus gave specific instruction to His followers to extend an outstretched hand to those in need. In numerous verses of Scripture, He created the framework for compassionate humanitarian ministry (Matthew 25:35-40, James 1:27). Some of the social services listed in the Bible include feeding the hungry, caring for the sick, clothing the naked, and ministry to the imprisoned. Throughout history, Christians have pioneered humanitarian organizations like hospitals, orphanages, adoption centers, shelters, treatment centers, food banks, and water projects.

In recent years, however, we have experienced a reverse trend. Much of the Church is becoming dependent on the state for its needs. Less than 7% of churches in America have an arm of compassion within their organization. That means many churches have abandoned the mandate of Jesus and, as a result, are losing their testimony within their communities. Residents no longer see the good works of Christ radiating from the church. Instead, they only hear continuous requests for their money.

Actually, statistics prove the government is ill-equipped to effectively carry out social services. This was clearly shown in the aftermath of Hurricane Katrina. It was Christian compassion ministries that were on the scene as first responders. Within a week, FEMA was relying completely on these ministries to organize, manage, and distribute goods and services to the victims in New Orleans. As the government lifted its assistance, compassion ministries increased their presence to help rebuild every facet of that community.

Currently, there are compassion outreaches that far outperform the efforts of our Government. Yet, because the church has lost control of this gate, compassion and social service ministries are often underfunded and understaffed. Their effectiveness is limited due to fiscal restraints. Often they are forced to alter their techniques and philosophies in order to qualify for state or federal funding.

Compassion Ministry distinguishes Christianity from every other religion.

The wholistic approach to healing pioneered by Jesus will always produce better results then any other method. Compassion ministry is what distinguishes Christianity from every other religion. Throughout history, wherever the Gospel has been preached, the quality of life in that place has improved.

There are three areas of life that are improved by the preaching of the Gospel — Personal Life, Social Life, and Spiritual Life.

Life Outreach International is an organization that digs water wells for communities in Africa for that lack clean water. This is an example of a compassion ministry that is saving thousands of lives and improving the quality of life for hundreds of thousands of families.[2]

Jesus gave the "gate of social services" to the Church, and we must continue to activate this gift. It is compassion ministry that distinguishes Christianity from every other religion.

> Let your light so shine before men, that they may see your good works, and glorify your Father which is in heaven.
>
> —Matthew 5:16

4. The Gate of Education

"Education is simply the soul of a society as it passes from one generation to another," said Gilbert K. Chesterton.[3] *"The church must teach or die"* is an old adage that reminds us that the Christian faith may always be only one generation away from extinction. In its ministry of education, a congregation is able to fulfill its scriptural commission to teach people in this generation the beliefs, traditions, faith, and lifestyles of the Christian community (Matthew 28:19-20).

For over three hundred years, the Church led this nation in education. This has been a major component of its overall success and prosperity. When prayer was removed from the public schools our educational system began to move from the top of the world report card, to the bottom.

The destruction or success of a nation can be found in its educational system. Today, there is a silent war being waged over the minds of the emerging generation.

Aristotle once said, *"All who have meditated on the art of governing mankind have been convinced that the fate of empires depends on the education of youth."*

Finance plays a vital role in the quality and direction of education. How important is education to national security and survival? A recent news article reported "Billions Spent by Saudi Royal Family to Spread Islam to Every Corner of the Earth."

> The destruction or success of a nation can be found in its educational system.
>
> ⸺ ❦ ⸺

The March 1, 2002, edition of the Saudi government English weekly *Ain Al-Yaqeen* extensively detailed the Saudi royal family's efforts to spread (Wahabi) Islam throughout the world. Recently, Harvard and Georgetown Universities each received $20 million from a member of the Saudi Royal Family, Prince Alwaleed bin Talal, the richest man in the Muslim world. The prince's motive? To establish strong seats in prominent American universities to help advance an Islamic agenda through education.

It is no coincidence that Islam is the fastest growing religion on college campuses. Meanwhile, Christian schools are closing more rapidly than they are opening, and liberal professors outnumber conservatives by an alarming ratio.

> Today's educational establishment increasingly seeks to marginalize or silence the parental voice.

The implementation of strong Christian education can only be accomplished through biblically-based curricula and church-governed schools. The Mandate of Psalm 78, clearly teaches that the primary responsibility for education rests on parents. However, today's educational establishment increasingly seeks to marginalize or silence the parental voice.

The core focus of education is our historical experience and our interaction with God in the course of that experience, but today's academic elites actually foster hatred for this aspect of our nation's history and seek its revision.

The education of children should also encompass God's laws, principles, and boundaries for wholesome living.

Clearly, the Church has lost its grip on the "gate of education" in America. The consequences of this have yet to be fully realized. *Most importantly, strategies of wealth creation and distribution must be developed to assist Christian schools to survive and thrive.*

5. The Gate of Government

William Patterson wrote, "Religion and morality . . . are necessary to good government, good order, and good laws." A simple glance at history informs us that a corrupt government can have devastating effects upon its people. Hitler, Stalin, and Saddam Hussein are prime examples of abusive government at work.

As a pastor, I'm bombarded by statements insisting upon the separation of church and state. They're almost always used by secular progressives, corrupt politicians, humanists, and atheists attempting to forbid any church influence in politics. For many years, pastors and congregations seemed hesitant to actively participate in politics until the 2000 election, when a grass roots conservative movement flocked to the polls.

The Truth About the First Amendment

There has emerged a serious distortion of the First Amendment to the Constitution in the evolving secularism that drives political correctness in America. This distortion regards the so-called *"separation of church and state."*

Here is what the First Amendment says:

> Congress shall make no law respecting an establishment of religion, or prohibiting the free exercise thereof; or abridging the freedom of speech, or of the press; or the right of the people peaceably to assemble, and to petition the government for a redress of grievances.

The Amendment is designed to protect the Church from the encroachment of government, as well as to protect the nation from a state-sponsored church, such as that the Pilgrims had fled in coming to America.

The term "separation of church and state" does not appear in the U.S. Constitution, but is based on a letter written by Thomas Jefferson to a church group seeking clarification about the relationship between church and government.

Modern political correctness, however, has twisted the Amendment's meaning to imply that the Church has little or no place in the public square.

Constitutional expert Hamilton A. Long says, *"The fundamental principle underlying the traditional American philosophy is that the Spiritual is supreme."*

> The term "separation of church and state" does not appear in the U.S. Constitution.

This is the fundamental presupposition of our constitutional system:

" ... all men are created ... Endowed by their Creator ..."

John Quincy Adams, Secretary of State, in a speech celebrating July 4, 1821, stated:

> "From the day of the Declaration ... They (the American people) were bound by the laws of God, which they nearly all, acknowledged as their rules of conduct."

Examining the Effects of Other Worldviews

We are sovereignly blessed of God in the fact that our founders placed the spiritual at the headwaters of our constitutional system, and specifically the spiritual as revealed in the Bible, otherwise this would have been a far different country.

Non-biblical views of mankind have profound impact regarding the relationship of the individual to the state, and ultimately lead to the following inadequate views of government:

Under Utilitarianism, the state decides what happiness is and what people must do to contribute to it.

"The greatest happiness for the greatest number"—Jeremy Bentham

Example: The humanist presupposition about education is that the child is the future survival of the state; therefore, the state can dictate how, where and when a child must be educated.

Imagine what our country might have looked like had our founders embraced the worldviews of Hinduism, Buddhism, Islam, or Animism:

Under Hinduism, there would have been no understanding of the concept that all people are "created equal." This is because in Hinduism, there are four castes, predetermined by one's birth.

Under Buddhism, there would have been no concept of unalienable rights, because there is no deity who grants the rights.

Under Islam, there would have been no 1st Amendment, guaranteeing freedom of religion and expression, because there is no separation between the law system and the organized religious system. Therefore, to be a member of the nation in the fullest sense, one would have had to be a member of the religious system (this is an issue Islam struggles with now).

Under Animism (New Age), there would have been no just law, since everyone and everything is god, and all law is relative.

Shaping America

This fundamental presupposition had profound impact on the shape of America in three areas:

First is the understanding of the citizen, the human being as one who is: *Created in the Image of God, and Endowed with unalienable rights from God that the state therefore cannot take away.*

Second, the understanding of the nature of law. Third, the understanding of the nature of government, especially in the application of law. Government exists to preserve the unalienable liberties. Government is to serve human beings, not human beings the government.

The American founders/framers believed that the spiritual is supreme. How did they arrive at this notion? From the Biblical Roots to which the founders had been exposed:

> For the kingdom is the Lord's, And He rules over the nations.
>
> —Psalm 22:28

> Blessed is the nation whose God is the Lord.
>
> —Psalm 33:12

> And He changes the times and the seasons; He removes kings and raises up kings …
>
> —Daniel 2:21

Righteousness must keep its grip on the gate of government so that the people may dwell in safety, peace, and prosperity.

> When the righteous are in **authority**, the people rejoice: but when the **wicked beareth rule,** the people mourn.
>
> —Proverbs 29:2 Emphasis added

I encourages congregations across the world to get involved in the political process and help nominate Kingdom minded candidates to office.

6. The Gate of Finance

This book is a comprehensive look at the topics of wealth and finance. Its purpose is not to build the riches of an individual, but to instill the worldview necessary for the expansion and proliferation of the Kingdom of God throughout the earth, using wealth as means.

> But thou shalt remember the LORD thy God: for it is He that giveth thee power to get wealth, that He may establish his covenant which He swore unto thy fathers, as it is this day.
>
> —Deuteronomy 8:18

Believers need to be on the forefront of economic change.

We can now clearly see the underlying flaws that existed in America's financial leadership. The economic crisis of 2008–2009 was the result of failed leadership in the gate of finance. America has been deceived by a financial establishment that has violated and abandoned the code of ethics and moral boundaries set forth in scripture.

A healthy economic structure must promote and require fiscal responsibility and proper stewardship over the wealth involved.

We are witnessing capitalism without Supreme Governance, and the result has been scandal and economic ruin.

This book and accompanying college course is designed for Christians to learn and activate the scriptural principles and laws that govern wealth, in order to lead in the gate of finance. Believers need to be on the forefront of economic change.

7. The Gate of Media, Arts and Entertainment

The power of mass media is a recognized force in turning the public eye. In the current cultural war, media is being used to propagate an immoral agenda. It is through the gate of media and entertainment that the minds and perceptions of an entire population are being shaped.

Propaganda vs Facts

Every culture is shaped by the consensus agreed to and propagated by its Establishment elite (mentioned earlier). This consensus becomes the propaganda that saturates the minds of people in the culture.

To understand propaganda and the role it plays in cultural formation, we must understand what propaganda is:

> **Propaganda** is an attempt to influence or form public opinion, and will distort misrepresent and conceal facts to accomplish its objective. Propaganda opposes objective truth. It utilizes the gate of media, arts, and entertainment, which are vital for the success of propaganda.

The worldview provided by the Bible is objective truth, resting on fact, which has been tested and proven true across many centuries.

German Nazi Party member Joseph Goebbels became Adolf Hitler's propaganda minister in 1933, which gave him power over all German radio, press, cinema, and theater. By exploiting mob emotions and pioneering methods of propaganda, Goebbels helped Hitler into power.

Based upon *Goebbels' Principles of Propaganda* by Leonard W. Doob, he lists Goebbels' nineteen propagandist tools that control public opinion. The list has become the *Holy Grail* for modern-day governments and political leaders throughout the world. Here are some of the tactics, which are employed by today's media and government officials.

> **Propaganda** must be planned and executed by only one authority. Propaganda must affect the enemy's policy and action. Declassified, operational information must be available to implement a propaganda campaign. To be perceived, propaganda must evoke the interest of an audience and must be transmitted through an *attention-getting* communications medium.

Propaganda opposes objective truth.

> **Propaganda** may be facilitated by leaders with prestige. Propaganda must be *carefully timed*. Propaganda must label events and people with distinctive *phrases or slogans*.

Propaganda to the home front must create an optimum *anxiety* level. Propaganda to the home front must diminish the impact of frustration. Propaganda must facilitate the displacement of *aggression* by specifying the *targets for hatred.*

As you read this list in light of the 2008 election, you can see the propaganda of both political parties and the media. Most of these tactics were exploited just on Sarah Palin in an attempt to discredit her record and achievements.

To resist propaganda, people must have two things: First, the ability to recognize propaganda as propaganda, not objective truth. Second, the ability to refute propaganda with truth.

We see these propagandist devices in Daniel's experience centuries ago in Babylon: The Chaldeans were the protectors and propagators of the consensus that formed Babylonian culture. (Daniel 1:1-5)

Idol Makers

This gate is not neutral when it comes to religion. For example, while there are few films attacking the foundations of Islam, Buddhism, Hinduism, or other religions, many do specifically target Christianity.

Believers need to be on the forefront of economic change.

Through literature, music, television and movies, like "The Da Vinci Code," the core beliefs of the Christian faith are under constant attack, both subtly and blatantly. The rising popularity of books on the occult, New Age thought and Atheism have also singled out Christianity as their main enemy. The so-called "New Atheists," like Richard Dawkins, Christopher Hitchens, and Eckhart Tolle, have sold millions of books in which they attack any resemblance to faith in God as idiocy and delusion.

Using the portals of our senses, media has access to the soul of an individual and the soul of a people.

It has been said, *"Give me the music of a generation, and I will possess it."*

During the Vietnam War, printing presses were parachuted in so that soldiers would be able to print liberating materials and distribute them throughout the country. The power of mass media was a recognized force in turning the public eye. In the current cultural war, media is being used to propagate an immoral agenda. It is through the gate of media and entertainment that the minds and perceptions of an entire population are being shaped. Music and music videos, TV, movies, magazines, and the Internet are flooded with foul language, sexual promiscuity, and crime.

Though in the last few decades the "gate of media" has been dominated by the forces of hell, this may be the greatest hour for the emerging generation within the Church to rise up and reclaim this gate. For example, the films "Facing the Giants" and "Fireproof" are great family films that were written, produced, and directed by brothers Alex and Stephen Kendrick, with their local church community.[4] This same community has made film production its focus of evangelistic ministry and is now impacting hundreds with their films.

I encourage young people and churches to activate their gifts and let God use them to impact this nation through the "gate of media, arts, and entertainment.

CHAPTER EIGHT

God & Prosperity

God and prosperity have become a topic of constant debate. The camps are so divided that most believers are forced to pick a side. If you believe that God desires you to be prosperous, then you are categorized within the *"prosperity group."* On the other hand, if you take the position that prosperity is a hindrance to spirituality, then you will adhere to what I refer to as the *"eternity group,"* a position birthed during the Puritan movement where earthly prosperity and property were resisted to secure *eternal riches.* Both groups have collected countless Scriptures, biblical stories, and life experiences to cement their position.

Most readers are still trying to figure out which stance I take, hoping to use this book as ammunition against the other. I feel like the poor soldier who, during the American Civil War could not decide upon a side. So to solve the issue, he put on blue pants and a red top. He then marched out to the middle of the field, where both sides proceeded to shoot him. At the risk of being shot by both, I will state, I am of neither group.

I recently received an e-mail from a friend who is a well-known national minister, which I believe it sums up the debate. It read:

Dear John,

I read your book, "Seven Women Shall Take Hold of One Man," on the way home from New York's LaGuardia Airport. Thank you so very much for this gift (the book) and your kind words written on the front cover. It was a joy to read because you have eyes that see. You aren't just "picking the berries," you are, "taking off your shoes."

I'm trying my best to put together your excellent and prophetic writing in this book with the upcoming publication of your next book, "Rich Church Poor Church." As I pursued your five key concepts to creating wealth, I wondered how this Kingdom-proclaiming man can deal with this issue of wealth also.

Mind you, I have no idea how you tie these two together for I, in my limited experience, have found the reverse to be true. If one pursues the kingdom of heaven with a reckless abandon, as you do, it ordinarily does not lead to the creating of wealth but to its very opposite - the loss of all things.

You know, "...foxes have holes and birds have nests but the Son of Man has no place to lay his head..." I am teachable in this area John. You seem to have found a way that keeps you from the sin of the "seeker-friendly" mentality that prostrates Christianity to the lowest possible denominator to attract seekers and not disciples.

You preach hard! You write hard! You fear God and not man! Yet, you also have a message about wealth building in God's church. Show me brother!

In my experience, if a person remains open-minded with God and the Scriptures, he or she will be shown revelations and mysteries that others cannot see. The first step is to leave your ideologies, prejudices, and opinions at the door. That is exactly what you must do with this book. Do not fear, you can always pick them up again when you are finished reading.

Critics allege that the Bible is full of contradictions and that the tension between prosperity and poverty is an example. However, the Bible includes many such exampless, and an examination of the whole of Scripture shows they're not contradictory.

For instance, Paul, in Romans, emphatically declares that a believer is justified by faith, and faith alone.

> What shall we say then that Abraham our father, as pertaining to the flesh, hath found? For if Abraham were justified by works, he hath whereof to glory; but not before God. For what saith the scripture? Abraham believed God, and it was counted unto him for righteousness. Now to him that worketh is the reward not reckoned of grace, but of debt. But to him that worketh not, but believeth on him that justifieth the ungodly, ***his faith is counted for righteousness.***
>
> —Romans 4:1-5 Emphasis added

On the other hand, James puts forth another view. He states that faith without works is dead, also referring to Abraham to substantiate his position.

> What doth it profit, my brethren, though a man say he hath faith, and have not works? Can faith save him? If a brother or sister be naked, and destitute of daily food, and one of you say unto them, depart in peace, be ye warmed and filled; notwithstanding ye give them not those things which are needful to the body; what doth it profit? ***Even so faith, if it hath not works, is dead, being alone.*** Yea, a man may say, thou hast faith, and I have works: shew me thy faith without thy works, and I will shew thee my faith by my works. Thou believest that there is one God; thou doest well: the devils also believe, and tremble. But wilt thou know, O vain man, that

faith without works is dead? Was not Abraham our father *justified by works*, when he had offered Isaac his son upon the altar? Seest thou how *faith wrought with his works, and by works was faith made perfect?* And the scripture was fulfilled which saith, Abraham believed God, and it was imputed unto him for righteousness: and he was called the Friend of God. Ye see then how that by works a man is justified, and not by faith only. Likewise also was not Rahab the harlot justified by works, when she had received the messengers, and had sent them out another way? For as the body without the spirit is dead, so faith without works is dead also.

—James 2:21-26 Emphasis added

> The Church has suffered many splits and divisions due to scriptural interpretations.

Both apostles quote the same spiritual father and patriarch, Abraham, to argue their point. If I did not have the benefit of viewing both arguments simultaneously, I may be persuaded to pick a side.

Suppose you were in Rome listening to Paul's eloquent scriptural position about justification by faith alone, and not of works. You would conclude that salvation is by faith alone. It would also lower the importance of works in your spiritual journey. On the other hand, those listening to James, the half-brother of Jesus, would be persuaded that faith apart from works is dead. You would hold works equally important to faith, if not more.

Over time, these positions could segregate into separate streams and possibly form opposing denominations. Both would start Bible schools and teach their positions to ensuing generations. Students would learn to debate their position using such tools as hermeneutics and linguistics. Both groups would refer to Abraham, and both would have numerous scriptural texts to reinforce their position.

This scenario has been repeated throughout history. The Church has suffered many splits and divisions due to opposing interpretations of Scripture. God and prosperity are part of the current debate. So then, who is right — Paul the greatest apostle, or James the brother of Jesus? The reality is that both men saw clearly.

Paul gazed into eternity and declared that salvation and justification are acquired only through faith. A person cannot be saved through good works, but must put faith and trust in Jesus Christ and Him alone. Only then is an individual justified. Paul's eternal and spiritual perspective shows that God imputed righteousness to Abraham based upon his faith.

> True God-ward faith produces works that are clearly seen by those who walk among us.

James, however, looks at faith and justification from an earthly or natural perspective — which doesn't necessarily mean carnal or fleshly. Rather, these words constitute a reference to the natural or earthly realm. James recognizes that faith is invisible and difficult to detect within an individual. In his day, most believers declared they had tremendous faith. James instructs that faith towards God, which you cannot see will produce fruit which is visible to those on the earth.

Paul teaches faith from an upward, God-ward, or vertical viewpoint. James teaches faith from a man-ward or horizontal view. These two positions are not contrary to each other. They are not even two positions, but one truth viewed from two different angles. You may say they are two sides of the same coin. Paul declares that your works on the earth are not a substitute for faith in God. James states that true faith in Christ has a horizontal effect on the earth and can be clearly seen, felt, and touched by man. *"Show me your faith,"* James says. You cannot, his words imply, unless you show the works of faith.

So then, true spiritual God-ward faith produces works that are clearly seen by those who walk among us. Separate the lion's den from Daniel and you cannot prove that he was a man of faith. Show me a man's works, and I will tell you of his faith.

The same is true of Meshach, Shadrach, Abednego, David, Rahab, Esther, and a host of others. Faith in God feeds the poor, clothes the naked, and visits the sick and imprisoned. Hebrews 11 records the exploits (works) of the heroes of faith.

In the same way, prosperity must be reconciled with spirituality. They are not opposites, but two sides of the same coin. Both ideas have numerous Scriptures to support their position. Yet, they are connected. For too long, believers had to choose one or the other. Only by journeying to the top of the coin can we view both sides clearly.

Money is a hot topic in the Bible.

The subject of prosperity has never been more critical than it is at this moment in history. Consider the current battle over our culture, moral values, family makeup, religious freedoms, educational institutions and political landscape.

Jesus taught about money more than any other subject.

The reality of religious censorship is being echoed throughout our nation for the first time in American history. Could this be the stepping-stone to religious extinction in America?

There is no question that God wants you to prosper. There are kingdom plans in place for your success and prosperity. Incalculable resources are needed to advance the Kingdom of God.

The answer to why the wicked prosper is that they are under the influence of someone who desires the destruction of all that is righteous, moral, and godly. Heaven is not silent in this battle. God aims to advance righteousness, moral values, purity and life.

Show Me the Money!

Money is a hot topic in the Bible. Jesus taught about money more than any other subject. Sixteen of the thirty-eight parables pertain to handling money and possessions. In the Gospels, an amazing one out of ten verses (288 in all) deals directly with the subject of money. The Bible offers five hundred verses on prayer, less than five hundred verses on faith, but more than two thousand verses on money and possessions.

There is no shortage of Scriptures declaring God's pleasure in the prosperity of His people. In fact, the propagation of the Gospel requires a bountiful war chest. The psalmist said:

Blessed is the man that walketh not in the counsel of the ungodly, nor standeth in the way of sinners, nor sitteth in the seat of the scornful! But his delight is in the law of the LORD; and in his law doth he meditate day and night. And he shall be like a **tree planted by the rivers of water,** that bringeth forth his fruit in his season; his leaf also shall not wither; and **whatsoever he doeth shall prosper.**

—Psalm 1:1-3 Emphasis added

The reference to the righteous man being like a *"tree planted by the rivers of water,"* means that God will provide him a continual source of sustenance. As the tree benefits from its roots accessing fresh water, making it large, healthy, and strong, so does the individual who walks in the same way as this man. In addition, his fruit will not be delayed, but will come in season. His leaf (*goods*) will not wither, and whatsoever he does shall prosper.

It took me many years to understand and accept that God takes *"pleasure"* in the prosperity of His servants. I have two young boys at home. When they are obedient and do the right things by their own initiative, I want to go out of my way to bless them. In addition, I desire for my sons to be prosperous in life. My wife and I continually make sacrifices in order to advance and secure their success. Once, the Lord spoke with me about this exact issue, and said, *"I, too, desire the prosperity of my sons and daughters."* That same day I read Psalm 35 in my personal devotional time. Verse 27 leaped off the page:

> The subject of prosperity has never been more critical than it is at this moment in history.

Let them shout for joy, and be glad, that favour my righteous cause: yea, let them say continually, Let the **LORD** be magnified, which hath **pleasure in the prosperity of his servant.**

—Psalm 35:27 Emphasis added

Jesus shared the same insight:

> Or what man is there of you, whom if his **son ask bread,** will he give him a stone? Or if he ask a fish, will he give him a serpent? If ye then, being evil, know how to give good gifts unto your children, **how much more** shall your Father which is in heaven give good things to them that ask him?
>
> —Matthew 7:9-11 Emphasis added

David reflects over his entire life and comes to this conclusion about prosperity:

> I have been young, and now am old; yet have I not seen the righteous **forsaken**, nor his **seed begging** bread. He is ever merciful, and lendeth; and his **seed is blessed**.
>
> —Psalm 37:25-26 Emphasis added

The Bible speaks of wealth and riches also:

> Praise ye the LORD. **Blessed** is the man that feareth the LORD, that delighteth greatly in his commandments. His seed shall be mighty upon earth: the generation of the upright shall be blessed. **Wealth and riches** shall be in **his house**: and his righteousness endureth forever.
>
> —Psalm 112:1-3 Emphasis added

David prayed for God to send provision and prosperity immediately:

> This is the day which the LORD hath made; we will rejoice and be glad in it. Save now, I beseech thee, **O LORD: O LORD**, I beseech thee, **send now prosperity.**
>
> —Psalm 118:24-25 Emphasis added

There is overwhelming proof that God desires you to be prosperous. However, if you believe that wealth and prosperity are a hindrance to your walk with God, I suggest you follow your convictions. This book is *NOT* an attempt to convince you otherwise. In fact, I believe wealth could be one of the most dangerous things an individual can contend with.

Paul warned that the love of money is the root of all evil *(1 Timothy 6:10)*. *"Love"* implies an obsession. The obsession of money is at the root of many of the most heinous crimes. From the poorest streets to the most affluent neighborhoods, countless people fall prey to the obsession of money.

Enron is an example of corporate millionaires needing just another million. This obsession caused them to risk family, career, company, clients and freedom — all for a little more money than they could have possibly spent. ***Money must never become an idol or obsession.***

Paul reveals a strategy for maintaining spirituality and prosperity.

Paul is not discouraging believers from active participation in wealth creation. In the same chapter of Timothy, he gives further instruction for those who are rich. He warns them on many levels to guard against social pride, arrogance, and greed. He gives them a strategy for maintaining spirituality and prosperity, saying:

> Charge them that are ***rich in this world,*** that they be not ***highminded***, nor trust in ***uncertain riches,*** but in the living God, who giveth us richly all things to enjoy; That they do good, that they be rich in good works, **ready to distribute** (wealth distribution), willing to communicate (generous); Laying up in store for themselves a good foundation against the time to come, that they may lay hold on eternal life.
>
> —1 Timothy 6:17-19 Emphasis added

To generate and maintain wealth, you must master money. If not, it may end up mastering you. We have been given authority to put all things under our feet. This includes greed, pride, haughtiness, anger, deceit, and many other such things. When it comes to wealth and riches, you must develop the attributes of humility, generosity, and meekness, which are the defenses to the things cited above that can destroy us. Paul stated,

"Everything is permissible for me" - but not everything is beneficial. "Everything is permissible for me" - ***but I will not be mastered by anything.***

—1 Corinthians 6:12 (NIV) Emphasis added

I do not mind going through trials, for there are lessons to be learned that cannot be acquired in any other fashion.

God desires His children to be blessed. Does that mean we will never experience trials, difficulty or pain in this life? This is one of the areas where I differ from those in the prosperity camp. I believe it rains upon the just and the unjust, and that life will throw us curves every now and then. Job stated, *"For the Lord giveth, and the Lord taketh away" (Job 1:21).*

The Apostle Paul said he experienced abundance and lack in life. Yet, through all these things God remains steadfast, consistent, and unshakeable. I do not mind going through trials and difficulty, for there are lessons to be learned in them that cannot be acquired in any other fashion. However, I also want to experience my seasons of blessings and prosperity as well. The seasons of harvest are designed to temper the seasons of lack.

Remember, God takes pleasure in your prosperity and success.

CHAPTER NINE

God, Judaism & Christianity

Some in the Christian community tag the subject of prosperity, wealth, and riches with negative connotations. That's why my aim is to present a fresh perspective on these topics. There's only one place to search for the history of economics and wealth creation, and that's the *history of the Jews*.

90% of global wealth is controlled by 3% of the population— that 3% is the Jewish people.

Clearly, the Jewish people have applied certain principles given by God that has produced continual success.

It's easier to establish the relationship between Judaism and Christianity than to debate prosperity and spirituality, because Judaism was the cradle of Christianity. Since I am not the first to connect the Church to its Jewish roots, let us take a glance from the plethora of Scriptures.

The Apostle Paul warns believers in Rome not to revile Judaism, as Christianity is connected to the same tree, *the Root of which is Jesus Christ Himself.* Both Judaism and Christianity share the same life-giving source. Paul describes the Church as a wild olive branch (*figurative of Gentiles*), and that they are given the opportunity to access the promises of God due to the temporary removal or blindness on the part of the Jews.

> For if the firstfruit be holy, the lump is also holy; and if the root be holy, so are the branches. And if some of the branches be broken off, and thou, being a wild olive tree, *wert graffed in among them*, and *with them partakest* of the *root* and fatness of the olive tree; *Boast not* against the branches. But if thou boast, thou bearest not the root, *but the root thee.* Thou wilt say then, The branches were broken off, that I might be *graffed in.* Well; because of unbelief they were broken off, and thou standest by faith. Be not high-minded, but fear; For if God spared not the natural branches (Jews), take heed lest He also spare not thee.
>
> —Romans 11:16-21 Emphasis added

Paul refers to this as a great mystery which Jews and Christians alike must come to understand. Simultaneously, he encourages believers to guard against arrogance, pride, and spiritual haughtiness.

> For I would not, brethren that ye should be *ignorant of this mystery,* lest ye should be wise in your own *conceits;* that blindness in part is happened to Israel, until the fullness of the Gentiles be come in.
>
> —Romans 11:25 Emphasis added

This is echoed throughout the New Testament. In Galatians, Jews who converted to Christianity tried to convince believers of the necessity to obey the Law of Moses and submit to the ritual of circumcision to perfect their faith. Paul argues that the covenant between God and Abraham is greater than the covenant between God and Moses. In addition, the Abrahamic covenant was made available to Jew and Gentile through faith in Jesus and not through obedience to the law. The Abrahamic covenant is superior because it is a spiritual covenant. These promises of God flow down through the spiritual seed of Abraham and not through the natural seed (*Jewish people*).

> That **the blessing of Abraham might come on the Gentiles through Jesus Christ;** that we might receive the promise of the Spirit through faith. Now to Abraham and his seed were the promises made. He saith not, And to seeds, as of many, but as of one, And to thy seed, which is Christ.
>
> —Galatians 3:14,16 Emphasis added

> For ye are all the children of God by faith in Christ Jesus. For as many of you as have been baptized into Christ have put on Christ. There is **neither Jew nor Greek,** there is neither bond nor free, there is neither male nor female: for ye are all one in Christ Jesus. **And if ye be Christ's, then are ye Abraham's seed, and heirs according to the promise.**
>
> —Galatians 3:26-29 Emphasis added

The Apostle Peter reveals that Christian women are the *"spiritual daughters"* of Sarah, the wife of Abraham.

> Even as Sara obeyed Abraham, calling him Lord, **whose daughters ye are,** as long as ye do well, and are not afraid with any amazement.
>
> —1 Peter 3:6 Emphasis added

Early in my walk with God, I became intrigued with Jewish history. I discovered that, without question, the biblical principles given to the Jews continue to be applicable for the believer today. Scripture after Scripture demonstrates the validity of applying the wisdom given by God to Israel. God provided Israel with patterns, principles, and strategies to elevate their power and influence amongst diverse nations.

> But thou shalt remember the LORD thy God, for it is He that giveth thee **power to get wealth,** that He may establish his covenant which He sware unto thy fathers, as it is this day.
>
> —Deuteronomy 8:18 Emphasis added

This scripture revolutionized my outlook on wealth, stewardship, and finance. Early on, I prayed for God to place riches in my hands. However, when I really understood this verse, I realized that God was not going to place a suitcase filled with money on my doorstep. Rather, He would give me the power (*capacity*) to create wealth.

> The biblical principles given to the Jews are applicable for believers today.

Unfortunately, people today are still looking for a quick fix for financial problems — waiting for the Publishers Clearing House van to arrive or to hit the heavenly lotto machine. However, Deuteronomy 8:18 declares clearly that God distributes the *power* (*capacity, means*) to become *wealth generators*. My father would always tell me, "*Give a man a fish, he eats for a day, teach a man to fish, he eats for life.*" I heard these words echoing in my ears as I discovered the meaning of this Scripture. God wants to teach you how to fish for finances.

The revelation of Deuteronomy 8:18 and my quest for financial independence led my research to the history of the Jews. As a believer and minister, I was well acquainted with the Old Testament. Yet, my study of the Old Testament Scriptures was through the lens of Christianity and the eyes of a Gentile.

You cannot be a serious student of the Bible without acknowledging the relationship between God and His beloved people — the Jews. At the age of twenty-three, during my first pastorate, I desired additional schooling. Unable to go away to Bible school due to my pastoral responsibilities I looked for other avenues. At that time, there were no correspondence courses available. Since my desired studies were in the areas of Jewish manners, customs, and history, I decided to look into available training from Jewish circles. This meant looking for Bible training from synagogues, Rabbinical schools, or from a willing Rabbi.

Finally, after numerous closed doors, I met a Rabbi of a local Synagogue who was sympathetic to my plight and desires, and he was willing to help. He had just finished his tour of duty as a military chaplain. His understanding of Christian beliefs, coupled with the fact that he debated Christian chaplains while in the military, created an intimidating environment for me. The Rabbi had an exceptional grasp of Christian doctrines, beliefs, theology, and history. Whenever possible, he would challenge my beliefs before the class by asking penetrating questions. He changed my name to Yanni, which is Jewish, and addressed me by it in class. I subjected myself to such an environment because it challenged me to know and understand what I believed to the point where I could debate, defend, and articulate my faith. In addition, the Rabbi had a burning desire to teach. I received more than I could have ever expected. He taught from the Torah, Talmud, Midrash[1] and many other Jewish sources with which I was unfamiliar. In learning about the customs, lifestyle, and beliefs of the Jews, I studied the Bible from a perspective I would not have learned from a strictly Christian education.

Jews and Prosperity

History shows that the Jewish people didn't always experience success, prosperity, and wealth. They've been dismantled as a nation, pillaged and robbed by the world, persecuted, killed, and trampled underfoot throughout Europe. They've suffered poverty and shame. The Jews were a people without a country for more than three thousand years. Yet, wherever they sojourned, they prospered and flourished. They possess a promise from God for success, influence, wealth, and riches.

Max I. Dimont, author, historian, and lecturer on Jewish history, chronicles over six thousand years of the Jewish people. He documents that for nineteen hundred years after Christ, Jews were invited to settle throughout Europe and reside as the middle-class. These European countries specifically desired the Jews to rebuild their economies, develop industry, open factories, and establish lending institutions.

Unfortunately, people today are still looking for a quick fix for financial problems.

The saga of Jewish success, innovation, persecution, and banishment are recorded within the pages of history.

From 500 A.D., Italy, France, and Germany invited the Jews to settle there. They were asked to found cities, create trade, and become the middle-class. During the 800's to 1100's, Jews organized merchant operations throughout Europe. In England, the Jews started money-lending activities and they became the bankers in all of Europe. They established the highest education standards. From 1100 to 1300, the

Crusades forced them to flee the Rhineland. Many soon settled in Poland and developed its economy.

Sadly, this was the time the first Talmud[3] burning. Jews were forcefully banished from England. They were persecuted throughout Europe from 1300 to 1500. Economically motivated persecutions began at this time. France, Spain, and Portugal banished the Jews. They then settled in the ghettos of Italy, Germany, Russia, Holland, and Central Europe. The Jews were dealt still more persecution from 1700 to 1800, intensified by the birth of psychological anti-Semitism.[4]

The amazing fact is that in every situation and climate, the *Jews flourished.* They started businesses, erected factories, and pioneered capitalism in foreign lands. They started in the ghettos, yet rose to the upper class in each nation. Sadly, once the Jews helped these nations prosper, they were asked to leave — many times by force.

Was this a coincidence? Were the Jews just lucky when it came to prosperity? I believe not. Once maybe, twice possibly, but four thousand years across several continents, under various civilizations, dealing with numerous economic conditions could not be viewed as coincidence. From Italy, France, and Germany to as far east as China, the Jews were able to succeed. I submit to you that the spiritual strength of Judaism within the lives of the Jewish people was the connection to the natural, social, and economic prosperity of the Jewish family no matter where they lived.

> The amazing fact is that in every situation and climate, the Jews flourished.

In every nation where the Jews resided, they rose to positions of influence and power in judicial systems, executive offices, and legislative branches of governments. Though the Jews were in the minority, they outmatched the majority because of their intelligence, industry, and spirituality. This was the result of a *series of innovative systems* the Jewish leaders created to ensure the perpetuation of the *Jewish way of life* while sojourning through the nations. These principles became the basis for the Talmud which was then used to govern Jewish communities everywhere in the world.

Four Foundational Practices of Jewish Culture

In the book "Jews, God, and History," Max I. Dimont, describes several concepts which have been essential to Jews around the world for centuries. From those concepts, I have identified the following four practices, which were foundational, not only for Jews, but also Christians in the early Church.

1. Universal Education

Jewish communities provided compulsory universal education, which made them literate.

Education, education, education — As community leaders we have a mandate to equip and educate the business sector as well as the congregation.

Included in this educational system was the area of finance. We see the quality of this education in the lives of Jews throughout the bible. Daniel, Shadrach, Meshach, Abednego were appointed to high positions in foreign nations because of their intellectual dexterity.

And the king spake unto Ashpenaz the master of his eunuchs, that he should bring certain of the children of Israel, and of the king's seed, and of the princes; Children in whom was no blemish, but well favoured, and *skilful in all wisdom, and cunning in knowledge, and understanding science*, and such as had ability in them to stand in the king's palace, and whom they might teach the learning and the tongue of the Chaldeans.

—Daniel 1:3-4 Emphasis added

Joseph displays a deep and broad based understanding of economics and commerce.

And *Joseph was the governor* over the land, and he it was that sold to all the people of the land .

—Genesis 42:6 Emphasis added

Let Pharaoh do this, and let him appoint officers over the land, and *take up the fifth part* of the land of Egypt in the seven plenteous years.

—Genesis 41:34 Emphasis added

And Pharaoh said unto Joseph, Forasmuch as God hath shewed thee all this, there is none so discreet and wise as thou art; *Thou shalt be over my house*, and according unto thy word shall all my people be ruled: only in the throne will I be greater than thou.

—Genesis 41:39-40 Emphasis added

Through the ministry of education, a congregation is able to fulfill the scriptural commission that we are to teach people in this generation the beliefs, traditions, faith, and lifestyles of the Christian community.

2. Worship of One Invisible God.

The Jews intellectual powers had been heightened because of their monotheism and their invisible God.

The Jews were surrounded by nations who believed that more gods meant more power. Conquering nations would acquire the gods of the nation conquered, simply adding them to their own worship.

It was common, even expected, that any given nation would have literally hundreds of tangible deities to call upon. It was in this cultural and spiritual atmosphere that Moses approached Pharaoh in the name of a single, invisible God — and was ridiculed.

By faith he [Moses] forsook Egypt, not fearing the wrath of the king: for he endured, as *seeing him who is invisible.*

—Hebrews 11:27 Emphasis added

However, their worship of an invisible God heightened their intellectual powers, allowing them to perceive things that no one else could. The Jews were uniquely equipped and trained by God to communicate and operate in the abstract and invisible realm.

God is looking to equip believers today in the same way, so that we do not need to place any trust in the gods of the culture around us: money, power, fame, etc. Our worldview and lifestyle must be impacted by the invisible realm of faith.

> Now faith is the substance of things hoped for, the evidence of things not seen.
>
> —Hebrews 11:1

The Bible declares that there are two different worlds coexisting at the same time — Visible and Invisible.

Unfortunately, most spend the majority of their time praying (*pleading*) to God about issues in the natural world. Invisible means unseen — not unreal. Invisible doesn't address your condition; it confronts your ability to perceive existence.

This invisible (*spiritual*) realm is actually more real than what we perceive and see. It is the parental world from which the visible world was created, birthed, or evolved.

Most spend the majority of their time praying to God about issues in the natural world.

> Through faith we understand that the worlds were framed by the word of God, ***so that things which are seen were not made of things which do appear.***
>
> —Hebrews 11:3 Emphasis added

WHEN YOU PRAY ABOUT A *visible* THING,
IT BEGINS IN THE *invisible* REALM.

When the Holy Ghost speaks to you (*stirs*) about something you have that you don't see yet – it's because in the invisible world it's yours. It's only a matter of time that it shows up in this realm.

Vision is the ability to see into the invisible realm, so that you can call forth those things God has given you.

3. Portable Tabernacle.

The Jews were not tied down to a specific place because of their "portable tabernacle". They could move with opportunity without giving up their unity.

For centuries they were called, "Opportunistic Jews." This refers to the practice of whole Jewish communities relocating to new geographical regions where they could capitalize on business and financial opportunities.

Hidden in the portable tabernacle was the idea that God is ever moving and would accompany and partner with the Jewish people wherever they lived.

What things are tying you down and hindering you from following God's destiny for your life? What opportunities have you missed because of an unwillingness to move?

For as many as are led by the Spirit of God, these are sons of God.

—Romans 8:14

4. Work Ethic

The Jews adhered to certain principles that governed their work ethic. These principles, contained in the Torah, regulated everything from the amount of time one should work, vacation and holiday time, health care, bonuses, and how conduct should be between employee and employer.

Six days shall work be done: but the seventh day is the sabbath of rest, an holy convocation; ye shall do no work therein: it is the sabbath of the LORD in all your dwellings.

—Lev. 23:3

The Jews considered the work itself as an investment and performed each task with dignity and excellence. By doing so, they outmatched their competitors in the top positions due to advantages in education, upbringing, and outlook.

The prevailing philosophies of the Gentile nations looked upon work as something reprehensible. These nations relied on immigrant workers to fill up their labor force. This was the practice from the pagan nations of Egypt through the Middle Ages. It was the slave ships of Africa which provided the workforce for early American agriculture. Currently, we have an increasing Mexican workforce employed to do the menial work that typical American citizens disdain.

There is an epidemic of believers on welfare.

Max Dimont states,

"When the Christians came to power, they had to enact laws prohibiting Jews from holding policy-making posts in order to avert the possibility of all-important jobs going to Jews by virtue of ability. It was only natural that success should earn its merited envy."[5]

If the Jews were going to survive as a people within a people, a nation within a nation, a state within a state, *and* provide self-discipline, they were going to need a creative and unparalleled social organizational system. According to Dimont, this is exactly what the Jewish leaders provided on several levels.

"Any time ten Jewish males over thirteen years of age lived within commuting distance; they have to establish a religious community." (*Minyan* in Hebrew)

He goes on to state:

"As soon as 120 males over thirteen years of age lived within commuting distance, they had the authority to establish a social community, including a court of their own to adjudicate those disputes among themselves that did not conflict with the laws of the nation within which they resided."

Notice it took 120 males to establish as social community with a court of their own. This number happens to be the exact amount documented in the upper room which established the community of Christianity.

This is not a coincidence considering numbers are very important to God and critical for proper biblical interpretation.

And in those days Peter stood up in the midst of the disciples, and said, (the number of names together were about an hundred and twenty,)

—Acts 1:15

In addition:

"Every community had to impose taxes upon itself in addition to those taxes demanded by the state. These taxes were to go toward making the Jew self-supportive so that at no time would there be any need to go to a pagan or Christian government for financial help. This money was used mainly for education and charity.

Every community was responsible for a school system, which had to provide universal education. This education was to be free to the fatherless, to orphans, and to all needy. It was compulsory for all boys, but it could not be denied to any girl who wanted to continue schooling beyond reading and writing. These laws specifically stated that teachers must make good salaries so as to make the profession attractive and honorable."

We see this example of Jewish education in the book of Esther, who was not just another pretty face. Based on her upbringing and education, Esther was a woman of wisdom, intellect, and knowledge. Unlike her competitors, she was a true conversationalist, communicating with depth and insight.

It is important to note that in this time period, women were not given the opportunity to receive an education. Jewish women were the brightest amongst the nations.

Her wisdom is seen in her maneuvers and strategy concerning Haman and his plot to destroy the Israelites. She also understood Parliament and with honor knew how to approach the King — her Husband.

In addressing compassion and charity, Dimont goes on to say;

No one could go hungry. Charity had to be provided with dignity to all needy and to anyone demanding it. No Jew must ever ask for charity from the state, only from his own Jewish community. From this date stems the Jewish custom of always taking care of its own needy. This is still a cardinal principle of Jew's all over the world.

Today, there is an epidemic of believers on welfare. They have become a burden to the state. There are ministers who prey upon welfare recipients looking to capitalize by selling them trinkets, miracles, and empty promises. We now have second and third generation children in America raised in welfare supported homes. Not only is this a detriment to the self-concept of the individual, it propagates feelings of uselessness within their homes. These practices are inconsistent with the principles laid out in the Word of God.

When I viewed these principles to which Jews all over the world have adhered for thousands of years, it challenged my philosophy and concept about success. It also questions about how the Church should operate within a community. Can you imagine what would happen if the Church in America began to function with these same principles?

Paul instructs the Church of Jesus Christ to apply the same rules that the Jewish leadership laid out for self-government and self-preservation. Take, for example, the practice of tithing. Because Jews understood the necessity for financial resources to remain independent, a self-imposed tax (*separate from the host nation's tax*) was placed upon them.

This type of giving was completely understood and never questioned. For this reason, Jews would never take a handout from the state. Even today, you will not find true Jews on welfare. To the Jews, the Talmudic principles provided the means for self-sufficiency.

These same Judaic principles are embedded within the teachings of Jesus and the writings of the apostles. The principles laid the foundation to which Christianity is built upon with Christ being the cornerstone (Ephesians 2:20). The Gospels and New Testament writings contain so many quotes and excerpts from Judaic sources that it would constitute a book of its own.7 Jesus, Paul, Peter, James, and John all gave instructions from Judaism such as taking care of the poor, hungry, destitute, and orphaned.

> Can you imagine what would happen if the Church in America began to function with these same principles?
>
>

The apostles must have been shocked at the practices of the Gentiles. Paul reprimands the Corinthian Church for not being able to self-govern and self-discipline its own affairs and disputes. Its members went outside the church to secular courts to handle legal matters involving church members.

Paul writes:

> If you have **legal disputes** about such matters, why do you go to **outside judges** who are not respected by the church? I am saying this to shame you. Isn't there anyone in all the church who is wise enough to decide these arguments? But instead, **one Christian sues another** — right in front of unbelievers!
>
> —1 Corinthians 6:4-6 (NLT) Emphasis added

As a former Pharisee and teacher of Jewish law, Paul was well acquainted with Talmudic principles. Apostle Paul, considered one of the most influential figures of his era, was known as the *"Pharisee of Pharisees."* Without doubt, he draws from the well of Judaic Biblical revelation and transfers it to Christian living. This is the marriage that produced the Judeo-Christian8 ethic, which became the basis for Western legal codes and moral values. This and many other Talmudic principles were brought into the Church through the Apostles. The Church has simply abandoned that wealth of wisdom in the 21st Century.

Two things are still true of the Jewish people today.

1. They take care of their own and never rely on the state or government.

2. You will never, never, NEVER hear Jews say they are to live in poverty — much less that their God does not desire them to have wealth and prosperity.

You will only hear that debate within Christianity. Only in churches will you find people arguing the difference between spirituality and prosperity — as though they cannot possibly coexist.

To the Jews, the natural offspring of spirituality is prosperity, success, wealth, and influence. *Shouldn't this promise apply to believers as well?*

CHAPTER TEN

God, Economics,
and Modern Capitalism

During my early quest for financial knowledge, the educational system produced only frustration. I believed the Bible to be the manual for stewardship and turned to the Church. Yet, no one talked about acquiring wealth for kingdom purposes. I only heard about giving. I thought, "What about receiving?" The Church is rich with theology, doctrine, and historical studies. However, the subject of acquiring, creating, and managing wealth is largely ignored. It's as if the faucet has been turned off when it comes to the topic of money.

My business background taught me the importance of systems, which are at the heart of productivity. Is the Bible just a book of wise sayings? Or is it a book of patterns, principles, strategies, and systems? I believe the latter to be true. Presently, economics is not part of church curriculum or education. Students graduate from Bible college having learned nothing about budgets, markets, cash flow, economics, interest rates, balance sheets, or banking. This must change if the Church is to be influential in the years to come. We have reached the point of needing a grass roots effort to educate the next generation of young believers, for they will inherit the failures and successes of this generation and shape the following culture.

It is naive to think that God takes pleasure in the humiliation and poverty of His people. The Scriptures declare that God expects fruit, productivity, multiplication, and prosperity from His servants. Adam was instructed to subdue, multiply, replenish, and take dominion over the earth. The "Parable of the Talents" teaches the importance of multiplication and profit. The word "talent" used by Jesus is a direct reference to finances. He rebukes the unjust servant for not putting the master's money in a bank where it would have at least earned minimal interest.

> It is naive to think that God takes pleasure in the humiliation and poverty of His people.

The Bible gives clear instruction for the accumulation of wealth. In the second part of this book, I lay out the "Twelve Biblical Laws of Wealth Creation." To me, the argument in churches about prosperity is nonsensical considering the Bible lays down the foundation for present-day prosperity, economics, and capitalism. For example, the framework for lending is found in the book of Deuteronomy.

> The LORD shall open unto thee His good treasure, the heaven to give the rain unto thy land in His season, and to bless all the work of thine hand: and thou shalt lend unto many nations, and thou shalt not borrow.
>
> —Deuteronomy 28:12

In Deuteronomy, God also declares His desired position for His people.

And the LORD shall make thee the head, and not the tail; and thou shalt be above only, and thou shalt not be beneath; if that thou hearken unto the commandments of the LORD thy God, which I command thee this day, to observe and to do them:

—Deuteronomy 28:13

Twenty-first century Christians are at a tremendous disadvantage considering the lack of education concerning finance. We have little expectation of receiving instruction on business, personal finance, or corporate economics from our churches. Thus, we are accustomed to separating our workplaces from our spiritual lives.

In the Jewish community, however, a Rabbi must be thoroughly versed in markets, interest, banking, trade, and economics. This is considered part of his Rabbinical training. Several years ago, I was looking for a complex to house our residential Bible school students. (This is our advanced training center for biblical studies and modern economics). My search led me to a property with sixteen rooms, which was being used as a dormitory for young Jewish men attending a Rabbinical Bible School. In negotiations for the property, I was allowed access on several occasions. What I found was very instructive concerning the Jewish training of emerging young leaders in their communities.

> The Bible laid the foundation for present-day prosperity, economics, and capitalism.

Certain rooms were furnished with computers, multiple monitors, high speed routers, Wi-Fi, and many other types of electronic equipment. My curiosity led me to ask why they needed such sophisticated systems. The response was that it was necessary to trade stocks in real time. What they were doing is known as "day trading," considered one of the riskiest ways to create wealth. However, for the trained trader, it could be very lucrative. The young men informed me they studied by night, learning all they needed to know about their faith, customs, and laws. Yet, simultaneously, they learned how to create wealth, to maintain financial independence, and teach members of their congregations to do the same. This was just one aspect of their training in economics. This was an eye-opener for me. Learning the concepts of wealth creation was actually part of their curriculum in Rabbinical school. These were nineteen to twenty-three year old young Jewish men learning the intricacies of using the stock market to generate wealth.

My thoughts about the need for a paradigm shift within the Church were solidified as I left that dorm. Most young Christian believers in that age group have little or no concept concerning portfolios, lending rates, leveraged purchases, or stocks and bonds. The contrast is staggering. The student in Judaic training is learning to create wealth through multiple streams of investing, while most Christian college students are running up their credit cards, stacking up a mountain of debt. According to numerous studies, credit card debt on campuses is out of control.

College students continue to succumb to credit card debt due to the industry's aggressive marketing tactics. According to a recent study by Nellie-Mae, *Sallie* a leading provider of student loans, an incoming freshman with zero debt can expect to be over $3,000 in debt in their first year. Upon graduation, the same student will likely be over $20,000 in debt. The study continued to state that credit card companies pursue college students because they are the least likely to pay off their monthly balance in full, thus fattening credit company's pockets with huge, ongoing finance charges. Credit card companies employ targeted marketing tactics to solicit students by renting tables on campus, stuffing offers in textbooks, and soliciting through physical and electronic mail.

> Credit card companies employ targeted marketing tactics to solicit college students.

Other studies, like "College Student Performance and Credit Card Usage," published by the Journal of College Student Development, have revealed that numerous universities have multi-million dollar partnerships with credit card companies that encourage students to apply.

Steve Trumble, president of American Consumer Credit Counseling (ACCC) states:

"Personal finance management is sorely needed, but generally not part of the typical college student's education. Many university curricula adequately cover the formal education but neglect to develop kids' life management skills. It's important that non-profit consumer credit organizations fill the gaps in student education."[1]

What contrasting stories when comparing Jewish and non-Jewish college students! You don't have to be a prophet to know which group will be best positioned to lead and which will be forced to follow. It breaks my heart to see God's children in this situation. I believe we are at the hour of change. However, we must remove the blinders to see this reality.

Currently, our ministry reaches college students across the nation with education and assistance for financial preservation and development. We provide free vouchers to college students attending seminars and numerous free curricula for them on our Web site. We provide students with the wisdom, knowledge, and resources about how to create income while attending college. Included is a list of top entrepreneurial ventures and business startups that can generate a substantial income while still in school. There are numerous examples of college campus wealth creation.

Michael Dell, for instance, has provided inspiration for millions of entrepreneurs to pursue their dreams of creating innovations. Dell is the son of an orthodontist and grew up in a Jewish family. He had his first encounter with a computer at the age of fifteen when he broke down a brand new Apple II computer and rebuilt it, just to see if he could. As a youngster, Michael did not excel scholastically. He attended college with the intention of becoming a physician. However, the road to financial success began out of his University of Texas dorm room in 1984 with just $1,000.00 and an idea to provide affordable personal computers to college students. The company became successful enough that, with the help of an additional loan from his grandparents, Dell dropped out of college at the age of nineteen to run PC's Limited, which later became Dell Computer Corporation, then ultimately Dell, Inc. Today, Dell's company has a net worth of over $30 billion.[2]

A church should be a place of empowerment and inspiration, and where God-given dreams are conceived, encouraged, and have the best opportunity of achievement, and where creativity and innovation are a part of Christian living.

In order for this to happen, a primary shift is needed within pastoral, ministry, and leadership training. Today, Bible students learn how to sing, lead worship, operate children's church, teach Sunday school classes, and Bible camps. They learn Hermeneutics, Greek, Hebrew, and similar subjects. They graduate prepared to teach apologetics and the harmony of the Gospels, but are unfamiliar with the workings of the very marketplace they must impact to succeed personally and lead their congregations in successful financial principles. The Church has an opportunity to fill this gap and provide financial education and empowerment to its members and communities.

Too often, churches approach the Lord's table like the Gentile woman satisfied with the mere crumb (Matthew 15:27).

> Beloved, know ye not that you are heirs of God, and that you have been given a seat at the table.
>
> —Galatians 4:7

We, of all people, should be sitting at the table — not just the dinner table, but also the conference table, the boardroom table, in addition to the tables of education, finance, and government.

Finance, economics, and wealth generation are simply not accepted as part of the core message of most churches today, when, in fact, the Church should understand and educate individuals about money, capitalism, trade, interest, budgets, OPM (Other People's Money), OPT (Other People's Time), startups, mergers, and acquisitions, to name a few.

The Birth of Capitalism

The Talmud laid the framework for capitalism[3] in its most productive, efficient and successful form. Whether people today recognize it or not, modern day capitalism was birthed out of the Word of God. Let me say it again. The Word of God provided the foundation for what we consider capitalism. We have noted in another chapter how the Bible's principles produce systemic prosperity in nations that embrace its truths.

Capitalism is not just buying low and selling high, or simply generating a profit. While profit is a goal of capitalism, it does not represent the full economic definition of capitalism. In order for true capitalism to flourish, certain elements and components must be in place.

Capitalism is commonly understood as a system of specific applications of certain established principles that govern wealth to create surplus wealth, which is then used to create "generational wealth." The components of this system are open markets, enforceable contracts, international judiciary, free movement of labor and money, open-wage working class, financial liquidity, feasibility of trade, ability to transfer and negotiate securities, and the accessibility of credit.

While these principles seem elementary today, in medieval days, they were considered strange and wicked. In the Middle Ages, before modern day capitalism, trade was always accomplished by the use of "concrete" economics, the exchange of money or goods on the spot. There was no such thing as a "promise to pay" or "promissory note." We get the expression "cash on the barrel head" from that type of exchange. Sailors arriving in port put barrels of goods like salt, grain, produce, etc., on the dock. Buyers literally put their cash on the flat top of the barrel. The seller took the money, and the buyer the barrel. The entire transaction was completed with the actual exchange of money for goods. Thus, there was a "concrete" or solid exchange with no credit or promise to pay another day, known as abstract economics.

> The Church has an opportunity to provide financial education and empowerment to its members and communities.

One well-known hypothesis of the "abstract" defines it as any object lacking a physical location, or a tangible physical existence, living or non-living. "Abstract" refers to concepts or ideas separated from embodiment. For example, "abstract words" are those like "truth" and "justice." They are real, but not concrete, since they do not possess a physical existence or location.

I will use abstract economics as a reference to all finances that have yet to become tangible or concrete. In many ways, concrete economics and abstract economics are simply two sides of the same coin. Concrete economics and our current economic system would collapse if it were to remove all that is abstract. Imagine, for example, going to the bank to apply for a mortgage. If the lenders are willing to loan you a certain amount of money, it will be based upon a specified return of interest and principal. For the bank, that return is supported by abstract economics. The bank will allow you to close on the loan and occupy the property though you've not yet made a payment. The bank's economic interest will be acquired over fifteen to maybe thirty years from the time of the closing. The strength of the bank's investment is the contract, which, along with the property, represents concrete economics while the interest payments are abstract, yet to be collected.

The concept of market, for instance, has long been debated on this point. Is the market a real, actual thing, or is it an abstraction? The answer is "both." The stock market is heavily influenced by abstract economics. The better the outlook for a company, the higher the stock price increase. A negative forecast about quarterly earnings or uncertain markets and economies could wipe out the value of a company stock.

In medieval times, this kind of thinking and these types of exchanges were unheard of until the Jews pioneered new and innovative methods of exchange based on credit, leveraging, and negotiation. They implemented a means of exchange where the buying and selling of debt was allowed. Because of their high moral code, Jews were comfortable dealing in the abstract, knowing another Jew would be bound by a code of behavior that would prohibit reneging on a promissory note or obligation.

The Capitalistic Jews

Until the Middle Ages, Jews were woven through the whole of each civilization where they lived. They were a part of the class system that prevailed in their resident countries. The Jews both contributed to and were affected by the culture around them. For example, there was an exchange and influence of Greek and Jewish philosophers upon their cultures. Before the Middle Ages, there was a merger of Jewish patterns, principles, and behaviors with the cultures and societies of which they were a part. The Jews were accepted, and their ideologies were embraced.

However, the Middle Ages are marked with an increase of Anti-Semitism, which prompted the removal of the Jews from the framework of the prevailing feudal systems. Feudal societies consisted of just three classes — the clergy, nobility, and serfs. This meant the Jews were left without a place in society.

This could have led to the extinction of the Jewish people. If they were not uniquely and specifically equipped by their God for this scenario, the Jews might not have been able to survive and thrive under these circumstances. Many nations under similar conditions were either absorbed into the existing culture or became completely extinct, never to reemerge.

In effect, the Jews were forced to carve out their own separate place or class in society. And that's exactly what they did. They formed the merchant class — a group that did not exist earlier. This new class was designed and equipped to exist in an abstract society. Needing finances to survive, the Jews later created a new economic system and an abstract economy to support it.

The Jews acquired patterns and principles from their God that enabled them to make a way where none existed. Consider that Jews throughout Europe were forced out of the framework of society, and you will see the undeniable miracle of God's providence for the Jewish people.

Interestingly, the Diaspora, or dispersion of the Jews from their homeland, which happened centuries earlier, actually positioned them for this particular time in history. They were scattered on three continents and established themselves in various corners of the known world. Yet, they had a common set of beliefs and principles that united them despite their geographical location. Looking back, one can see that the seeds of capitalism were planted by creating a people who could operate in the abstract, occupying positions in various countries and on various continents, yet able to trade and operate with a concrete set of rules and regulations they believed were handed down by God.

> The Jews acquired patterns and principles from their God that enabled them to make a way where none existed.

Creating a merchant class became the clear choice for the Jews. Since they were dispersed in various parts of the world, they could supply goods, luxuries, and commodities desired by people throughout the known world. It's reasonable to ask, "Why didn't anyone else do this?" The answer is simple: there was absolutely no system of security or protection to engage in those types of trades. In that day robbing, pillaging, thieving, and pirating were common practices. You might entrust a shipment of your cargo to a ship master only to have him keep your goods and establish himself in another part of the world.

The Jew, however, was bound by Talmudic law, and could not operate in that fashion. The Talmudic law provided a way for the Jew to establish easy credit arrangements. In addition, it required the honoring of all debts, and the establishment of a system for business between nations — all of which facilitated international capitalism. If I desired to trade goods in another part of the world, I would be foolish to do business without some type of protection. The only place to receive that type of security was to deal with the Jews, who now formed the merchant class. He could guarantee through the Talmud that my cargo was safe because it would be traded between Jews on both ends.

Max I. Dimont eloquently describes this by writing:

> In order for such international capitalism to flourish, several conditions must first be met: Governments must enforce all international agreements, must protect the flow of free trade, must allow the exchange of one another's currencies, must enforce contracts, must protect foreign investments, and must guarantee against the expropriation of property. The Diaspora created just such conditions for the Jews, and the Talmud provided the legal framework for them.

> The Diaspora Jews, though dispersed over three continents and in three civilizations, represented but one law. They were organized as "states within states" with the permission of the various Gentile governments of the countries in which they lived. These "Jewish states" were governed by the laws and ethics of the Talmud, and they were knit by the Talmud into a commonwealth of Jewish nations. In the Talmud, then, the Jews had an international law, which regulated their moral, ethical, and business conduct, as well as their religious life. The parts of the Talmud that deal with torts, trade regulations, damages, real estate, commerce, the sanctity of oaths, and the enforcement of contracts made the Talmud an ideal system of international law to regulate the far flung enterprises of the Jews. Rabbis had to know not only ritual observances, but commercial regulations as well. Through the Talmud, the Jews had an international law that regulated business conduct between Jew and Jew, between Jew and state, and between Jew and non-Jew. The Talmud held that a Jew was under an even greater obligation to honor all commitments to non-Jews.[4]

Jews thus possessed a worldview that prevented them from separating their spiritual and merchant lives. Their economics were never to be separated from their adherence to Talmudic principles. There was a prevailing understanding that the Jew would not violate the Talmud. In fact, if there was a discrepancy a person merely had to go to that particular Jew's community, find his Rabbi, and set the facts before him. If the Jew had violated Talmudic law, he would be reprimanded and possibly cast out of the synagogue or Jewish community. In addition, the Rabbi would see to it that the person who was cheated would be repaid in full. These principles of honesty, integrity ,and responsibility made the Jews the only merchant class that could be trusted completely.

> Our modern banking system has its roots in the Talmud.

In addition, Jews set up informal clearinghouses where loans could be obtained and notes negotiated. People desiring investment opportunities, while not being an actual part of the commercial transaction, could put up money and participate in the profits of the business indirectly. In effect, the concept that evolved into today's stock market was birthed by the Jews.

Many modern banking principles sprang from these early ventures established by the Jews. In fact, it is accurate to state that much of our modern banking system has its roots in the Talmud. There was a time when the Jews were the only people engaged in lending money. The Church viewed money-lending as usury instead of banking. Usury carries the connotation of lending money at exorbitant rates — which, by the way, is exactly what credit card companies are doing today.

The Jews viewed lending differently. The Talmud forbids usury — the taking of excessive interest. In fact, it compares usury to murder. The Talmud was ethical centuries ago in the same way Christian bankers are today. It encourages the lending of money to aid in business and commerce and required the Rabbis to set the permissible rates of interest. This ensured reasonable interest rates and eliminated Jewish lenders from controlling or hiking rates.

When the Jews were asked to vacate much of Europe, non-Jews and Christians replaced them in money-lending. Their practices were so unfair and rates so stifling the people begged the ruling powers to bring back the Jews so money-lending could return to a fair, just, and reliable practice.

The point is clear! The Jews clung to the Talmud and followed God's plans and purposes within the world.

I challenge Christians today with the following statements: the Word of God is as important, effective, and powerful in today's marketplace as it was thousands of years ago. It is the instrument that lays out the instructions for believers to generate wealth in agreement with the blessed plan and provision of God.

CHAPTER ELEVEN

The Poverty Paradigm

I don't know when or where it happened. Some say it was during the Medieval Period, others refer to the Puritan movement as the birthing place. However it happened, the Church adopted a "poverty mentality." This is the greatest hindrance to biblical prosperity. This notion is so ingrained in much of the Church's teaching that it has become a stronghold.

The Apostle Paul understood the power of false ideologies and vain philosophies. He gave specific instructions to the Church to free itself from their grip when he wrote:

> For the weapons of our warfare are not carnal, but mighty through God to the pulling down of strong holds, ***Casting down imaginations***, and every high thing that exalteth itself against the knowledge of God, and bringing into captivity every thought to the obedience of Christ;
>
> —2 Corinthians 10:4-5 Emphasis added

This verse gives insight into human psychology. Many an individual's problems are from flawed thinking. Paul understood that dominant strongholds could reside within an individual's thought-life. "Stronghold" is as much a military term today as when originally penned.

A "stronghold" defines an area that is most prone to revert to enemy control. It describes an arm of resistance also known as an "insurgency." If not completely conquered, it will rise again. This is exactly the situation in Iraq. While our soldiers defeated the Iraqi army, they could not completely defeat the opposition. As I write, throughout Iraq, there are cities that contain "strongholds of resistance." Immediately after U.S. military presence is reduced, those "strongholds" retake these territories.

To reconcile spirituality and prosperity, we need a paradigm shift.

Paul uses this term to explain the importance of displacing our old ways of thinking. Many believers have trouble maintaining long-term success or experiencing breakthrough because they still have strongholds in their lives that have never been eliminated. When such people are weak, stressed, overwhelmed, or emotionally drained, these areas begin to dominate them. Paul experienced the liberating power of Christ in his own life. Remember, before coming to Christ, Paul amassed an impressive list of credentials, including being a Pharisee and instructor of the Mosaic Law. He described himself as "circumcised the eighth day, of the stock of Israel, of the tribe of Benjamin, a Hebrew of the Hebrews, as touching the law, a Pharisee; concerning zeal, persecuting the church; touching the righteousness which is in the Law, blameless" (Philippians 3:5-6).

Paul was ingrained with doctrines, ideologies, philosophies, and other concepts of thinking. If anyone understood the importance of displacing old ways of thinking, it was Paul.

Writing to the Church at Rome, he says:

> Be not conformed to this world: but be ye transformed by
> the renewing of your mind, that ye may prove what is that
> good, and acceptable, and perfect, will of God.

> —Romans 12:2

The Bible is about transformation, which happens when we renew our minds. So then, if we are to reconcile spirituality and prosperity, we will need a "paradigm shift." As Keith Green said, "Going to church doesn't make a person any more a Christian than going to McDonald's makes them a hamburger."

Exposing the Poverty Spectrum

The conventional definitions of "poverty" do not capture the true sense of the word. They are one-dimensional, focusing only on the economic state. Every example refers to "poverty" as:

> Poorness, impoverishment (the state of having little or no money
> and few or no material possessions), a financial and economic
> condition; want, deprivation; the state of one who lacks a usual or
> socially acceptable amount of money or material possessions.

According to these definitions, we can spot "poverty" by the car it drives, type of house in which it lives, side of town it comes from, amount of money it makes, and clothes it wears. This definition provokes opinions and prejudgments against a person based solely on income and possessions. Today, like in former days, these mind-sets have become powerful cultural prejudices that affect every level of society.

If poverty is the state of having little or few material possessions or one who lacks a "socially acceptable or usual amount" of money, then the billionaire can view the millionaire as impoverished, and the community in the suburbs can see those of the city as poor. You may be thinking, "No way." Yet, this is exactly what is taking place in today's culture. I recently watched an interview with a well-known billionaire who commented about having to deal with the numerous "poor millionaires," as he put it. Are these not the mind-sets that plague our present society?

So then, let me propose a more accurate definition, one that is multi-economical, multi-cultural and free from outward appearances:

Poverty is NOT the state of not having. Rather, "Poverty" is the FEAR of not getting, which causes you to hold on tightly to what you have. Poverty is not a state of being, it is a state of mind.

This definition is supported by biblical economics. Proverbs provides its foundation when it says:

> There is that scattereth, and yet increaseth; and there is that withholdeth more than is meet, but it tendeth to poverty. The liberal soul shall be made fat, and he that watereth shall be watered also himself.
>
> —Proverbs 11:24-25

The Living Bible puts it this way:

> It is possible to give away and become richer! It is also possible to hold on too tightly and lose everything (come to poverty). Yes, the liberal (giving) man shall be rich! By watering others, he waters himself.
>
> —Proverbs 11:24-25 (TLB)

Poverty is NOT the state of not having. Rather, it is the FEAR of not getting.

———◦◦◦———

I find this definition to be true in life. My wife and I were invited to Haiti for our honeymoon. We stayed at a mission complex that educated close to one thousand kids and fed more than three thousand per day. The entire mission staff knew we came on our honeymoon. Their accommodations were wonderful. They prepared a bungalow for us with many amenities. At night, we joined the staff at the mission director's home for dinner and fellowship. Though they were not rich in earthly possessions, they were rich in ways that could not be measured. This is true about so many dealings and experiences I've had with people throughout my life.

Simultaneously, some of the most impoverished people in the world are those who are the richest. This "poverty mentality" permeates the wealthiest people and communities in our nation. Poverty usually brings along its cohorts: greed, deception, manipulation, haughtiness, arrogance and covetousness. I have seen Poverty alive and well in the poorest of places, as well as in the richest. Money in many ways exposes or magnifies our character flaws and personality defects.

King Solomon, the wisest and perhaps richest king ever to have ruled, witnessed something very disturbing in his day.

> There is a sore evil, which I have seen under the sun, namely, riches kept for the owners thereof to his hurt.
>
> —Ecclesiastes 5:13

Poverty thrives on fear. During recessions, bearish markets, uncertain economies (including threats of terrorism, war, and impending duress), people are more prone to come under the grip of poverty.

Breaking the Back of Poverty

Once, while attending temple service, Jesus stood by the offering basket. When I first read this, I thought, "This is an odd spot for Jesus to stand." Maybe the next time you're at church He will be sitting beside you, watching as you thumb through your wallet or pick through your pocketbook preparing to give in the offering. On this day, Jesus took notice of a particular woman who gave more than all the others. Yet, no one else paid her any mind.

> And Jesus sat over against the treasury, and beheld how the people cast money into the treasury: and many that were rich cast in much.
>
> —Mark 12:41

"Much" refers to the money being offered. Jesus must have seen large offerings put into the basket. What would you consider large — fifty thousand, a hundred thousand, or maybe a million dollars. How about Warren Buffett, who gave $37 billion to the "Bill and Melinda Gates Foundation?" In an interview with all three at the New York Public Library, Mr. Buffett told reporters, "There is more than one way to get to heaven, but this is a great way."[1]

I am amazed at how many people believe large donations and good works will give them a free ticket to Heaven. If that were the case, then only the rich and wealthy would get in. That sounds more like a yacht club or an exclusive membership to a private getaway. Thank God, Heaven isn't for sale, for someone wealthy would've bought it, put up a casino, built penthouses, and then let no one else inside.

Surely, Jesus must have been impressed at these huge donations. Then someone gave an amount so incredible Jesus called over His disciples.

> And there came a certain poor widow, and she threw in two mites (about 50 cents), which make a farthing. And he called unto him his disciples . . .
>
> —Mark 12: 42-43a

The disciples must have been thinking, *Two mites, what's the big deal about that? Jesus must be confused, that is the least amount given in this crowd.* Yet, Jesus will reveal to them how God calculates giving. He says:

> Verily I say unto you, that this poor widow hath cast more in, than all they which have cast into the treasury: for all they did cast in of their abundance; but she of her want did cast in all that she had, even all her living.
>
> —Mark 12:43b-44

Money exposes or magnifies our character flaws and personality defects!

Many think they can impress God with the size of their gift. However, Jesus tells us God looks at what remains. In fact, what's left over tells the true value of what was given. This woman, though lacking in earthly goods and possessions, was not gripped by the power of poverty. Others gave out of their abundance with plenty left over. She gave out of her need and lack and had nothing left over. Giving ten thousand dollars while still having millions left in the bank is not sacrificial giving. Based upon what was left over, this woman gave a gift that measured greater than all others. She gave all she had.

Poverty is not a "state of being," but a "state of mind." Jesus took notice of an individual who had every reason to hold tightly to what little she had. Yet, she overcame the pull of poverty by releasing her grip. Poverty is not the state of not having. It is the FEAR of not getting, which causes you to hold on tightly to what you have. This is an area of our lives we must monitor, especially if we are to increase financial wealth and experience long-term success.

CHAPTER TWELVE

The Biblical Blueprint for Release

When I began searching the Bible for a better understanding of biblical finance, I was stumped by a few of the stories. Was Jesus actually instructing us to give away all our possessions? When you combine *"The Widow's Mite,"* with the story of *"The Rich, Young Ruler,"* it is difficult to suggest otherwise. However, my perspective broadened the more I researched the Scriptures.

The key to understanding these stories is found in the Old Testament, specifically at the house of *"The Widow of Zarephath."* It's important to read the preceding story that leads up to this miracle, for it will provide additional insight.

And Elijah the Tishbite, who was of the inhabitants of
Gilead, said unto Ahab, As the LORD God of Israel liveth,
before whom I stand, there shall not be dew nor rain these
years, but according to my word. And the word of the LORD
came unto him, saying, get thee hence, and turn thee eastward,
and hide thyself by the brook Cherith, that is before Jordan.

—1 Kings 17:1-3

Elijah steps into the Palace of Israel and declares to King Ahab that,
according to his word, a drought will begin, lasting years. Upon his
departure, Elijah receives a word from the Lord, Who tells him to leave
quickly and go to the brook Cherith. Now comes the part that is especially
important to us:

And it shall be, that thou shalt drink of the brook, and I
have commanded the ravens to feed thee there. So he went
and did according unto the word of the LORD, for he went
and dwelt by the brook Cherith, that is before Jordan. And the
ravens brought him bread and flesh in the morning, and bread
and flesh in the evening; and he drank of the brook.

—1 Kings 17:4-6

Notice what this verse states:

"I have commanded the ravens to feed thee there" (vs. 4).

"*Commanded*" in the original language means:

To set things in order, put things in place; to decree, command,
order, arrange, organize; it means to put persons or things into
their proper places in relation to each other; a straightening out
so as to eliminate confusion.

God is saying He has made proper arrangements for Elijah's provision.
According to His Word, the ravens have been instructed to feed Elijah,
so every morning and evening the ravens brought Elijah fresh bread and
meat. Maybe they swooped down into the King's palace and took fresh
food right from Ahab's table. This shows God always has a plan to take care
of His faithful. In difficult or lean times, He has a brook and birds at His
command. David said, "I have been young, and now am old; yet have I not

seen the righteous forsaken, nor his seed begging bread" (Psalm 37:25).

Just as Elijah was basking in his beautiful oasis, the brook dried up. Has your blessing ever dried up? I cannot count the times this has happened to me. In my early walk, I would pray that God would fix it. Often, churches stay in an old movement that has dried up. Their people gather and tell stories of the time God visited or when the brook was full and the birds fed them. Elijah does none of the above. He gets another word from the Lord with new instructions. It says:

> Often, churches stay in old movements that have dried up.

> And the word of the LORD came unto him, saying, arise, get thee to Zarephath, which belongeth to Zidon, and dwell there; behold, I have commanded a widow woman there to sustain thee.
>
> —1 Kings 17:8-9

Elijah is instructed by God to go to Zarephath where He has arranged all the necessary provisions for Elijah through a widow. The same word "commanded" is used that described the arrangement of the ravens that fed him at the brook. Elijah is probably thinking, "This is easy."

> So he arose and went to Zarephath. And when he came to the gate of the city, behold, the widow woman was there gathering of sticks; and he called to her, and said, Fetch me, I pray thee, a little water in a vessel, that I may drink. And as she was going to fetch it, he called to her, and said, Bring me, I pray thee, a morsel of bread in thine hand. And she said, As the LORD thy God liveth, I have not a cake, but an handful of meal in a barrel, and a little oil in a cruse: and, behold, I am gathering two sticks, that I may go in and dress it for me and my son, that we may eat it, and die.
>
> —1 Kings 17:10-12

Elijah arrives at Zarephath and finds a different situation than at the brook Cherith. The widow tells him she only has enough breadcrumbs and oil to cook up a mouthful. She is preparing the last meal for her and her son. They are at the point of starvation and death. Most of us would have responded one of two ways. First, we might conclude we have the wrong widow woman, and simply say, "Oh, I'm sorry, I must be looking for someone else." The other option is to question God and His instructions. I would have been moved to give her an offering or put her on the church's benevolent fund.

However, Elijah discerns that something is restricting the provision of God. Just as God had commanded the ravens to feed him, the Word of the Lord had made all the necessary arrangements for this widow to have more than enough. What was holding back the blessing? Elijah identifies the grip of "poverty" as the culprit. This stronghold of poverty needed to be broken in order for a release to happen.

The FEAR of not getting was causing the widow to hold on tightly to what she had. So Elijah gives her instructions that would shatter the obstacle of poverty and allow the provisions of God to flow.

> And Elijah said unto her, Fear not; go and do as thou hast said, but make me thereof a little cake first, and bring it unto me, and after make for thee and for thy son. For thus saith the LORD God of Israel, The barrel of meal shall not waste, neither shall the cruse of oil fail, until the day that the LORD sendeth rain upon the earth. And she went and did according to the saying of Elijah: and she, and he, and her house, did eat many days. And the barrel of meal wasted not, neither did the cruse of oil fail, according to the word of the LORD, which he spake by Elijah.
>
> —1 Kings 17:13-16

The two instructions from Elijah were: first, get hold of your fear, a crippling emotion causing anxieties, depression, discouragement, exhaustion, panic attacks, shakes, sleep disorders, and many other disabilities. The Apostle Paul takes this into the next realm by stating that fear, apart from a psychological or emotional illness, can be a spirit.

> For God hath not given us the spirit of fear; but of power, and of love, and of a sound mind.
>
> —2 Timothy 1:7

Today, the widespread effects of fear are evident throughout the world. Fear is the instigator of global terrorism and the root of poverty. When I first took notice of the "poor church" message and how prevalent it had become in Christianity, I realized that simultaneously there was and is an epidemic of fear troubling believers. This is not a coincidence, because fear thrives on poverty. If we are going to be kingdom wealth builders, we must get a grip on our fears.

The second instruction Elijah gave the widow was to release what was in her hand. In essence he was saying, "Let go, and let God." The tighter she gripped what little she had, the tighter poverty gripped her. Elijah told her to prepare her meal, but to give him (give away) the first portion. You might be thinking, "How could he ask that poor widow woman for her last meal?" That's exactly what the culture thinks. It points its judgmental finger at the Church, continually criticizing its giving practices. If Elijah had been more concerned about public opinion, he would not have given her proper instructions. That decision would have set off a ripple effect, allowing poverty to destroy the widow's house and eventually take her life and her son. In addition, Elijah would have lost the provision of God.

This reminds me of the age-old method of catching monkeys still utilized throughout Africa and in the mountains of India. This sure-fire strategy is so simple it's quite comical. Villagers rely on their understanding of a monkey's behavior. They carve out pots with long necks or simply use tall glass jars with a small opening the size of a monkey's open hand. They place a few shiny stones or banana on the bottom. The monkeys, eager to collect their prize, put their arms into the neck of the jar and grab hold of the treasure. Once in their hand, they continue to tighten their grasp. However, they are unable to pull their "tightfisted" hand through the narrow neck. They sit holding their treasure, gleaming with excitement, yet unwilling to release their grip for fear of losing their treasure. Because they will not give up the banana in their grasp, they remain immobilized, and the villagers simply pick them up. The only thing the monkey has to do is "Let Go," and it would be free.

> The tighter
> she gripped
> what little
> she had,
> the tighter
> poverty
> gripped her.

This is exactly the effect poverty has on individuals. It traps us! Jesus took notice of the poor widow who sowed her last two mites because her act of giving freed her from the grip of poverty. This was a lesson for the disciples on how to break the stronghold of poverty.

Vital Lessons from Jesus about Poverty

Another vital lesson about poverty came when the "Rich Young Ruler" approached Jesus with his question:

> . . . Good Master, what good thing shall I do, that I may have eternal life?
>
> —Matthew 19:16

Here is a wealthy young man looking to do a good deed in order to possess eternal life. One who has servants that clean the house, wash the chariots, feed the horses, and cook his dinners. It seems fitting to want to buy a ticket to Heaven.

Jesus instructs the rich young man to obey the commandments. For most of us that would have been enough, but not for this young man. He has an additional question: "Which commandments?" Somewhere along his short life he came upon a belief that he is not obligated to do everything that others are required to do. Maybe it's because when restaurants are booked he is still given the best of seats. He rarely waits in line for anything, especially when a tip can move him forward. He was saying to Jesus, "Yes, the commandments are to be followed, but which ones do I need to follow? Isn't there a way around some? What good thing can I do to bypass the long list?"

Incalculable blessings and provisions flow when we loose what's in our hand.

Jesus questions his observance of the commandments by reciting the first six. There is a strong hint that this man is not Jewish, possibly a Roman. I state this because of the order in which Jesus approaches the commandments. The first four commandments are religious in nature, constituting a series of commands about the recognition of God. Only the last six relate to moral behavior in a society and deal with actual behavior toward other humans. The latter (second tablet) are common to almost all religious systems and are seen in many religious and secular law codes, including the "Pagan Roman Laws" at the time of Christ.

> The young man saith unto him, All these things (second tablet) have I kept from my youth up: what lack I yet?
>
> —Matthew 19:20

Jesus gives this rich young ruler one last instruction, moving him from the second tablet to the first. Because of the young man's arrogance, Jesus conceals the two great commandments, "You shall have no other gods before me," and "You shall not make for yourself any idols in the form of anything." Jesus prepares to expose the serious blind spot through which the man's wealth had become a god and idol in his life. Who was possessing whom?

> Jesus said unto him, If thou wilt be perfect, go and sell that thou hast, and give to the poor, and thou shalt have treasure in heaven: and come and follow me. But when the young man heard that saying, he went away sorrowful: for he had great possessions.
>
> —Matthew 19:21-22)

The reason Jesus instructs the rich young ruler to sell all his possessions was that he was under the power of poverty and didn't know it. This instruction is not meant to set a standard or precedent. Jesus, like Elijah, knew that the only way to be free from a poverty stronghold is to let go of what is in your hand.

These stories set forth the principle of overcoming poverty. It is ironic that the poor widow is actually the richer of the two. Do you realize that incalculable blessings and provisions flow when we loose what's in our hand? It causes God to release what's in His hand.

The stewardship practices of the Church should be based upon the Word of God and not the world's opinions. I have learned that the laws and principles of God operate differently than those of man.

For my thoughts are not your thoughts, neither are your ways my ways, saith the LORD. For as the heavens are higher than the earth, so are my ways higher than your ways, and my thoughts than your thoughts.

—Isaiah 55:8-9

Giving is the great breaker of poverty. You break the grip of poverty by responding in the opposite manner. When it says grip tighter, and you are overcome with the fear of losing what you have, let go and let God. Put your trust in a loving Savior who will never leave nor forsake you. This is what Solomon witnessed in his day.

It is possible to give away and become richer! It is also possible to hold on too tightly and lose everything (come to poverty). Yes, the liberal (giving) man shall be rich! By watering others, he waters himself.

—Proverbs 11:24-25 (TLB)

The Macedonian Example

You break the grip of poverty by responding in the opposite manner.

The Apostle Paul also attested to the stronghold of poverty in his day. Paul had been writing and traveling to the churches of Asia Minor requesting funds for the Jerusalem Church for they were under intensifying persecution and in desperate need of support. In a letter to the Church of Corinth, he challenges them with the example of a group of believers in Macedonia who were under a severe trial of extreme impoverishment. Paul is moved on many levels by the response of the Macedonians to his request. Their economic situation was severe, and they possessed little to offer.

And now, brothers, we want you to know about the grace that God has given the Macedonian churches. Out of the most severe trial, their overflowing joy and their extreme poverty welled up in rich generosity.

—2 Corinthians 8:1-2

Paul did not expect the Macedonians to give this offering considering they themselves were in great need. He states they were in extreme poverty! However, poverty had lost its grip through the rich generosity of these believers. Like the two widows in the previous stories, they gave beyond their ability.

> For I testify that they gave as much as they were able, and even beyond their ability. Entirely on their own, they urgently pleaded with us for the privilege of sharing (giving) in this service to the saints.
>
> —2 Corinthians 8:3-4

Paul's initial response to these believers was "I can't take any money from you. It doesn't sit well with me. No, I won't allow you to give." His position was actually empowering poverty. This suggests that Paul at this point is unacquainted with the principles that break poverty. When the Macedonians are denied the opportunity to give, they plead their case in, what Paul records as, "urgency." They believed this was a divine opportunity to break poverty's hold on their people, churches, and community.

The Macedonians did what all believers should do: they sought the Lord about how and what to give.

> And they did not do as we expected, but they gave themselves first to the Lord and then to us in keeping with God's will.
>
> —2 Corinthians 8:5 (NIV)

As Paul writes this letter to the Corinthians, he's had a year to reflect on the Macedonian gift and time to seek the Lord and study the Scriptures. His insight is recorded in the remaining verses of chapters eight and nine and summarized in the following verses:

> But this I say, he which soweth sparingly shall reap also sparingly; and he which soweth bountifully shall reap also bountifully. Every man according as he purposeth in his heart, so let him give; not grudgingly, or of necessity: for God loveth a cheerful giver.
>
> —2 Corinthians 9:6-7

Paul states a powerful promise for those led of the Lord and willing to release what is in their hand. God will make all grace abound to them so that every need is met — not just financial, but physical and spiritual also. Money cannot buy everything we need. This is a promise we cannot do without.

> And God is able to make all grace abound toward you; that ye, always having all sufficiency in all things, may abound to every good work: As it is written, He hath dispersed abroad; He hath given to the poor: His righteousness remaineth for ever.
>
> —2 Corinthians 9:8-9

The Trip That Changed My Perspective

When I first discovered these principles, I was hesitant to teach them. Like Paul, I believed if people held onto what little they had, it was understandable. Then came a trip overseas, which changed my view. Several years ago I was in Cape Town, South Africa, ministering in open crusades and training pastors. In one large meeting, I felt such heaviness and a dark oppression in the atmosphere. Whenever you travel to foreign places, you're at a disadvantage considering your lack of historical knowledge concerning the people, their hardships, setbacks, trials, and triumphs. You must rely on the prompting of the Holy Spirit to be fruitful.

The Gospel is good news to all people, especially those held captive by destructive forces.

I sensed God quickening my spirit to speak on "Breaking the Stronghold of Poverty." My initial response to this prompting of the Spirit was questioning. I always thought an atmosphere of joy was more favorable when dealing with the topic of money. Clearly, that was not the situation. I wrestled with this instruction all the way to the pulpit. As I opened with prayer, I knew I was to minister this message. No matter what the outcome, I would be obedient to God's direction.

I preached amidst oppression. I never received an "Amen," "Hallelujah," hand clap, or even a positive nod. It was the fastest I ever moved through a sermon, barely pausing, and hardly making eye contact because of the possibility I might get discouraged.

At the close of the message, God gave me an unusual instruction for the altar call. I called the ushers to the front and asked them to form a straight line, each holding an offering basket. I then instructed the pastors and altar workers to form another line at the opposite side of the stage, prepared to pray. Then I asked the congregation if there were any who wanted to break the stronghold of poverty over their lives, families, or churches.

Before anyone could respond I said, "Wait, I have one instruction. In order to be free from poverty, I want you to go first to the ushers and release the money you have tonight into the offering baskets. Then walk to the other side of the altar, where the pastors will anoint, and pray a prayer of release over your life and household."

Hundreds came forward to the altar that night. I will never forget it.

I went back to my room still wondering about the overall outcome of the meeting. I would soon have the answer, because the next morning I was training about two hundred pastors, some of whom had been present the previous evening.

That morning I witnessed the faithfulness of God to His people. The meeting was packed with additional pastors and leaders. There was a buzz in the air and countless testimonials of financial breakthrough. During the remaining seven days of that trip, and for almost a year afterwards, I received more than a thousand reports declaring the works of God in the finances of the people who came forward that night. From that time forward I have never been hesitant to give instruction about biblical finance.

The Gospel is good news to all people, especially those held captive by destructive forces. This is so important that it is a part of the mission statement of our Lord and Savior Jesus Christ.

> The Spirit of the Lord is upon me, because He hath anointed me to preach the gospel to the poor; He hath sent me to heal the brokenhearted, to preach deliverance to the captives, and recovering of sight to the blind, to set at liberty them that are bruised, to preach the acceptable year of the Lord.
>
> —Luke 4:18-19

CHAPTER THIRTEEN

What about the Ninety?

For too long, tithing has been the focal point of financial education within the church. The message most often given is *"be faithful in your tithes, and God will open the windows of Heaven and pour you out a blessing."* This is usually followed by a warning taken from the book of Malachi — *"Will a man rob God."* I do not believe calling a congregation robbers and thieves during the offering is the best motivator for creating cheerful givers.

As Paul wrote in 2 Corinthians:

> Every man according as he purposeth in his heart, so let him give; not grudgingly, or of necessity: for God loveth a cheerful giver.
>
> —2 Corinthians 9:7

Paul's whole message in this section is that the prospect of giving should produce an attitude of joy. Yet, many believers have not been given proper teaching on giving. Therefore, opportunities to give are met with resistance and uneasiness.

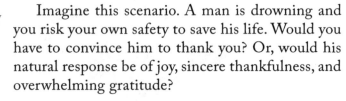

The customary teachings on giving have led to confusion and overall financial frustration.

Imagine this scenario. A man is drowning and you risk your own safety to save his life. Would you have to convince him to thank you? Or, would his natural response be of joy, sincere thankfulness, and overwhelming gratitude?

When I instruct at wealth creation seminars, people are amazed that I can teach for an entire day on finances and not mention tithing. This is because I believe that tithing is not the blueprint for wealth and prosperity, rather, an act of obedience that sets the foundation for the principles of sowing and reaping.

With that said, let's look at the design for giving, and within that framework you will see the component of tithing and how it fits.

I feel that many believers have become "weary in well doing" when it comes to giving. Many have been faithful with their tithes for years, but have grown tired because their "ship has never come in." The customary teachings on giving have led to confusion and overall financial frustration. Too often in my travels, I come across frustrated individuals who say, "I'm consistent, I'm faithful, but things never change."

When you receive your paycheck, the government takes a portion off the top. They consider it theirs due to your responsibility to pay a tax they instituted. Unfortunately, you receive very little residual benefit from paying taxes, so it becomes a painful experience. Many of these same feelings carry through to tithing.

Many in the Body of Christ teach that our paycheck is from the Lord. This is inaccurate, since we are required to work the field and earn our own living. The Apostle Paul was clear on how the Lord viewed our responsibility to work.

But if any provide not for his own, and specially for those of his own house, he hath denied the faith, and is worse than an infidel.

—1 Timothy 5:8

For even when we were with you, this we commanded you, that if any would not work, neither should he eat.

—2 Thessalonians 3:10

Therefore, our paycheck is the result of our own labor. Let me make this point very clear. A person's paycheck is compensation for work provided to their employer. The paycheck solidifies the mutual transaction between the employer and employee. God is not the employer. However, in order for multiplication to happen, God asks that I present him an offering from the fruit of my labor.

God's universal law requires that He be put first in all things. When adhered to, it produces manifold blessing.

The Bible tells us that all firstfruits are holy to the Lord.

And all the tithe of the land, whether of the seed of the land, or of the fruit of the tree, is the LORD'S: it is holy unto the LORD. And concerning the tithe of the herd, or of the flock, even of whatsoever passeth under the rod, the tenth shall be holy unto the LORD.

—Leviticus 27:30, 32

So then the tithe, as a form of firstfruit, is holy to God, and when He receives His 10 percent, He sanctifies the remaining 90 percent.

And now, behold, I have brought the firstfruits of the land, which thou, O LORD, hast given me. And thou shalt set it before the LORD thy God, and worship before the LORD thy God:

—Deuteronomy 26:10

The Bible provides three forms of firstfruits — they are firstfruits of income, of increase, and a whole first-fruit offering at the beginning of each year. The tithe is a form of first-fruit because it represents the first part of our paycheck every pay cycle. Many believers view paying their tithes as sowing seed. Unfortunately, the tithe is not seed, rather it represents the first portion, which should be reserved for God.

The act of tithing does not produce increase. Some people may get confused or outraged at that statement, but according to Malachi, this is absolutely true.

> Will a man rob God? Yet ye have robbed me. But ye say, Wherein have we robbed thee? In tithes and offerings. Ye are cursed with a curse: for ye have robbed me, even this whole nation. Bring ye all the tithes into the storehouse, that there may be meat in mine house, and prove me now herewith, saith the LORD of hosts, if I will not open you the windows of heaven, and pour you out a blessing, that there shall not be room enough to receive it. And I will rebuke the devourer for your sakes, and he shall not destroy the fruits of your ground; neither shall your vine cast her fruit before the time in the field, saith the LORD of hosts. And all nations shall call you blessed: for ye shall be a delightsome land, saith the LORD of hosts.
>
> —Malachi 3:8-12

If all we do is pray—and not act—after the curse is broken, we have no reason to expect fruit.

This portion of Scripture must be examined closely to gain the proper understanding. Our tithe sanctifies the remaining 90 percent so that it can produce fruit. By giving the 10 percent, the "windows of heaven" are now opened on the remaining 90 percent so that it can be invested and sown into fertile ground. Many individuals stop at the tithe and eat the remainder or their "seed" through mortgage payments, car payments, vacations, and the other expenses of life. When churches become obsessive with the tithe, it causes their congregations to become consumed with it as well. Many are taught through osmosis that financial increase will occur based solely upon the tithe.

There needs to be a radical shift in the church from the 10% to the 90 percent. Believers and churches are being held back from financial prosperity by focusing strictly on the tithe. The tithe only removes the curse. So, if nothing is done with the remaining 90%, even the most faithful tither will be stuck in the same place, year after year, never capitalizing on the blessing of God. They may not suffer lack, but they will not break into prosperity.

This principle can be illustrated in the story of Hannah in 1 Samuel. Hannah was barren and consumed with her inability to conceive. She wept before the Lord to have the curse removed, and she was healed. However, once the curse was broken, Hannah had a responsibility to receive seed from her husband in order to conceive. If all she did was pray and did not act after the curse was broken, she would have had no reason to expect fruit.

The book of Malachi records that God will "open you the windows of heaven, and pour you out a blessing, that there shall not be room enough to receive it." Many believers stop here, satisfied with this undefined blessing. They fail to interpret the Scripture in its full context. The following verses define the four specific blessings God releases in response to our obedience.

1. He will "rebuke the devourer" for our sakes (Malachi 3:11).

God will not allow the enemy of our soul to "kill, steal, and destroy" the affairs of our lives.

2. He will not be able to destroy the fruit of our "ground" (Malachi 3:11).

The fruit of the ground is a common phrase throughout the Old Testament that refers to wages earned. This promise states that God will protect and stretch your income in times of difficulty.

3. Your vine shall not cast her fruit before the time (Malachi 3:11).

This simply means that God will ensure that the timing associated with your financial endeavors will be perfect. Timing is critical to create and sustain wealth. Often the timing of an investment is more crucial than the investment itself.

4. "All nations shall call you blessed: for ye shall be a delightsome land (Malachi 3:12)."

This final blessing shows the magnitude of God's favor on those who abide by the Laws of the Harvest. As Joseph was promoted from the pit to the palace, so God will cause our success, influence, and reputation to be known locally, nationally, and internationally.

These verses hold the keys to sowing and reaping. They reveal God's desire to position us to bear fruit in our finances. In light of proper interpretation, it makes sense that we should be "cheerful" givers. How exciting to know that God will bless our financial endeavors once we give Him the first part. We can give cheerfully knowing that God's promises are true and never fail when we act in obedience.

> For all the promises of God in him are yea, and in him Amen, unto the glory of God by us.
>
> —2 Corinthians 1:20

It is beneficial for us to work in concert with God's blueprint for sowing and reaping. Since the tithe sanctifies the remainder, it is our responsibility to allocate a portion of the 90% in places it can be multiplied. A great starting point is to separate an additional 10% above the tithe and place it in avenues of wealth creation.

The Four Laws of the Harvest

Agriculture is the most common analogy used in Scripture to illustrate biblical finance. Terms such as sowing and reaping, harvest, good ground, fruit, and fertile soil are examples of basic principles in finance. A few years ago, I sat with a farmer to get more familiar with the process of planting and harvesting crops. From that discussion, I gained four specific practices a farmer must incorporate to have a successful harvest. The integration of these practices in my personal finances have produced a tremendous harvest.

1. No Farmer Plants Unknown Seed

A harvest first begins with the seed. A farmer will always identify a specific seed that he is going to plant. He evaluates the quality of the seed and plants it with an expected harvest. He would never purchase an unknown seed. I find that many believers throw seed around, not knowing what it's supposed to yield. I can throw a bunch of money in the Stock Market, but if I don't research the investment and become knowledgeable of the market, I've sown a recipe for disaster. Additionally, once a farmer has identified the seed, he is extremely liberal in distributing it over his fields.

Likewise, New Testament writers instruct believers to give "bountifully" and not "sparingly." Imagine if the farmer approached his field with the philosophy, It's not how much I sow, but the thought that counts. What type of harvest do you think he would produce?

As Solomon noted in Proverbs:

> The liberal soul shall be made fat: and he that watereth shall be watered also himself.
>
> —Proverbs 11:25

2. His Harvest Always Dictates His Sowing

If you go to any garden store and pick up a packet of seeds, the information on the back would give you the necessary conditions the seed needs to produce a proper harvest. In the same way, a farmer understands that the expected harvest will dictate the process he must follow in sowing that seed. Knowing the harvests in our lives will provide us with wisdom and instruction. If I know I need a specific return from an investment, I'm not going to place seed in something that can't generate that return.

This holds true in harvesting good relationships, ministries, and businesses. Knowing the desired outcome in these areas will help you nurture them accordingly.

3. A Farmer Never Mingles Crops

As seen in the parable of the wheat and the tares, mingled crops will draw from the same source of nutrients to survive, and therefore both suffer. In business practices or in any partnership including marriage, it's never wisdom to mingle unrighteous

159

seed with righteous seed. Sowing seed in unrighteous fields will never produce a healthy harvest. The believer should not expect his seed to be blessed in a Las Vegas Casino, lottery, or any other similar soil.

4. A Farmer Never Plants Without Having His Crop Sold

Farmers understand the market value of their crop. In order to reduce risk, they will pre-sell their crops to protect against a negative turn in the market. In this way the profit is secured in case the crop is wiped out. Likewise, it's important for us to always understand the true value of any potential investment, and to always develop an exit strategy in case of disaster. In measuring the risk, it's critical we identify a "worst-case scenario" and plan accordingly. If you cannot get out of something, then maybe you shouldn't get into it.

In the mortgage industry, a lending institution will protect profit on a loan by issuing a pre-payment penalty to the borrower in case they sell early. The penalty protects the lender's profit in the transaction and restricts the borrower from selling. Knowing that, we also need to protect ourselves and maneuver around pitfalls that can eat up our harvest. Equity traders will purchase "a stop-loss" to protect their investment from an unexpected drop in share price. The "stop-loss" serves as an exit strategy that will automatically sell the shares if the stock drops to a predetermined level.

By giving to God, we have the joy of experiencing true security. God will create such blessing and favor over the 90 percent that, when sown properly, will lead to magnificent fruit. God is longing for the Church to benefit from sowing their seed money. I am convinced that creating a lifestyle of sowing according to this foundational truth will lead to continual cycles of unimaginable prosperity in your life.

CHAPTER FOURTEEN

The Crucial Power of Position

Position is crucial to wealth transference. It is important that you familiarize yourself with the *"crucial power of position."*

I didn't understand this concept until I got older. In my early years, I had an abundance of zeal. I wanted to make some waves. Do you remember when you were a kid making waves in a pool by spreading your hands and jumping up and down? After a while, it becomes so tiring you can't lift a thing. It is impossible to maintain those waves for any length of time, even when others are helping. Making waves in life produces the same effect. It will cost you energy, time, and *lots of money.* I had plenty of zeal, but lacked wisdom. The Apostle Paul took a hard look at his youthful zeal and concluded:

When I was a child, I *spake* as a child, I **understood** as a child, I **thought** as a child: but when I became a man, **I put away childish things.**

—1 Corinthians 13:11 Emphasis added

> You must learn that catching waves is far less strenuous.

After years of *making waves,* I soon learned that *catching waves* is far less costly, time-consuming, and utilized my energy more efficiently. I needed only to locate a wave and *position* myself correctly. The wave created the momentum to keep me moving. Position is the secret to catching waves. This principle is embedded within the Kingdom of God. Many individuals have run out in front of God and involved themselves in a project, or launched some plan, then asked God to bless it as an afterthought. This is nothing more than making waves in the Kingdom pool.

There is a way that seems right to a man, but in the end it **leads to death.**

—Proverbs 14:12 NIV Emphasis added

We must learn to inquire of the Lord *first* to find out the things He has already blessed and go where He Himself is "making the waves."

In all thy ways acknowledge him, and he shall **direct thy paths.**

—Proverbs 3:6 Emphasis added

There is safety, provision, protection, and direction for those who learn to **position** themselves under the mighty hand of God.

The Crucial Power of Position

The theme of "position" runs throughout the Bible. Have you ever heard the phrase *"being at the right place at the right time?"* It has to do with being favorably positioned, which is vital to almost every aspect of life.

Position plays an essential part of ministry, leadership, success, economics, wealth creation, marriage, family, and relationships. Thus, every year I take time to analyze my current positions regarding my future goals, projects, and projections. Not a year's gone by that I haven't made critical shifts *(repositioning)* within my life, family, ministries, and the companies I oversee to be properly positioned for success.

Many people desire success, peace, happiness, healthy marriages, wholesome relationships, and many other honorable things. However, they fail to **position** themselves properly. You cannot catch a plane sitting in the train station. Don't get mad at the ticket person or the conductor, because they can only give you what they have available. God has prepared perpetual blessings, promises, favor, miracles, and anointing for those who will position themselves correctly. One such blessing is found in Psalm 133, which says:

> Behold, how good and how pleasant it is for **brethren** to dwell **together in Unity!** It is like the precious ointment upon the head, that ran down upon the beard, even Aaron's beard: that went down to the skirts of his garments; As the dew of Hermon, and as the dew that descended upon the mountains of Zion: **for THERE** the LORD **commanded the blessing**, even life for **evermore**.
>
> —Psalm 133:1-3 Emphasis added

These verses tell us God has commanded a perpetual blessing to flow down upon the place of unity. The phrase *"for there"* refers to a specific place. This Psalm provided vital instructions for me during the initial stages of planting our church. For two years we experienced supernatural growth, followed by times of discord. When we finally were able to remove the division, it unintentionally removed a portion of our attendance. Lack of attendance was followed by lack of funds. This roller coaster started to take a toll on me, both spiritually and physically.

> Position plays a major role in guiding you to the place of Blessing.

Then one day the Lord whispered this Psalm to me. He instructed me to position myself at the place of unity, along with the core leadership and those willing to follow, because *"there"* He commanded the blessing to flow. As I shared this word with our leadership, we were challenged to regard unity above ministry, position, ideologies, personal preferences, or anything else pertaining to oneself.

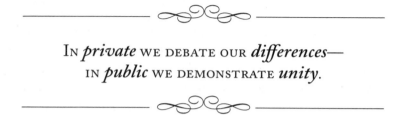

In *private* WE DEBATE OUR *differences*—
IN *public* WE DEMONSTRATE *unity*.

We established an open-door policy for offences amongst leaders, using Matthew 18:15 as our guide. We progressed to the point of penning out a list of attitudes and behaviors that might open the door to discord — The *Unity Declaration*, was signed by leaders and ministry workers. This is a powerful document against the attacks of carnality. It starts like this;

We, the leadership of Calvary Life, both labor and strive to preserve Unity as the upmost ambition — only to be eclipsed by our devotion to Jesus, our Savior and Head of this Local Church.

The results were miraculous. Leadership raised the bar and set the example. We positioned ourselves under the "banner of unity," held it in great esteem and others followed.

The *"crucial power of position"* played a major role in guiding us to the place of blessing. Since then, we have witnessed the favor of God on our ministries, families, and finances. I consult with pastors from all over the nation on strategic planning for marketplace ministry, wealth empowerment, strategies, and biblical economics.

Many who contact our offices are in financial straits. Church giving is declining and leaders can't figure out why. For others, there's a necessity to raise the level of giving due to expansion projects. In either case, unity plays a crucial role. In each situation where giving had decreased, the root cause was a lack of unity — whether in the leadership team in situations in which some are in disagreement with the direction, or through a breakdown of communication between the congregation and the corporate vision. In churches with unity in the vision or expansion project, there is sacrificial giving by the congregation, usually with more than ninety percent participation.

I submit to you that unity is a stepping-stone towards prosperity just as discord is the slippery slide to poverty.

Do you know what the number one consumer of family prosperity is? It's not the high cost of education, energy bills, or rising credit card debt. All these make the list, but the top spot is held by divorce, the nation's leading destroyer of wealth, prosperity, and generational blessings *(inheritances)*. Much of the cycle of poverty can be traced to divorce, adultery, cohabitation without marriage and similar lifestyles. More than sixty percent of all marriages will end in divorce. Sadly, these statistics correspond to those inside the Church.

History concurs that the way of the family is the way of a nation and its society. One major component of wealth transference is *"generational wealth."* When God bestows prosperity, His intent is that it be transferred through the generations.

> A good man leaveth an inheritance to his children's children:
>
> —Proverbs 13:22 Emphasis added

Divorce redirects this flow of prosperity away from the family. The untold effects of divorce are seen in properties that are liquidated, wealth split and squandered, the added expense of child support and alimony, the high cost of legal fees, and the emotional stress upon everyone connected to the family.

When children are a part of the equation, there's an additional list of consequences. They suffer the aftermath of being robbed of the protection of a safe loving home where they are protected and covered by their mother and father. Children of divorce are often cheated out of intimate adolescent development and needed social skills.

In each situation where giving had decreased, the root cause was a lack of unity.

—⁓ఄ⁓—

Numerous studies have shown that children *positioned* in households with *"one man and one woman"* committed to each other in marriage have the best chance for *economic, emotional, and spiritual stability* in their lives.[1] Children of divorced parents are being cheated of *family finances.* The *inheritance* and *generational wealth* potential that should be passed down the family line is shipwrecked.

Secular humanists like Margaret Sanger and Thomas Dewey successfully changed the paradigm of the American people to a *one-generational, self-centered society* dependent on a *"messianic state"* in competition with God and the Bible.

The story of the Prodigal Son in Luke 15:11-32 shows that what motivated the backslidden son to repent and come back home to his family was *economics*. His economic ability was connected to his *father's wealth*. If this happened today, the prodigal son would have by-passed his family and gone to the local welfare office for state aid — the *messianic state*.

We live in a time when believers must stay *positioned* under the safety, provision, protection, and direction of God. This will ensure their ongoing financial well-being and enable them to *be positioned* for a present-day transference of wealth.

CHAPTER FIFTEEN

The Wealth of the Wicked

"Wealth transference" is very much a biblical term and theme. Yet, in the Church, this word has been taken grossly out of context. Charlatans, heretics, and extremists prey upon and distort topics that are separated from their biblical roots. Millions watch late-night televangelists selling the idea that God is getting ready to transfer riches into their hand — all they need to do is sow a seed, make a financial vow, or give a gift to their ministry. Don't get me wrong, I believe in the power of giving as stated in previous chapters. However, *"Giving to get"* is not a blueprint for wealth creation and prosperity.

What usually follows is the Scripture phrase from Proverbs 13:22, *"The wealth of the wicked is laid up for the just."* This verse is quoted with charismatic emotion. Listeners are prompted to think of people with big homes, nice cars, and fancy clothes. *"These things,"* they say, are getting ready to be transferred to the believer. Think about this for a minute. All I need to do is sow a seed, and the possessions of the unrighteous will be put in my hands. The question has to be asked: *"Should I view the unsaved with predatory intentions?"* Should I covet their possessions, or win their souls? The Apostle Peter describes the attitude of God towards the sinner:

> The Lord is not slow in keeping His promise, as some understand slowness. He is patient with you, **not wanting anyone to perish**, but **everyone** to come to **repentance**.
>
> —2 Peter 3:9 (NIV) Emphasis added

> The question has to be asked: "Should I view the unsaved with predatory intentions?
>
> ────

The Apostle Paul dealt with dangerous false teachers in the early church. He responded by writing letters of rebuke and correction, first to the charlatans, and then to the Body of Christ for *listening to* and *partaking in* such error. Within his correction, he established and taught proper doctrine to replace the false.

Today, we just ignore it. Worse, we position ourselves at the opposite spectrum so no one will link us with the frauds. In his letter to the Galatian Church, Paul asks, "Am I therefore become your enemy, because I tell you the truth" (Galatians 4:16).

Jesus declared that truth leads to freedom when He said, "And ye shall know the truth, and the truth shall make you free" (John 8:32).

Because so many churches avoid the subject of wealth and prosperity, believers have become the target of false teachers and are forced to look for answers from sources other than the Bible.

To get an accurate interpretation of Proverbs 13:22, one must read the whole text. The verse contains two subjects, or themes, connected by the conjunction *"and."*

A good man leaveth an inheritance to his children's children:
And the wealth of the sinner is laid up for the just.

—Proverbs 13:22 (NIV) Emphasis added

This verse is referring to generational wealth transference *(inheritance, children's children)*. It compares the inheritance of both, a good man and an unrighteous man. According to the verse, a good man's inheritance is kept secure and intact for his future generations. This is consistent with the promises of God.

Praise ye the LORD. Blessed is the man that feareth the LORD, that delighteth greatly in his commandments. ***His seed shall be mighty upon earth***: the **generation** of the upright shall be blessed. ***Wealth and riches*** shall be in his house, and his righteousness endureth forever.

—Psalm 112:1-3 Emphasis added

However, it is not so for the unrighteous man. His inheritance will be *spoiled* and *forfeited* to the *righteous*. His seed will not benefit from his wealth. The historical data and general experience of people across history show this to be the common case. The prosperity of corrupt individuals, or from ill-gotten means, seldom reaches to the third generation.

Proverbs 13:11 helps give an accurate interpretation of verse 22:

Dishonest money dwindles away, but he who gathers money little by little makes it grow.

—Proverbs 13:11 (NIV) Emphasis added

These verses illustrate a principle about the moral conduct, character and values of a person. Webster defines a "principle" as:

A fundamental *law*, or *doctrine*: a rule or *code of conduct,* an underlying faculty or endowment; example — *"such principles of human nature as greed and curiosity"* (EMPHASIS ADDED).

God relates, interacts, and covenants with mankind through a system of patterns, principles, and promises. These are meant to govern, empower and enhance our lives. The Bible is the believer's handbook for this system. *"The wealth of the wicked is laid up for the just"* is a principle, not a promise.

This Scripture is not meant to be prayed or claimed, but to govern our lives as a biblical code of conduct. A *"promise,"* on the other hand, is defined by Webster's:

> As a ***legally binding declaration*** that gives the person to whom it is made a *right to expect or to claim* the performance or forbearance of a specified act: a reason to expect something: a ground for expectation of success, improvement, or excellence (Emphasis added).

To achieve long-term success in life, we must organize and structure our lives after the *patterns* modeled by God, we must govern our lives by the *principles* of God, and we must take hold of and claim the *promises* of God. By doing this, we will secure and prosper our lives, families, heritage, and those we lead.

Parable of the Talents

There is even a more immediate warning to be acquired from Proverbs 13:22. For it is God and not man that determines *who* and *what* a *sinner* is. Taking this into consideration and our current topic of wealth transference, let us read *"The Parable of the Talents"* in Matthew 25.

> For the kingdom of heaven is as a man traveling into a far country, who called ***his own servants***, and delivered unto them ***his goods***. And unto one he gave five talents, to another two, and to another one; to every man ***according to his several ability***; and straightway took his journey. Then he that had received the five talents went and traded with the same, and made them other five talents. And likewise he that had received two, he also gained other two. But he that had received one went and ***digged in the earth, and hid his lord's money***.
>
> —Matthew 25:14-18 (NIV) Emphasis added

This parable gives insight and instruction on the topic of biblical wealth transference and financial stewardship. The characters in the parable include the *"master"* who represents Jesus, and the servants, representing believers. The far country is Heaven, in which Jesus is presently dwelling and making intercession for us (Romans 8:34). The goods symbolize the wealth of the Kingdom of Heaven, including the anointing, gifts of the Holy Spirit, financial prosperity, wealth, and riches. The word "delivered" means to transfer, entrust, or inherit. This parable illustrates that Jesus is transferring His possessions to the believer to equip and empower him or her to carry out the Master's business in this world until He returns.

The amount given to each servant was determined by *their capacity* to handle money, possessions, and responsibility. This is a vital point. Just as present-day lenders evaluate a potential borrower's capacity to handle money, earn income, pay loans on time, maintain good credit scores, and many other factors, so does the Kingdom of Heaven.

> To achieve long-term success in life, we must structure our lives by the *patterns, principles* and *promises* of God.

I learned many years ago that God won't bless a mess. Many people want God to give them prosperity and success, yet they expect God to build a skyscraper on an outhouse foundation. This is why building wealth is a journey and not an event.

We must practice and educate ourselves with the biblical laws of wealth creation and stewardship in order to increase our capacity to handle wealth.

A future day of reckoning is also described in this parable:

> "After a long time the master of those servants returned and *settled accounts with them.*"
>
> —Matthew 25:19 Emphasis added

Many in the Church desire to see the day when God will judge the nations. However, the Scriptures warn that judgment begins *first* in the *house of God*.

> For the time is come that judgment must *begin at the house of God*: and if it first begin at us, what shall the end be of them that obey not the gospel of God?
>
> —1 Peter 4:17 Emphasis added

In the parable, the first two servants *put the master's money to work* and *doubled* it, or received a **hundredfold return.**

> The man who had received the five talents went at once and **put his money to work** and **gained** five more. So also, the one with the two talents **gained** two more.
>
> —Matthew 25:16-17 Emphasis added

This was not the situation for the third man, who had received only one talent. He buried the money, fearful of losing it, and gripped it all the more. This is a clear symptom of someone bound by poverty.

> But the man who had received the one talent went off, **dug a hole** in the **ground** and **hid** his master's money.
>
> —Matthew 25:18 Emphasis added

Look at the language the master uses with this servant:

> His lord answered and said unto him, Thou **wicked** and slothful servant, thou **knewest** that I reap where I sowed not, and gather where I have not strawed: Well then, you should have put my money on deposit with the **bankers**, so that when I returned I would have received it back **with interest**.
>
> —Matthew 25:26-27 Emphasis added

He calls the man a wicked servant, the same citation spoken in Proverbs: *"the wealth of the sinner (wicked) is laid up for the just" (Proverbs 13:22).* For years, this verse has been interpreted to refer only to the wicked outside the congregation of believers. Yet, Jesus warns us He will include the unprofitable servant in this group. The parable also depicts the transference of the *"wealth of the wicked servant"* to the righteous.

The parable also illustrates *two major* wealth transferences within the Kingdom of God. First, there is transference between the Lord and His servants, which is available for every believer. Just as Jesus transferred talents to His servants in the parable, so He is fulfilling this same transaction today with believers.

The other wealth transference will take place within the body of Christ. It will take place between unprofitable servants, ministries, and ministers, and those who are good, faithful, and profitable. Yes, this is happening right now. Denominations, churches, and ministries that have become unfaithful and unprofitable are on the decline. God is transferring wealth within the Church so quickly that most have been caught off guard.

Jesus commanded the wealth of the wicked servant to be taken from him and added to the account of the good and faithful servant. This servant was a wealth generator. It is important to understand that there is more to biblical economics than just sowing, if that were not the case, the wicked servant did well by sowing his talent into the ground. However, farmers do more than just sow, they also produce a crop and reap. Many in the Church today want to reap a harvest, yet rarely sow or labor in the field. It is easy to get upset about how the rich servant *(the one with ten talents)* got richer, with God Himself adding to his net worth. This complaint is echoed today, *"The rich get richer and the poor get poorer."* In a sense, this parable is saying just that.

> **Take the talent from him and give it to the one who has the ten talents.** For **everyone who has will be given more**, and he will have an abundance. Whoever does not have, even what he has will be taken from him.
>
> —Matthew 25:26-29 Emphasis added

Duncan C. Manzies states:

> *Profit is a must. There can be no security for any employee in any business that doesn't make money. There can be no growth for that business. There can be no opportunity for the individual to achieve his personal ambitions unless his company makes money.[1]*

Jesus' parable does not guarantee a constant "open heaven," or an unending flow of prosperity in my life, but suggests I will experience seasons of prosperity and transference. It then becomes my personal responsibility to multiply, or create additional resources from the wealth. There is no welfare system in the Kingdom. If I am faithful to produce increase, then I will receive added wealth exponentially from the Lord.

Chapter Sixteen

The Emerging Generation
of Wealth Builders

The topic of "wealth transference" has been featured on numerous financial, business and market news programs. Until recently, it was the new buzzword in economics. The concept, in some form, has been around the Church for many years. However, "modern economics"[1] and the Bible do not always look at the subject through the same lens.

The term has a broad range of definitions. Depending on who you talk to, you may get a variety of explanations. Wealth transference has been referred to as wealth distribution or wealth redistribution. In economics, redistribution is the transfer of income, wealth or property from one group of individuals to another group or groups of individuals.

The phrase redistribution of wealth specifically refers to assets being seized from one entity and redistributed to another entity in order to achieve economic equality (e.g. land being taken from feudal lords and given to serfs). Common methods of redistributing wealth are welfare, nationalization and taxation.

All political and economic systems facilitate the transfer of wealth, including capitalism, communism and socialism. Some proponents of redistribution argue that capitalism results in unequal wealth distribution. They also believe that money should be redistributed to benefit the poorer members of society, and that the rich have an obligation to assist the poor, thus creating a more financially egalitarian society.[3]

On the surface this sounds like noble concept, similar to the Robin Hood story. Wealth redistribution is packaged and sold to the public through rhetoric and propaganda as a system that will benefit the majority while only affecting the ultra rich. This is another example of political deception. In reality what the government is practicing is income redistribution, which adversely affects every worker. *Wake Up!* As long as you are working and earning a paycheck, your income is being redistributed in the form of taxation — without your consent!

On the other side, communism and socialism's versions of redistribution are likened to government-controlled acquisition. These systems strongly oppose entrepreneurship and business enterprise. I recently spoke to business leaders in Bulgaria, where capitalism is still regarded as an evil word. In order to change their perspective, I simply asked them three questions; do you believe in the right to land ownership? Do you believe in the right to earn wages and experience income and occupational advancement? Do you believe in the right to participate and invest in open market economies? The response was a unanimous "yes" — to which I responded — "welcome to Capitalism!"

Though it has flaws, Capitalism is the only system that positions a nation and its people for economic success.

Generational Wealth

Many economists and financial consultants view the process of accumulative stored wealth passing from one person to another as wealth transference or inheritance. Inheritance includes the passing on of property, titles, debts, and obligations upon the death of an individual.[4] The government and IRS recognize wealth transference and seek to transfer wealth from the jurisdiction of the family to the state through the death/inheritance tax instituted by left-wing politicians.

Let me to introduce the term "generational wealth" to assist us in getting a better understanding of wealth transference.

Generational wealth is found in both, biblical and modern economics. The term refers to resources passed from one generation to another. Two things separate this from "inheritance." First, transference is not contingent upon death. The majority of examples suggest that generational wealth must be passed between two living generations. Secondly, generational wealth is not restricted to money and property, whereas, inheritance is limited to the passing on of property, titles, debts, and obligations.

> All Biblical wealth creation is intended for generational transference.

To begin the journey of building wealth, you must start thinking generationally. All biblical wealth creation and accumulation is with the intent of generational transference. From the very start of the Bible, we see God created every living thing with a generational pattern. In every tree is a forest. in every kernel a harvest. in every fish a school. in every man and woman a child. God designed the next generation to be the seed within every living thing. The commandments to be fruitful, multiply, and fill the earth and sea was given to ensure the release of future generations after their own kind.

> And God created great whales, and every living creature that moveth, which the waters brought forth abundantly, after their kind, and every winged fowl after his kind: and God saw that it was good. And God blessed them, saying, Be fruitful and multiply, and fill the waters in the seas, and let fowl multiply in the earth.
>
> —Genesis 1:21-22

After God created Adam and Eve, He placed them in the garden, and the bible says, "He blessed them." Part of that blessing was to be activated only when the next generation was released.

> And God blessed them, and God said unto them, Be fruitful, and *multiply*, and *replenish* the earth, and subdue it:
>
> —Genesis 1:28 Emphasis added

Abraham's journey established the geographical boundaries and generational inheritance of his seed, while King David invested his influence and riches in a generational throne through his son Solomon that flowed all the way to Christ.

> And the LORD appeared unto Abram, and said, unto *thy seed* will I give this land: and there builded he an altar unto the LORD, who appeared unto him.
>
> —Genesis 12:7 Emphasis added

In many ways, God deals with humanity, as a whole, in our respective generations. God kept a whole generation of disobedient Jews in the wilderness until they all passed away. Then He chose Joshua to lead the emerging generation into the Promised Land.

The most sought after blessing in the Bible was for God to place His favor upon a man's lineage. Jehu secured the future of his children, grandchildren, great grandchildren, and great-great grandchildren with his obedience to God.

> And the LORD said unto Jehu, Because thou hast done well in executing that which is right in mine eyes, and hast done unto the house of Ahab according to all that was in mine heart, thy children of the *fourth generation* shall sit on the throne of Israel.
>
> —2 Kings 10:30 Emphasis added

Jacob coveted the blessing of his father Isaac because he understood what that generational blessing would do for him and his family. So much so, that he was willing to deceive to obtain it.

The Jewish people understand that wealth is created and obtained for the sustaining and survival of the generations. This type of stewardship is considered sacred, and ensures the perpetuation of their economic and spiritual heritage.

Generational Failure

There is a stark contrast in how Jews have viewed wealth in comparison to the rest of the world. The Jews view wealth as a tool to be passed to future generations, while most of the world views wealth as a tool to get what they want—now. Unfortunately, many Christians have also fallen into this category and missed God's intent for their personal legacy of wealth for their descendants.

Until recently we were poised to witness what was deemed the largest transference of wealth in U.S. history. It was to occur as the World War II generation passed on their wealth to the Baby Boomer generation. Some estimates surpassed $136 Trillion in transferred wealth. However with the recent economic crisis, much of that wealth has evaporated as the stock and housing markets plummeted in the past two years.

> Many Christians have missed God's intent for their personal legacy of wealth for their descendants.

Instead, we have witnessed what may be the biggest violation of this principle of generational wealth in history. The greater crisis for America was not the economic turmoil brought on by the sub-prime mortgage failure or the credit default swaps, but by the lack of emphasis and care given to develop a sound strategy to solve the problem.

The 2008 & 2009 economic stimulus packages lacked any provision for the ensuing generations that will inherit trillions of dollars of debt and a crippled economy — rather then wealth and the hope of a better future. Our government has spent two generations of future prosperity, throwing it at a problem, hoping something will stick or work — All this with NO Fiscal Responsibility. The Federal Reserve used to stand for fiscal responsibility, high employment and low inflation. Now, it seems their top priority is just printing money.

The extraordinary spending displayed by the government failed to address the root problems in the system and revealed two critical yet fundamental flaws prevalent in both political parties.

1. It proved the current and past administrations, and our elected officials do not understand how to create wealth.

Successful economies have always been centered on the foundation of creating wealth. Through business, entrepreneurship and innovation, created wealth has resulted as the staple of a healthy economy. High employment, consumer spending, and expanding business (not government) are all characteristics of a wealth creating structure.

Our government has never been, nor is structured for the purposes of wealth creation. When initially formed, the constitution set the guidelines to protect and enable its citizens to flourish in an open market economy. It is not designed to be a business. This is clearly seen by its failed programs and business attempts such as the United States Postal Service — which posted a whopping $5.1 billion postal deficit in 2008, and a $2.8 billion loss in 2009. Lest we mention public education, welfare and the biggest bust of them all—social security. If this were my business I would be losing sleep, worried about my ability to care and provide for my family or going to jail. Yet, the government seems undaunted— Why? Because, you, the taxpayer, will pay for this and all other spending ventures and shortages.

It's one thing to create wealth, but another entirely to be a good steward over the wealth we have.

Not only has the government failed to run a profitable business, but it shows a blatant disregard for existing business as seen in the initial stimulus package, which only allocated 8.5% of its $750 billion to small businesses.

As the government fails to pay its bills, they only have three ways to access additional revenue: They can steal it—through taxation and redistribution; they can print it—which will lead to an extraordinary inflation and devaluing of our national currency; or they can borrow it—which will continue to grow our national deficit.

According to a recent study, Federal policies have pumped more newly printed money into the economy in the last two years, then ever before in history. Even throughout the Great Depression and into World War II very little new money was printed. In this recent spiral, the United States Treasury has revealed that since October 2008, the US has increased its money supply by close to 70%. We have almost doubled the amount of money in the financial system!

What does this mean for the economy? Unfortunately this will lead to massive inflation and possibly hyperinflation—which is always an economic death knell. Hyperinflation is defined as inflation exceeding 50% per month! The basic economic law of supply and demand simply states that when there is a large supply of an item or commodity, the value of that item decreases. It's no different with a nation's currency. As the Federal government continues to flood our economy with new money, the weaker our currency will be in the world economy.

Printing, borrowing, and spending money are all dangerous substitutes for creating it. A recession or depression is difficult for any economy, but the inability to create wealth and blatant disregard for those who do, will prove to be America's greatest tragedy.

2. An Incredible Lack of Stewardship Principles

In an attempt to maintain the status quo, the federal government has sacrificed the future prosperity of America and the potential success of ensuing generations. It's one thing to create wealth, but another entirely to be a good steward over the wealth we currently have. Despite any argument one would make, the government of the United States has consistently shown a lack of stewardship as evidenced by our national debt and federal budget deficit.

As of December 2009 the total US federal debt topped $12.2 Trillion.[5] This number is so astronomical it almost seems fictional. However, it is very real and extremely precarious for America's long-term success. The national debt is the total amount of money owed by the federal government to creditors. These creditors include states, corporations, individuals and foreign governments. Basically, we have borrowed money from other countries to help finance our lifestyles in this country.

The other word we hear often is the federal budget deficit. The federal budget is exactly as it sounds. It's a big spreadsheet of all government income and expenses for the year. While the budget has been consistently negative for quite some time, in 2009 it will see historical levels. According to a recent article the Congressional Budget Office revealed that 2009's budget deficit was already nearly $1.7 Trillion and new projections for 2010- are just as bad.

All these numbers simply prove that the federal government spends much more then they receive. No sound business could continue with expenses greater than income, year after year. Our Government simply does not operate with sound business practices. Might I say, "Government spending is out of control."

Proper stewardship often requires short-term sacrifices and disciplines for a long-term progress. We have done the opposite by sacrificing long-term success for short-term comfort. In fact, a culture of debt has been spawned. You could say that the state of a government is a good indicator of the state of the people it governs. An indebted country will have indebted citizens, which is exactly what we have. According to money-zine.com, consumer debt in 2008 was $2.6 trillion and the average household in 2008 carried nearly $8,700 in credit card debt.[6]

In order to reverse these trends, revenue must be increased. Since we already established that the government doesn't know how to create wealth, they will do only what they know – increase taxes. While raising taxes will increase revenue for them, it will in turn slow consumer spending and therefore the economy.

So what does this mean for America's future leaders? The next generation that lead this nation will be left responsible for our irresponsibility. Instead of wealth, they will inherit trillions of dollars of debt, high inflation, and a weakened position in the world.

Thomas Jefferson said "I sincerely believe that banking establishments are more dangerous than standing armies ... and that the principle of spending money to be paid by posterity under the name of funding is but swindling futurity on a larger scale."

> Release always brings increase. God wants to flow through you, not just to you.

What we have done, as a country, is a great injustice and a major violation of biblical and economic principles.

A good man leaveth an inheritance to his children's children: and the wealth of the sinner is laid up for the just.

—Proverbs 13:22

Thinking generationally is the pattern and blueprint for wealth, prosperity, and blessing. The design and pattern of God is to ensure that the supernatural "power of release" is activated through generational transference. Keep in mind, "release always brings increase," and God wants to flow through you, not just to you.

The Emerging Leadership

Generational wealth consists of more than money, but encompasses the philosophies, moral values, and leadership of a culture. It is vital that these positive components be passed to ensuing generations.

According to estimates, the last generational transference was during the 1940s and 1950s. A people united by a common cause and values characterized the 1940s. In his book "The Greatest Generation," Tom Brokaw tells the stories of America's citizen champions who came of age during the Great Depression and the Second World War and went on to build modern America. He states this generation was united not only by a common purpose, but also by common values — duty, honor, economy, courage, service, love of family and country, and, above all, responsibility for oneself.[7] Unfortunately, most of what this generation stood and fought for has been lost today.

A common sign of a generational transference is a shift in the landscape of leadership in the spheres of community, business, government and church. It was during the 40's and 50's that a new generation came to power.

For instance, John F. Kennedy was born May 29, 1917. At the age of thirty, he was elected to the U.S. House of Representatives from Massachusetts. Being elected at this young age was unheard of. He served from 1947 to 1960, first as a member of the House of Representatives, and then in the U.S. Senate. He was elected the thirty-fifth president (Democrat) of the United States in 1960, at the age of forty-three. He was assassinated at the young age of forty-six on November 22, 1963, in Dallas, TX.

Church leadership is also going through a changing of the guard.

President Kennedy was not the only young leader to emerge during that period. Consider Martin Luther King, Jr., born January 15, 1929. He was the most famous leader of the American Civil Rights Movement, a political activist, a Baptist minister, and one of America's greatest orators. In 1953, at the young age of twenty-four, King became pastor of the Dexter Avenue Baptist Church in Montgomery, Alabama. In 1957, at age twenty-eight, King was instrumental in founding the Southern Christian Leadership Conference (SCLC). In 1959, at age thirty, he wrote *The Measure of a Man*, from which the piece *What Is Man*—an attempt to sketch the optimal political, social, and economic structure of society—is derived. Dr. King organized and led marches for African-Americans' right to vote, desegregation, labor rights, and other basic civil rights. Most of these rights were successfully enacted into United States law with the passage of the Civil Rights Act of 1964 and the Voting Rights Act of 1965.

In 1963, King was among the leaders who organized the historic March on Washington. There, he delivered his speech "I Have a Dream," which electrified the crowd and much of America. It is regarded, along with Abraham Lincoln's Gettysburg Address, as one of the finest speeches in the history of American oratory. He was thirty-four years old. President Kennedy, who opposed the march, met King afterwards with enthusiasm, and repeating King's line back to him — "I have a dream" — nodded his approval. In 1964, at the age of thirty-five, King became the youngest man to be awarded the Nobel Peace Prize. Sadly, on April 4, 1968, King was assassinated in Memphis, Tennessee at the age of thirty-nine.[8]

This was a unique time in history, as leadership shifted to an emerging generation and produced some of America's most outstanding leaders. Today, this identical shift is taking place. We haven't witnessed such an enormous influx of thirty-three to forty-six year olds in every sphere of leadership for sixty years. The last two elections have produced the greatest number of under-forty-five year old candidates in history, from both sides of the aisle.

Church leadership is also going through a changing of the guard. The landscape of Christian leadership, from the national platform to the local congregational body, is being dominated by the emerging generation. The voice of Christianity is getting younger. Take, for example, John Bevere, Andy Stanley, Ed Young Jr., Ron Luce, Craig Groeschel, Rob Bell, Mark Driscoll and Joel Osteen, just to name a few.

> The number of senior pastors ages twenty to thirty-eight in Protestant churches has doubled in just two years.

According to a report by the Barna Research Group, the number of senior pastors ages twenty to thirty-eight in Protestant churches has doubled in just two years from about 22,000 to more than 45,000, and these young pastors are making significant changes in their ministry approaches when compared to those who went before them.[9]

There is a global shift as well within Italy, Germany, Britain, Canada, Africa, and most of Europe. They are all reporting the same shift in national leadership. And for the first time in Asian countries the baton is being passed to the next generation — at times with much resistance.

CNN Money reports: Change is slowly coming to the world of Japanese politics. While the country's political system undergoes evolution, the political players are also changing — and it's often a matter of age. Think of Japanese politicians as the 70-somethings and the 50-somethings.

The changing of the guard underway is bringing with it a change of perceptions and a gradual shift in priorities. You can see the shift in Prime Minister Hashimoto's Liberal Democratic Party — in the way the LDP's leadership is getting younger. [10]

Understanding that generational wealth consists of more than just money, but also the philosophies, moral values, and leadership of a culture, it becomes vital that Judeo-Christian beliefs and doctrines are passed on to emerging generations.

Peter Drucker wrote: "Every so often throughout Western history, a sharp transformation has occurred. In a matter of decades, a society altogether rearranges itself – its worldview, its basic values, its social and political structures, its arts and its key institutions. Fifty years later, a new world exists. In addition, the people born into that world cannot even imagine the world in which grandparents lived and into which their own parents were born.

Failed leadership always leads to crisis for the generation that follows.

I believe we are living in one of those rare points in time, a period of total transition. The old worldview (modernism) with its trappings is dying and another (postmodernism) is struggling to be born. The consequence is a massive shift in our culture, sciences, society, and institutions. This change is enormously greater than the world has ever experienced before. We are living at a frightening point of absolute and chaotic discontinuity. It's a time when you will hear members of one generation say to the upcoming generation, "We always did it this way." The reply from the new generation is, "Yes but times have changed." The true leader will coalesce the best of both without alienating either one.

The original intent of teaching history in schools was to provide lessons from those who went before us, who have labored, fought, sacrificed, planted, discovered, pioneered, and built. Their examples and experiences can provide a clear path for future generations. Today, we have a revisionist movement attempting to rewrite history, and redirect us from that path — right before our eyes. The problem with revisionist history is that it masks the TRUE lessons that could be learned from the factual reporting of what took place.

History has proven that failed leadership always leads to crisis for the generation that follows. Out of that crisis emerge young leaders with the resolve to grab hold of the prevailing problems and issues that are crippling that nation, and bring significant changes.

Invaders of the Culture

The Church and its cultural irrelevance has become a major issue in the twenty-first century. There are some topics about which the Church is no longer considered to possess any insight or wisdom. In fact, the Church should be most able to instruct the culture in how to adapt to any circumstance. King Solomon noticed a unique thing about wisdom. He stated that wisdom was calling from the streets and public squares looking for any to listen.

> Wisdom calls aloud in the street, she raises her voice in the public squares;
>
> —Proverbs 1:20 (NIV)

So then, if Biblical wisdom isn't declared and taught in the sanctuary, it's substitute will be heard from the secular public arena. Today, the secular progressives have captured street wisdom in the public square. They have become the "mind molders" of our current culture — a position formally held by the Church for over two hundred years in America. How can the Church invade the marketplace and let the wisdom of the Bible influence our culture again? I believe the answer is to equip a new generation of young men and women who have an aptitude for learning and possess a strong faith.

The Book of Daniel records the incredible example of four Hebrew boys exiled in Babylon. To the Jews, Babylon was a secular society, lacking the teachings, principles, and truths of God (Torah Scriptures). This is a direction America is quickly moving toward.

Every civilization is supported and defined by its culture. There are at least six traits that are commonly found in every culture both past and present. They

> If Biblical wisdom isn't declared and taught in the sanctuary, it's substitute will be heard from the secular public arena.

are — beliefs, customs, languages, institutions, arts and literature. Christianity, like Judaism is a culture containing all six of these traits. The Christian belief system should function as a culture within a culture. This is exactly what we see throughout the last 2000 years of history. The culture of Christianity has helped shape and mold every known civilization. However, lately we've allowed Christianity to be defined as a religion, when it is not!

These Hebrew boys were able to stay faithful to their God and Jewish culture. They were quickly promoted to influential positions in a completely secular society. These young men possessed certain qualities that set them apart from their counterparts. Those qualities are listed in the book of Daniel.

> . . . showing aptitude for every kind of learning, well informed, quick to understand, and qualified to serve in the king's palace. He was to teach them the *language* and *literature* of the Babylonians.
>
> —Daniel 1:4 (NIV) Emphasis added

Though educated in Babylon's public schools Daniel, Meshach, Shadrach and Abednego rejected secular indoctrination and severed the Babylonian King using their convictions of Judaism. This should be the prayer of every Christian parent who sends their children to public schools—to reject evolution and moral ambiguity and become a witness to the world.

We must remember the words of Jesus:

> *. . . for the children of this world are in their generation wiser than the children of light.*
>
> —Luke 16:8 Emphasis added

America is in a war, and I'm not referring to the war against terrorism. Rather, a silent war is raging between the cultures. In his book "Culture Warrior," Bill O'Reilly defines this war and analyzes the competing philosophies of the traditionalist and secular-progressive camps. He declares that America is in the midst of a fierce culture war between those who embrace traditional values and those who want to change America into a "secular-progressive" country.[11]

The election of President Obama is evidence of this value war. President Obama has been applauded for his ability to capture the hearts of a younger generation of voters. Like never before in history, young people mobilized to help elect possibly the most liberal President this country has ever seen.

As this younger generation moves to the forefront, the Church is desperate for mentors of quality and aptitude to help them impact this culture.

A final note to this chapter — there is a tremendous need for education and empowerment classes to be made available at local churches on "biblical economics, wealth creation, management and the distribution of wealth and resources."

These types of ministries will not only attract believers, but will provide an evangelistic opportunity to gather non-believers from the local community to churches. Churches providing these services will experience incredible growth. Great things can be accomplished for the Kingdom through this type of cross-pollination. If the Church plays no role in this area, it is likely to experience the decline of yet another sphere of influence as it moves deeper into the twenty-first century.

CHAPTER SEVENTEEN

Thriving in My Economy

I would like to address the economic crisis of 2008-2009, considering it will have an effect on global markets and international workers for many future generations.

The U.S. economic crisis has contributed to a global recession, and many wonder if life will ever be the same. I sure hope not! We did not get into this situation by accident, or bad karma. Nor is this the judgment of God, which most prophets of doom declare at the mention of bad news.

Instead, this crisis is the consequence of violating certain principals, outlined in this book, which govern the creation, accumulation and perpetuation of wealth. Like the law of gravity, God has woven into the fabric of life specific laws that govern wealth. Violate them, and sudden economic disaster is unavoidable.

Hopefully, we're learning who **not** to call during an economic crisis! Ever wonder what happened to all the financial professionals, economists, forecasters, bankers and brokers who appeared to be brilliant prior to the collapse? How could they have missed a financial collapse of this magnitude? It is because anyone can manage money when the economy is in a raging bull market. But when the markets turn downward, you better have sound principles dictating your strategy or you will see loses mount. Now as a solution, many top "experts" have instructed individuals to remove their money from investments and put it under their pillows—as if "hoarding" is a viable solution for any financial problem.

> God always gives believers an advantage in every circumstance, including finances.
>
>

And let's be honest, turning to the government for financial wisdom is like another sequel to "Dumb and Dumber." When words like "stimulus" and "bailout" are used in any proposed economic strategy, the long-term impact is not promising. These two strategies are in direct opposition to each other. It's like a sinking sailboat trying to catch a good headwind, when there are obvious holes needing to be patched.

Wall Street and the government have left Americans, and the world, short on answers and long on questions. Many are asking, "How long is this crisis going to last? How do I prepare myself for an uncertain future?"

Believers are wondering: Is there a difference for faithful followers of Christ?

I must remind you of Jesus warning that "…. the rain falls on the just and the unjust alike (Matt. 5:45)." However, God always gives believers an advantage in every circumstance, including finances.

Sadly, many believers have not been equipped for financial success. For the most part, we have "trusted the experts" and neglected personal fiscal responsibility and proper financial education.

We live in a time when economics is not part of Church teaching or curriculum. Finance has been over-spiritualized and limited to giving and receiving. This is true even at the Seminary level. Students graduate from Bible College having learned nothing about budgets, markets, cash flow, economics, interests rates, balance sheets, or banking. The subject of acquiring, creating and managing wealth is largely ignored. For the most part we have been "catching up" rather than, like the Jews, "setting the pace."

The Biblical Pattern Of Cycles

I want to reveal the most important pattern in the Bible concerning success, productivity, and increase. It is so fundamental God interwove this pattern into every aspect of Jewish life. It has shaped the Jewish perspective on finance since the creation of the Torah. Jews throughout the world have used it to succeed in all economic endeavors, no matter what the financial climate. This pattern is a central component of their financial education.

First, consider that the majority of the Bible is written by Jews and uses manners and customs supported by Jewish thought. Jesus himself was a Rabbi, and the Apostle Paul—a former Pharisee—instructs believers, let the mind of Christ be in you (Phil. 2:5). What kind of mind was in Christ? Definitely, it is a mind shaped and influenced by Jewish manners, customs and theology. Without an in-depth understanding of this viewpoint, much is lost or, worse, misinterpreted.

Jewish thinking differs from Western thought. The widespread saturation of "Greek Thought" followed the success of Greece while under the reign of Alexander the Great. Alexander understood long-term victory and integration of conquered nations could not be accomplished through the sword — this would only maintain or contain an enemy. Conquer the mind and Greece would have a friend and ally. The influence of Alexander far outlived his short life through the education centers he built throughout his vast kingdom to train captives in Greek thought.

> For the most part we have been catching up rather than setting the pace.

The Greek philosophers Socrates, Plato, and Aristotle solidified Greek thought throughout the known world and that thought still influences people in the 21st century.

I would like to point out two central concepts of Greek thought that still persist today. First, the Greeks taught that the gods were in constant change. This transformation was the effect of man's progression and evolution. The gods desired to be worshiped, entertained and revered, but not necessarily obeyed. Greek intellect was the guiding light of man and all that pertained to his life. The Apostle Paul refers to this

> People get into trouble because they live with the assumption that their current economic situation will never change.

in 1 Corinthians 1:22, saying the Greeks seek wisdom rather than signs.

Second, history was on a time line, with events, one after another. The Western (Greek, Hellenistic) mindset is based upon linear progression. It begins at one point in time and progresses in a straight line towards the future. Very little value is placed on the past or future. The major emphasis of this type of thinking is on the "Now." You can see this type of mentality still influencing our western government. Both the Bush and Obama administrations showed a blatant disregard for lessons learned from the Great Depression. Plus, a reckless spending policy that is consuming the wealth of two ensuing generations, crippling their future. All so we can maintain our current lifestyles - Now!!

In comparison, the Jewish mindset is cyclical in nature. Time is continually repeating itself. The patterns of cycles are woven throughout the entirety of Jewish life. There are cycles of the Sabbaths, cycles of feast days, cycles of festivals, cycles of New Moons, cycles of new years, cycles of Jubilee and cycles of Torah reading. This is the basis of the cornerstone Jewish teaching from birth to death, "The Cycle of Life."

We find cycles embedded within creation — making it a pattern for life itself. Perhaps the best- known verse that speaks of cycles is found in Genesis 8:22,

> While the earth remaineth, seedtime and harvest, and cold and
> heat, and summer and winter, and day and night shall not cease.

This scripture informs us that while the earth remains as it was created, it will experience seedtime and harvest. More important, this cycle will not cease! To fail to understand this pattern is to encounter continual difficulty. Agriculture in the Bible is analogous to economic productivity. The Jews understand this verse to declare that everything in life has cycles, including markets, economies, people, relationships, and political environments.

Yes, life is lived in cycles. Throughout history, one thing has remained constant, and that is change. You cannot alter the seasons or their timing – you must adjust to them. Congress and Wall Street are attempting to stop

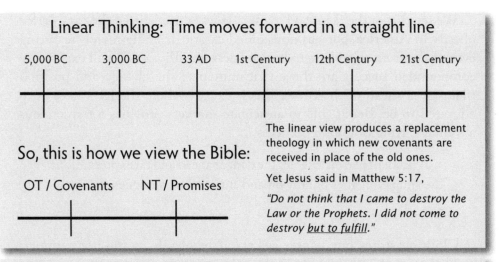

Linear Thinking: Time moves forward in a straight line

5,000 BC   3,000 BC   33 AD   1st Century   12th Century   21st Century

So, this is how we view the Bible:

OT / Covenants   NT / Promises

The linear view produces a replacement theology in which new covenants are received in place of the old ones.

Yet Jesus said in Matthew 5:17,

"Do not think that I came to destroy the Law or the Prophets. I did not come to destroy <u>but to fulfill</u>."

However, the Scriptures present a Cyclical (Hebraic) way of thinking which is critical to understanding the Bible.

In Rabbinic teaching, covenants, feasts and the Torah are built upon and supported by each other.

God taught the Jews through cycles—of Sabbath, of feasts, of years, of new moons, or Torah and of Jubilees.

It is interesting to note that when David says, *"He leads me in paths of righteousness..."* the word for "paths" actually comes from the Hebrew root '*agol*,' meaning to be round or a cycle. This is a familiar phrase to the Hebrew people. He is saying YHVH leads us in cycles of righteousness (yearly return of the feasts of YHVH).

a natural cycle of retraction from taking place. This bailout will prove to be the most costly mistake in U.S. history. The most our government can salvage is delaying the inevitable. The bailout is based on linear thinking which sacrifices our future security and prosperity in order to maintain our current lifestyles.

People get into trouble because they live and operate on the assumption that their current economic situation will never change.

Individuals and organizations that will survive economic downturns are those that realize everything is subject to change. Those that will experience sustainable success are those that respond to changing markets. They are flexible and adapt their businesses, product lines or employment to the current trend.

We see this in the fast-food market. It was once labeled the catalyst for obesity in America, but has now added calorie-friendly menus featuring everything from salad bars to healthy desserts. Those that will experience compounded success are those that anticipate the change and position themselves ahead of the curve. This is exactly where the Jews have been educated to be. Being able to anticipate markets provides a tremendous advantage. King Solomon observes,

> A prudent person foresees the danger ahead and takes precautions.
> The simpleton goes blindly on and suffers the consequences.
>
> —Prov. 27:12

Clothing stores buy winter jackets at wholesale in the hot summer; and below-cost bathing suits in the cold winter to resell at a premium to consumers who need it now.

This is an opportune time to buy undervalued stocks, underpriced real estate, or to change vocations or employment to future industries such as green energy, information technology and education.

Today, while economists and so-called government experts are baffled, confounded and confused by the global economic crisis, many Jews are harvesting an economic windfall. They expect cycles of expansion and cycles of contraction. They know well the story of Joseph and how he advised Pharaoh to store up grain for seven years in a time of plenty so that they would have provision in a time of lack. The key difference is they are not surprised by the current economic crisis. They have been prepared because they were taught to anticipate this circumstance long before the signs became apparent.

This type of financial education is needed in the church. With millions of Americans facing economic hardship, and a global recession on the horizon the Church must be a light with answers.

Today, Christians are facing panic and fear, wondering if they will survive this unstable time. At the same time, Jews are praising God for the opportunity to thrive during this economic crisis, as they have done in previous periods. What is it that causes Jews to flourish in troubled economies? The simple difference is they know how to utilize biblical strategies to prepare for every circumstance.

Get ready to be positioned for success and prosperity as you learn the twelve universal laws of wealth creation outlined in the final section of this book. Apply them and you will never be caught off guard for the rest of your life!

Section Three

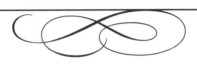

Twelve Biblical Laws of Wealth Creation

THE MIDAS TOUCH

In Greek mythology, Midas is popularly remembered for his ability to turn everything he touched into gold, out of which the phrase "*The Midas Touch*" was coined. In the corporate world, someone who consistently demonstrates the ability to prosper and flourish is often said to have "*The Midas Touch.*" Unlike King Midas, everything you touch will not turn to gold. We do not live in a fairy-tale world, and there are no magic formulas. However, for those who are diligent to learn and apply *The Twelve Biblical Laws* and remain faithful to God, they will capture numerous opportunities to prosper and lay a foundation for consistent profit and success.

I would like to warn you that these laws should never be used to create wealth for ungodly purposes or to promote immoral endeavors. Many may ask; "what is a universal law?" Here is a brief definition:

Universal Law/Principle — A principle embedded in creation that always succeeds and never fails; is applicable and present everywhere and in all cases; pertains to all existing things. (i.e. laws of gravity and lift)

If something fails once, it is a *theory*. If it fails often, it is *hypothesis*. If it never worked in the first place, it is *evolution*!

The Power to Gain Wealth

"The State giveth and the State taketh away." That's the attitude of millions of Americans when it comes to prosperity. It's contrary to both Scripture and the original intent of the United States' constitutional system.

It wasn't just any faith that led to prosperity.

From the beginning — *reflecting biblical principles* — the nation's founders declared that our rights, including those of work and wealth, were given by the Creator, not the State.

They knew what the State could give, the State can also take away.

Sadly, many Americans have slowly succumbed to a mentality that holds the State as the source of their prosperity. They vote for politicians who will tax and give away, tax and give away. Many become dependent on government for their existence.

There was no tax on income in the original Constitution. Government would defend the people and "provide for the general welfare." Revenue for its limited tasks would come primarily from duties on imports. Then, in 1916, the government was faced with financing its engagement in World War I, and the income tax was instituted. In 1943, embroiled in another conflict — World War II — President Roosevelt decided that withholding tax from every paycheck would be quicker than requiring people to pay annually. Thus, the immediate taking of taxes became part of the legal system of our country. The measure was supposed to be temporary to deal with wartime needs, but it was never reversed. Now the government takes its share right off the top, *before* it gets to the hands of the people who earned it.

Taxation is one of the many tools by which government gains control. It's the source of many woes in a society — especially when a government spends frivolously and squanders the peoples' money, or spends money on causes contrary to personal values.

The Bible's way of prosperity is vastly different and infinitely better. In fact, it's proven. For example, *The Christian Science Monitor* posed this question in an article: "Do Europeans work less because they believe less in God?"[1] The report dealt with Harvard studies aimed at discovering if there is "a link between religious belief and economic performance."

The answer was a clear *yes*.

- In 2003, Harvard researchers studied 60 nations, and found there was a link between economic prosperity and a belief in the biblical idea of hell.

- History Professor Niall Ferguson found that a decline in the hours the average European works coincided with a decline in faith.

- But it wasn't just any faith that led to prosperity, Ferguson concluded. "This divergence . . . coincides with a period of European de-Christianization and American re-Christianization."[2]

- Though the *Christian Science Monitor* column didn't deal with it, the economic surge in China, many argue, is because of the increase in biblical values, arising from the ministry of the hundreds of thousands of house churches.[3]

While the Bible's prosperity teachings have been twisted, abused, and misused to justify personal greed, its truths do indeed lead to abundance. Prosperity results from pushing forward and breaking out of economic bondage. The worldview presented in the Bible is that of forward movement and freedom. Forgiveness makes it possible for us to break away from past mistakes. Jesus said He had come explicitly to set captives free (see Luke 4:18).

Prosperity, THEN, IS NOT THE INVENTION OF *politicians* OR *economists*.

Just because a doctrine is abused doesn't mean it should be neglected or abandoned.

Accountability and stewardship are vital in wealth-building, and the Bible presents these as core principles. A steward, as the Bible shows, is a person who manages someone else's property or finances. The steward has the authority to administer the possessions of the person for whom he works as an agent. In biblical times, as now, stewards ran the household, or enterprise. While the steward had authority, he also was accountable for how he managed his master's wealth.

Eliminate the biblical ideas of accountability and stewardship, and you have a workplace characterized by slothfulness, low productivity, high conflict, and continual employee turnover.

Many nations are finding this out the hard way, as the Harvard studies show. Some segments of the Church have had as much difficulty talking about money and economics as others have had talking about grace. The doctrine of grace has been de-emphasized in various periods because of the fear it would lead to an amoral lifestyle. So there are churches that say nothing about the link between biblical truth and prosperity because they fear they will cultivate "name it and claim it," or "health and wealth" Christians. However, just because a doctrine is abused doesn't mean it should be neglected or abandoned.

Money is power, and its highest use is the advancement of God's Kingdom.

Jesus Himself said, "The thief comes only to steal and kill and destroy; I came that they may have life, and have it abundantly" (John 10:10). That abundance extends to both the here and now, as well as Heaven.

God's covenant includes prosperity and the generation of wealth. His foundational covenant people, Israel, were to:

" . . . remember the LORD thy God: for *it is* He that giveth thee ***power to get wealth***, that He may establish His covenant which He sware unto thy fathers, as *it is* this day.

—Deuteronomy 8:18 EMPHASIS ADDED

This covenant originated with the patriarch Abraham. God's blessing produced prosperity beyond measure. The Bible records the increase of his household, his servants, his cattle, his land, and much more.

This blessing is not only personal, but also corporate. It extends to all those who are willing to adhere to the provisions of the covenant. That is, if individuals and nations followed God's principles of wealth generation, they would find prosperity inherent in God's Kingdom. Prosperity is *systemic* within the Kingdom. That is, the biblical laws and principles about wealth constitute a coherent system that repeatedly produces prosperity. Allow that body of truth to shape one's personal view of finance, and prosperity "happens," as revealed in the Harvard studies cited earlier. Those same principles can be applied to national economic policies as well.

> Money is power, and its highest use is the advancement of God's Kingdom.

Joseph adhered to God's Word. He didn't seek wealth, but sought to honor God in everything, no matter what the personal cost, and prosperity resulted. Joseph was found faithful as a steward of Potiphar's wealth and was later given stewardship for the national economy of Egypt.

The Bible reports it like this:

And the LORD was with Joseph, and he was a prosperous man; and he was in the house of his master the Egyptian. And his master saw that the LORD was with him, and that the LORD made all that he did to prosper in his hand. And Joseph found grace in his sight, and he served him: and he made him overseer over his house, and all that he had he put into his hand. And it came to pass from the time that he had made him overseer in his house, and over all that he had, that the LORD blessed the Egyptian's house for Joseph's sake; and the blessing of the LORD was upon all that he had in the house, and in the field.

—Genesis 39:2-5 Emphasis added

Even when Joseph was thrown into prison under the false accusation of attempting to seduce Potiphar's wife, God blessed him with abundance (Genesis 39:20-23).

Joseph had a personal commitment to God that resulted in a lifestyle of discipline and hard work. That's the foundation on which The Twelve Biblical Laws of Wealth Creation are established.

Like the law of gravity, these laws are unshakable. From ancient times to the modern world, these laws of prosperity have governed and protected wealth.

It has taken me a lifetime to discover these twelve laws. It has been a journey of difficulty, trial, success, and failure. If you choose to ignore these laws, you will not be able to create wealth, nor sustain your existing wealth. If you follow them, they are the foundation upon which all wealth is built and sustained from generation to generation.

Law One

The Law of First Things First

"We do what we value and we value what we do,"[1] says church growth expert Bill Beckham.

Priorities constitute a value system that arranges all the affairs of a person's life. If you want to understand someone's true values, study their daily schedule and checkbook stubs. These speak much louder about genuine priorities than a voice that proclaims how much it treasures this or that.

Our priorities arise from our value system. They are gauged by the amount of time, energy, and material resources we allocate to our activities and the order in which we do them. A father may claim he is committed to his family, but if he allocates no time, energy, or resources to his children, then I would say his desire is more an aspiration than a priority.

Life can be fulfilling, successful, and prosperous if we learn to put "first things first." To accomplish this, the Bible lays out a clear set of priorities.

FIRST PRIORITY – GOD

Jesus states this priority clearly when He says in Matthew 6:33, "seek first His kingdom and His righteousness, and all these things will be added to you." The context of "all these things" refers to the accommodations and necessities of life with which some are obsessed. When you are a follower of Christ and place God and His Kingdom as the main priority, He will ensure that you are both sustained and blessed.

> Leadership is stewardship, and it must begin with family.

When God provided Israel with the Ten Commandments He instructed the people in the Law of First Things First, by reserving the top spot for Him. How then can we know that God is first in our lives? I suggest that you analyze the time allotments of your week. Create a log of how many hours you spend — with your family, at leisure, at work, at church, or in prayer. That information should tell you if God is your first priority. A meager two hours a week spent at church, when there are 168 available, does not indicate that God has the primary position in an individual's life.

There is a direct connection between making God and His Kingdom the priority and the provision of "all things." When we put God's purposes first, He provides the resources to accomplish whatever He calls us to do.

We don't prioritize God and His Kingdom to get wealth, but material resources flow as the result of making that commitment.

SECOND PRIORITY – FAMILY

Family is high on the list of qualifications for leadership in the church. In fact, caring for one's family is a qualification for a man to be an elder. Conversely, he who cannot govern well in his family fails the test of leadership. Paul writes in 1 Timothy 3:4-5 that the elder "must be one who manages his own household well, keeping his children under control with all dignity, but if a man does not know how to manage his own household, how will he take care of the church of God?"

If a person doesn't give his family the correct priority, it reveals a weakness in his view of what's important. Leadership in the church or in any entity can be a passion quencher. A CEO can become so absorbed in establishing and sustaining a company that he or she forgets the importance of establishing and sustaining his or her spouse and children.

Leadership is stewardship, and it must begin with family.

There is an epidemic of neglect in modern American families. Many would object to being accused of giving low priority to their spouse and children. They would argue that they provide toys, trips and trinkets galore. Yet, the statistics show that for many people, family is low on the list of things they deem important.

In the book Family-Based Youth Ministry, Mark DeVries writes:

> With one in four young people now indicating that they have never had a meaningful conversation with their father, is it any wonder that 76 percent of the 1,200 teens surveyed in *USA Today* actually want their parents to spend more time with them? [2]

Andree Alieon Brooks, a *New York Times* journalist, in her eye-opening book *Children of Fast-Track Parents*, describes her interviews with scores of children and parents who seemed to "have it all."

> "If there was one theme that constantly emerged from my conversations with the children it was a surprising undercurrent of aloneness — feelings of isolation from peers as well as parents despite their busy lives."[3]

My father was committed to earning a living for our family. He was a disciplined hard worker. However, what we needed most was not his paycheck, but *him*. We needed Dad to toss a baseball with us and to be with us on those rocky roads we all travel in the process of growing up. But, most of the time he was at work.

Prioritization of family is a central law of wealth building primarily because spouses, children — even aging parents — constitute a segment of stewardship. Financial success hinges on the effective management of assets. If one has a problem seeing members of his or her own family as "assets," it's unlikely he or she will have a proper regard for the management of money.

THIRD PRIORITY – MINISTRY

Many years ago, Elton Trueblood distinguished between vocation and the work we do to earn our living. Trueblood called the wage-earning job your "other vocation." A person's true vocation, Trueblood wrote, is his or her ministry.[4]

> The Church is only as strong as its families and that the way of the family is the way of the Church.

Every individual's personal ministry should be focused on the advancement of God's Kingdom in this fallen world. Early in my Christian walk, I was not given these priorities in the proper order. I was told that our priorities should be arranged with ministry being placed before family. This teaching remains as a gross error within the Church. Many Christian leaders experience divorce and are still allowed to function in ministry as if nothing happened. Statistics inform us that the Church is suffering from family dysfunction, experiencing a 58% divorce rate among its members. It has been said that the Church is only as strong as its families and that the way of the family is the way of the Church.

However, ministry still must be an important priority in our lives. Paul opens Ephesians with the urging that we "walk worthy of the vocation wherewith ye are called" (Ephesians 4:1). The Greek word translated "vocation" literally means "a calling to." Your vocation is the ministry purpose for which God put you in the world.

In the Twenty-first century, God is challenging His children to exchange meaningless talk for a meaningful walk. Mission asks the question, "What on earth are you doing?" There is a present-day epidemic of people who do not know their mission and purpose for life. Now we have second and third generation children who are being raised without purpose in mind.

Could this be the reason for sleepless nights, depression, and anxieties? Could this be the missing link causing difficult and broken relationships, teenage rebellion, and drug and alcohol abuse? Fulfilling your purpose is so important that Jesus Himself had a mission statement. He stated in the Gospel of John that He came that we may have life and life more abundantly.

Jesus modeled a life of purpose. In the book of John He stated:

> I have glorified thee on the earth: *I have finished* the work which thou gavest me to do.
>
> —John 17:4 Emphasis added

It is difficult to finish the work if one never starts it. In her masterful book, *The Path,* Laurie Beth Jones notes that in World War II, if an unidentified soldier appeared suddenly in the dark and could not state his mission, he was shot without question.

According to Acts 20:24, Paul desired that above all things he might finish his course with joy. In 2 Timothy chapter 4:7, while handcuffed to a guard and awaiting execution, he said *"I fought a good fight, I have finished my course, I have kept the faith."*

Richard Leider and David Shapiro wrote in *Repacking Your Bags,* that according to research, the number one fear of people is living a meaningless life.[5]

This concern is echoed in Philippians where Paul explained:

> Holding forth the word of life; that I may rejoice in the day of Christ, **that I have not run in vain, neither labored in vain.**
>
> —Philippians 2:16 Emphasis added

How important is a purpose and mission statement? Well, it answers the age-old questions: Why am I here? Why do I exist? And what should I be doing?

A mission statement will assist you in two ways.

1. It Defines "What" I Am Doing

Jesus had an amazing effect on the people with whom He came into contact. It was as if destiny was looking right at them. This is especially seen with the calling of the apostles.

And he saith unto them, Follow me, and I will make you fishers of men. *And they straightway left their nets, and followed him.* And going on from thence, He saw other two brethren, James the son of Zebedee, and John His brother, in a ship with Zebedee their father, mending their nets; and he called them. And they *immediately* left the ship *and their father,* and *Followed him.*

—Matthew 4:19-22 Emphasis added

Why would they instantly drop their nets, leave their ships, and follow Him? It is because they felt a sense of purpose and mission in Jesus that motivated their decision. Far too much of what is going on in the Church and in the world has not come from a mission, but is a reflection of the human ego left unchecked.

2. It Helps Me Get through Difficult Times and Make Critical Decisions

And we know that *all things work together* for good to them that love God, to them who are the *called according to His purpose.*

—Romans 8:28 Emphasis added

There are Corporate retreats designed to help companies and other organizations develop purpose and mission statements that cost thousand of dollars, as Laurie Beth Jones notes in *The Path.*[6]

Employers are investing more in executive coaching, mentoring and career development. Assessments probing for strengths and weaknesses drive up costs of human resource development. All this, as Jones observes, are attempts to help people get purpose and direction for their lives.

God has a specific purpose and assignment for every believer. Paul stated in:

> Who hath saved us, and called us with an holy calling, not according to our works, but according to his own purpose and grace, which was given us in Christ Jesus before the world began.
>
> —2 Timothy 1:9

Viktor Frankl did pioneering work showing that Nazi concentration camp inmates who could hold on to a sense of meaning for their lives had a higher survival rate than others.[7] Frankl spent five years in Auschwitz and other infamous camps.

He discovered that people with the greatest chance for survival and sanity were those who had,

- A sense of life-meaning

- Purpose and goals

- Strong faith in God and the fact there was a divine plan for their lives

- High intellectual content in their minds and a capacity for reflection

- Those who clung to the bonds of their loved ones

All this adds up to the fact that a personal life mission is critical for a person's ability to endure and even advance in the face of trials, tests, and challenges.

If you don't put First Things First, then you may end up like Samson, who fell asleep in the lap of Delilah and lost his strength. Samson's poor decisions were a result of him not sticking to God's purpose and mission in his life.

Having a personal mission statement guides our decisions, because it keeps us on a path that leads to a specific destination. For instance, there are certain investments that I will not consider purchasing because they do not fit my mission statement. Some opportunities, while attractive, still may divert the plans of God for my life.

Unfortunately, many people end up wasting years and money going in directions that ultimately don't fit their mission. Mission is critical for having an efficient and effective life.

To begin to create wealth in your life for the Kingdom of God, you must have your priorities in proper order. Max Lucado says, "Undefined priorities are at the root of much of our success-or-failure frustration." I have found that when you practice The Law of First Things First and put the three aforementioned areas in their proper order, all secondary priorities fall right into alignment.

Law Two

The Law of Generosity

Philanthropy is on the rise in the United States. One reason is people are catching on to the link between giving and receiving.

Paul Newman, the acclaimed actor, started a company, Newman's Own, Inc. Paul Newman and Newman's Own donate all profits and royalties to charities and compassion organizations. Since its inception in 1982, Newman has given away some $200 million to thousands of charities.[1]

Arthur C. Brooks, of Syracuse University, wrote a book, *Who Really Cares: The Surprising Truth About Compassionate Conservatism.* There he revealed findings that "religious conservatives donate far more money than secular liberals to all sorts of charitable activities, irrespective of income."[2]

Fortune Magazine reported that of the top twenty-five philanthropists in our nation, only four inherited fortunes. Eighty percent attributed their generosity to religious backgrounds. And all were givers even before they became wealthy.

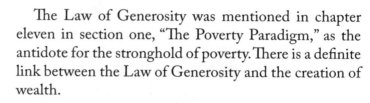

For the Law of Generosity to be applied, it must be a lifestyle and not just an act of giving.

The Law of Generosity was mentioned in chapter eleven in section one, "The Poverty Paradigm," as the antidote for the stronghold of poverty. There is a definite link between the Law of Generosity and the creation of wealth.

In its purest sense, giving is a spiritual concept. God, within His very nature, is the Giver of all good things. The gift of salvation through the sacrifice of His own Son is the foundation of the entire Christian faith. As a result, there is a principle embedded in the universe that applies to physics, human relationships, money, and all facets of living: REAPING IS LINKED TO SOWING. Stingy sowing leads to a meager harvest. Generous planting results in a bountiful garden. Paul mentions this principle in his letter to the Corinthians:

> Now this I say, he who sows sparingly will also reap sparingly, and he who sows bountifully will also reap bountifully. Each one must do just as he has purposed in his heart, not grudgingly or under compulsion, for God loves a cheerful giver. And God is able to make all grace abound to you, so that always having all sufficiency in everything; you may have an abundance for every good deed . . .
>
> —2 Corinthians 9:6-8

This verse is revealing that giving is actually an accelerator to accessing "all grace." Every aspect of grace shall abound toward you if the Law of Generosity is activated in your life. It is the skeleton of wealth. God will ensure that "all grace" will abound toward you. Grace for your family, your ministry and mission in life, grace for your endeavors, and grace for wealth creation will be given if you abide by the Law of Generosity.

Generosity is multi-generational. The emerging generation must learn the value of money and the principles surrounding it. This was at the top of John D. Rockefeller's priority list in raising his children. In the book, *"Kids on Cash"* authors Ken Davis and Tom Taylor explain how billionaire Rockefeller taught this principle to his children:

> "John D. Rockefeller, Jr., was certainly not trying to save money when he decided to pay an allowance to his five sons. According to Nelson, "We got 25 cents a week and had to earn the rest of the money we got." To earn part of that extra money he raised vegetables and rabbits . . ." "We always worked," according to Nelson. All the boys were required to keep personal daily account books. They were required to give 10 percent of their income to charity, to save 10 percent, and to account for all the rest. They had to balance their account books every month and be able to tell what happened to every penny they earned. Nelson went on to serve as governor of the state of New York for many years, and, ultimately, became vice president of the United States. One of his brothers, David Rockefeller, chairman of the Chase Manhattan Bank, says, "We all profited by the experience — especially when it came to understanding the value of money."[3]

Please note that Rockefeller required that his children give the first 10 percent of their earnings to charity. Sound familiar? Rockefeller understood that the Law of Generosity created a lifestyle that God could bless. He understood that by having a generous outlook on life and teaching his children to do the same, he was creating a legacy of continual reaping as well.

Generosity is multi-dimensional and refers to more than just money. For the Law of Generosity to be applied, it must be a lifestyle and not just an act of giving. A lifestyle is a commitment to live a certain way that transcends a motivated moment of generosity. This is exactly what Jesus was referring to when he instructed his disciples:

> Give, and it shall be given unto you; good measure, pressed down, and shaken together, and running over, shall men give into your bosom. For with the same measure that ye mete withal it shall be measured to you again.
>
> —Luke 6:38

Notice Jesus didn't specify "what" we should give. Jesus was indicating that whatever you gave, you would get back "pressed down, shaken together, and running over." Give of your time, your energy, your prayers, and you'll receive back what you gave, but multiplied. Giving affects every area of your life.

If I come home from work and give my wife an attitude, I'll be sure to get it back, "pressed down, shaken together, and running over!"

I was amused by a recent story I heard. A woman was out shopping one day and decided to stop for a cup of coffee. She bought a bag of cookies, put them into her purse, and then entered a coffee shop. All the tables were filled except for one at which a man sat reading a newspaper. Seating herself in the opposite chair, she opened her purse, took out a magazine, and began to read. After a while, she looked up and reached for a cookie, only to see the man across from her also taking a cookie. She glared at him; he just smiled at her, and she resumed her reading.

Moments later she reached for another cookie, just as the man also took one. Now feeling quite angry, she stared at the one remaining cookie — whereupon the man reached over, broke the cookie in half and offered her a piece. She grabbed it and stuffed it into her mouth as the man smiled at her again, rose, and left.

The woman was really steaming as she angrily opened her purse, her coffee break now ruined, and put her magazine away. There was her bag of cookies, unopened! All along she'd unknowingly been helping herself to the cookies belonging to the man with whom she had shared the table.

The Law of Generosity must be a lifestyle. You don't give to get, you give to bless, and by continually giving, God will honor your lifestyle by causing men to give into your bosom.

> There is that scattereth, and yet increaseth; and there is that withholdeth more than is meet, but it tendeth to poverty. The liberal soul shall be made fat: and he that watereth shall be watered also himself.
>
> —Proverbs 11:24

Years ago a Sunday school in Philadelphia was overcrowded, much like some of our children's departments today. A little girl was turned away. She began, that day, to save her pennies to help the Sunday school have more room. Two years later, she died. They found a pocketbook by her bed with 57 pennies and a little scrap of paper with a note saying to help the church build a bigger Sunday school.

The pastor of that church, Dr. Russell Conwell, used that note to make a dramatic appeal to his congregation. People's hearts were touched. One realtor gave the church a piece of land. He said he just wanted a down payment of 57 pennies.

The local newspaper picked up the story, and it was carried across the country. The pennies grew, and the results can be seen in Philadelphia today. I've never been to that spot, but I'd like to go see that church. It seats 3,300 people with a large Sunday school department. I'd like to visit Temple University and Good Samaritan Hospital which came about as a result of that initial effort. I'd like to visit the room at Temple University where that little girl's picture is on the wall with the reminder that she gave 57 cents with amazing results.[4]

> You don't give to get, you give to bless.

A life of generosity is a circle that will produce exponential fruit in our life and have unimaginable benefits in the lives of those around us.

LAW THREE

The Law of Time

Time management is big business because it leads to big dividends. The American Management Association notes that:

> In today's harried, frantic business world, superior time management is critical for individuals and organizations. Greater productivity, improved results, and reduced stress — these are just some of the benefits that successful time management confers. Yet, research conducted by Proudfoot Consulting indicates that unproductive time for the average U.S. worker amounts to 33 days per year. Clearly, effective time management continues to elude many of us.[1]

Stephen Covey writes that time management is crucial for the productive lifestyle of highly effective people. So we have Palm Pilots, Blackberries, Outlook, pocket calendars, flow charts, atomic clocks, and a host of other gadgets to help us make time our ally.[2]

The person living under kingdom authority knows stewardship goes beyond material possessions to include the stewardship of time.

Time management was very much on Moses' mind when, in desperation, he received important counsel from his father-in-law. Moses was exhausted from trying to mediate between snarling opponents, solve the problems of scores of anguished people, and give counsel to the mournful. His father-in-law, Jethro, suggested he appoint "captains" — today we would consider them mid-level managers — to distribute the workload. However, the real issue was managing time.

This concept is at the heart of Psalm 90:12, where Moses prays, "So teach us to number of our days, that we may apply our hearts unto wisdom." The Hebrew word translated "number" not only means to assign sequence, but to "allot" and "appoint." Thus, the prayer is focused on the wise use of time.

Moses is wondering how he can get the very best out of life. He's conscious of the fact that time is marching on. Israel's leader wants every moment to count. God alone has the number of our days, and only God can enable us to maximize the precious time we have.

The kingdom man or woman lives in the consciousness of this truth:

> You do not know what your life will be like tomorrow. You are
> just a vapor that appears for a little while and then vanishes away.
>
> —James 4:14 (NAS)

Foolish people believe they will live on the earth forever, or that time is an unlimited commodity. Wise people are those who recognize the brevity of opportunities and commit themselves to seizing every moment.

Time Strategy for Success

For many, the approach of a new year and its uncertainties can be an overwhelming thought. As the ball drops in Time Square many will make resolutions that will be broken quickly.

I'm constantly looking for parcels of time that can be used effectively. The truth is, I'm happiest when I'm getting more than one thing accomplished at the same time. I try to look for ways to multiply the increments of time that make up my day.

For example, the demands of being a pastor, consultant, and CEO can gobble up my whole twenty-four hours like those carnivorous smiley faces on old Pac Man games. Yet, I'm also a husband and father, and the time I have with my wife and growing children is zipping by. I must use every precious allotment of that time.

Many years ago, I developed a time strategy to maximize each year. If I look at a whole year in advance, I get overwhelmed. But when I break the twelve-month period into manageable segments, order emerges. Paul gained tremendous insight from athletic competitions throughout his epistles. Paul referenced runners, boxers, wrestlers, and marathoners in providing his readers with valuable principles for life. A few years back, in the last game of the regular season, the New York Giants mounted a huge second-half comeback, to win the final spot in the playoffs. During the post game interview, Head Coach Jim Fassel was asked if he believed his team could overcome the deficit after the rough start. In response, the coach revealed his full game strategy. I was amazed to hear in essence the same time strategy now being applied to football.

> When I break the twelve-month period into manageable segments, order emerges.

He believed that if he divided a game into four quarters and approached each quarter as a game in itself, then the team could possibly lose one or even two quarters and still be victorious. With that game plan, he motivated his team at half-time to forget the two previous quarters and to go out and play the best two quarters of the year — then at the end of the game, they would be positioned for success.

Coach Fassel used the art of *time management* to adopt an effective strategy for each game. In the same way, we must employ an effective time strategy to manage our life effectively.

For over twenty years my approach to the new year has been the same — divide, and then sub divide. At the beginning of each year, I take our core leadership away for two days to seek the Lord and lay out the plans, quarter by quarter. Every new year is divided into four manageable quarters. Then those quarters are divided into individual months to which goals, tasks, and deadlines are assigned.

This process is repeated within each organization that I oversee. Failure to do this, inevitably cost us wasted time, deferred blessing and missed opportunities. During this time we review our vision, mission, and purpose along with assessing our goals by asking, "What is God calling us to accomplish this year?"

> For I know the plans that I have for you, declares the Lord, plans to prosper you and not to harm you, plans to give you hope and a future.
>
> —Jeremiah 29:11 (NIV)

Don't despair if a quarter doesn't meet your expectations, for there will be other quarters in which you will excel beyond your dreams and bring balance to your pursuit. As you continue to sow good quarters, you will begin to receive compounded dividends from previous ones in years past. A bad year is one in which we've not governed any quarters. It saddens me when I see people give up on an entire year because the first three months haven't gone well. It's vital to remember that there are nine more months ahead!

> We must not trust in luck or chance for the success of our lives. God is in control of my destiny and time.

Some may question, "Is this limiting the spontaneity of the Holy Ghost?" My response is that very little in the Bible is spontaneous. God revealed to Abraham the path by which he would walk, to Joshua the land in which he would be victorious, and even Samuel was sent by God to anoint David king years before he would sit on the throne.

We must not trust in luck or chance for the success of our lives. God is in control of my destiny and time. Luck and chance are the lazy man's excuse for the undisciplined and unplanned life. There is a saying, "If you aim at nothing, you'll hit it every time."

TIME WAS CREATED SO THAT *purpose* COULD BE FULFILLED.

Failure is a result of poorly managing your time. "Time is money," goes the old adage, and we could add, "bad time management is a loss of money."

Time Maximizer

During business conferences or training sessions I sometimes spend an entire day on this subject. Also, since the initial release of this book we've been asked for more of the techniques we use on time management — all of which have been added to the accompanying curriculums.

PROJECT MANAGEMENT (Example)

List all of your current projects. Make separate lists for home and work related projects.

Assign priority levels to each project, using a scale of 1–5:

1 = Must complete this month

2 = Must complete this quarter

3 = I will schedule this when higher priorities are completed

4 = Someday I will get to this, if I can

5 = Discard! These are projects that will take valuable time, energy and resources away from more important projects.

ACTION STEPS:

Determine who is responsible for each project, and what is needed for completion.

1. **Personal Projects**: Set realistic time markers, or mini-goals to track your progress from start to completion.

*Do not set completion date first — follow the Action Steps process. This ensures a realistic completion date.

Example: To complete this curriculum, my entire team collaborated on a comprehensive project path (our sub-projects and goals), which was then submitted to our publisher. The publisher then committed their team to accomplish the goals as detailed by our project path. Every individual was able to track their responsibilities and understand their role in relation to all the other components of the project as a whole.

Time-markers, or milestones, can be weeks, months, or longer, depending on how much time a project will need.

Sub-projects are simply a way to break down a complex project into smaller, more manageable tasks. For example, suppose a current project is to revitalize your home office. A sub-project might be to update your file system or replace your folders.

2. **Projects to Delegate**: When you delegate a project to someone else, you still need to set milestones. Determine the following:

   - Who is responsible for this task?

   - What is the time frame for completion?

   - Is this task part of a greater project? If so, Integration is necessary. How does this individual task integrate with the entire project — who or what is dependent on the completion of this task?

3. **Projects to Discard**: This analysis is vital to achieving greatness — deciding what projects are worth your time and are in accordance with your personal calling. Whether an individual, company, or ministry, there must be a willingness to sacrifice many good things in order to become great at a few things.

When you contemplate taking on a new project, ask yourself; *Can I do a great job at this?* If the answer is no, discard it.

It's important to understand the value of time and consider OPT (other people's time). Because I value time, I don't like to waste anyone else's. If I'm wasting someone else's time, I'm squandering mine as well. So, in every interaction, whether a family evening, a staff meeting, or a conference, I want to maximize the time others are giving to the occasion. As a result, my time gets maximized, too!

If life is measured in terms of time, then time wasted is life abused.

Being too preoccupied with past failures also wastes your time. "Don't let yesterday use up too much of today," said Will Rogers.[3] The day is a span of time nobody is wealthy enough to waste. The stewardship of time means considering the minutes as precious.

It's been said that if you take care of the minutes, the hours will take care of themselves. So, as the sayings go:

Take time to Work - It is the price of success.

Take time to Think - It is the source of power.

Take time to Read - It is the foundation of knowledge.

Take time to Laugh - It is the music of the soul.

Take time to be Courteous - It is the work of a gentleman.

Take time to Pray - It is the Christian's vital breath.

God's truths are universal. Investment strategists understand how time can make you money or lose it for you. They advise clients to invest for the long haul. Though markets may experience short-term fluctuations, the long-term investor will experience success.

Unfortunately, many of us squander not only our money, but our time as well. Studies from the University of Maryland and the California Air Resource Board show this. In studies of people eighteen to sixty-four years old, the research indicated that, on average, people spend their minutes each day like this:

Sleeping - 461 minutes

Working - 211 minutes

Watching TV - 121 minutes

Doing Housework - 101 minutes

Traveling - 78 minutes

Eating - 69 minutes

Socializing - 48 minutes

Recreation - 31 minutes

Caring for children - 28 minutes

Dressing - 28 minutes

Washing and grooming - 25 minutes

Reading - 24 minutes

Conversing - 24 minutes

Thinking or relaxing - 9 minutes[4]

It's evident many people squander their precious allotments of time — and with it, their wealth.

To use your time wisely, think of a person wandering in a vast desert. He has a map and GPS system that tells him where he is and how far it is to the next oasis. The desert explorer has a canteen of water, and carefully portions out his drinks so that every drop is used wisely. If he is diligent and uses the guidance provided and uses the resources wisely, he will succeed. If not, he will most certainly fail.

Time management is a law that governs the fruit of our lives in the accumulation and creation of wealth. How we manage the Law of Time determines the productivity and ultimately, the prosperity of our lives.

LAW FOUR

The Law of Intellect

The Law of Intellect governs our capacity to reason, plan, comprehend ideas, think abstractly, and learn. This law is applicable to every aspect of life including wealth, health, relationships, success, security, and longevity. Intellect is inclusive of three specific levels. They are: knowledge, wisdom, and instruction.

- ✳ Knowledge - the accumulation of facts

- ✳ Wisdom - the application of facts

- ✳ Instruction - direction calling for compliance

These three levels are expounded on throughout the Bible. All throughout Scripture, you'll find that the combination of wisdom, knowledge, and instruction always produces wealth, riches, and prosperity.

God says in Proverbs 8:10-11:

> "Receive my *instruction* and not silver, and *knowledge* rather than choice gold. For *wisdom* is better than rubies; and all the things that may be desired are not to be compared to it." Emphasis added

"Wisdom," says Proverbs 8:21, "endows" those who love her with wealth and fills "their treasuries." The Scripture clearly teaches that wealth accompanies wisdom and knowledge. No wonder Benjamin Franklin said that the best place to put your money is in your head!

Many people believe that their financial problems are due to lack of money. Yet, more money usually means more problems. In most cases it's not more money that's needed, but rather the wisdom to handle more money.

THE PURSUIT OF WISDOM

Proverbs instructs us in the pursuit of wisdom.

> Wisdom is the principal thing; therefore *get wisdom:* and with all thy getting *get understanding*.
>
> —Proverbs 4:7 EMPHASIS ADDED

This Scripture gives insight that wisdom is the heartbeat of the Law of Intellect. It was Solomon's passionate pursuit of wisdom that assisted him in answering the critical question of God, "Ask what I shall give you" (2 Chronicles 1:7).

As you begin your pursuit of wisdom, you will discover four types of wisdom essential for building wealth:

1. Scholastic Wisdom

There is no prize in God's courts for stupidity. Throughout history, the Church has been populated with groups of people who disdain or perhaps fear academics. The Bible, however, calls for a life of continual learning. It is far from anti-education. It is, in fact, a collection of books revealing the highest level of education possible. It's the study of discipleship. But it's not just theology we are to study. God's Kingdom people are to "understand the times" (1 Chronicles 12:32).

There is value in understanding the broadly revealed truths of God in nature and society so that they can be applied for good. We should always be seeking to fill our minds with truths that can bear fruit in our lives.

Scholastic wisdom is gained from the study of mathematics, the sciences, history, and language. We see that Daniel and his friends were well-rounded in their education. So much so that they were selected by the Babylonian king to be prepared for high-ranking governmental positions.

> In most cases it's not more money that's needed, but rather the wisdom to handle more money.

> Children in whom was no blemish, but well favored, and skillful in all wisdom, and cunning in knowledge, and understanding science, and such as had ability in them to stand in the king's palace, and whom they might teach the learning and the tongue of the Chaldeans.
>
> —Daniel 1:4

> As for these four children, God gave them knowledge and skill in all learning and wisdom: and Daniel had understanding in all visions and dreams.
>
> —Daniel 1:17

Moses received the highest level of education Egypt had to offer.

> And Moses was learned in all the wisdom of the Egyptians, and was mighty in words and in deeds.
>
> —Acts 7:22

Likewise, Paul was learned in Talmudic, Greek, and Roman studies. Clearly, scholastic wisdom was a contributing factor to their overall success.

2. Professional Wisdom

Scholastic wisdom sets the foundation for professional wisdom. Professional wisdom is gained by following the educational track for known professions. Doctors, lawyers, accountants, and the like must apply themselves to gain specific professional wisdom to step into those positions and receive "continued education" to excel. Successful businessmen will tell you that they must constantly gather new knowledge to remain competitive in an ever-changing marketplace.

I rely on those who possess professional wisdom to give me counsel and direction for success. Believers should not be discouraged, but rather encouraged to gain professional advice for their life. More Christians should follow the necessary paths to fill these professions so that God can use them to be providers of this type of wisdom.

3. Financial Wisdom

Many have wrongly interpreted 1 Timothy 6:10 which says, "The love of money is the root of all evil." They read the passage as saying "*money* is the root of all evil." People with that mind-set think it is selfish and greedy to become a wise investor. They disdain the study of economics, financial markets, stocks, bonds, and other elements of wise investing. They miss the fact that it is the *love* of money that becomes idolatry. Money itself can and should be used mightily for God. Genuine disciples must include financial wisdom in their range of studies.

4. Spiritual Wisdom

This is the crowning wisdom. It alone has the ability to integrate all the other aspects of wisdom. It gives them cohesion and unity. "For the LORD gives wisdom; From His mouth come knowledge and understanding. He stores up sound wisdom for the upright," states Proverbs 2:6-7. Physicists, since Einstein, have sought the "unifying field" of everything in the universe. Spiritual wisdom brings every fact, every element of truth, and every law of the visible and invisible into one great statement of truth and reality.

Knowledge is the understanding and perception of facts and data. Wisdom is the capacity to know what to do with the information. Someone may have great knowledge, but lack wisdom. The truth is: information is useless without the wisdom to know how to apply it. A person with much knowledge but little wisdom will contrive plans that are flawed and destined to fail. Wisdom, then, is knowledge rightfully applied.

Scripture tells us that spiritual wisdom is controlled and distributed by God. This truth is seen in Daniel 12:4. There, after God's messenger has enabled Daniel to see into the future, the angel tells Daniel, "**shut up the words, and seal the book**, even to the time of the end: many shall run to and fro, and knowledge shall be increased."

We are living in a time when people rush "to and fro," bursting with knowledge, but lacking wisdom. For example, we have volumes of books written by experts about marriage and family. There are countless marriage seminars, workshops, and private counselors, yet divorce soars and dysfunctional families fill our land. Without wisdom, knowledge is incomplete.

> Information is useless without the wisdom to know how to apply it.

However, wisdom can be hindered where there is no knowledge. God says in Hosea 4:6, "My people are destroyed for lack of knowledge. Because you have rejected knowledge, I also will reject you from being my priest. Since you have forgotten the law of your God, I also will forget your children."

It is taught in the Body of Christ that Joseph was promoted from the pit to the palace because of his interpretation of Pharaoh's dream. When in actuality he was promoted because he was able to give Pharaoh a complex, organizational system to survive the upcoming famine.

> Now therefore let Pharaoh *look out a man discreet and wise*, and set him over the land of Egypt. Let Pharaoh do this, and let him appoint officers over the land, and take up the fifth part of the land of Egypt in the seven plenteous years. And let them gather all the food of those good years that come, and lay up corn under the hand of Pharaoh, and let them keep food in the cities. And that food shall be for store to the land against the seven years of famine, which shall be in the land of Egypt; that the land perish not through the famine.
>
> —Genesis 41:33-36 Emphasis added

Many in the Body of Christ are dreaming when they should be receiving wisdom and knowledge to make their dreams a reality. Pharaoh recognized that Joseph manifested a type of wisdom not seen in any Egyptian. As it reads:

> And Pharaoh said unto Joseph, Forasmuch as God hath shewed thee all this, *there is none so discreet and wise as thou art*:
>
> —Genesis 41:39 Emphasis added

Christ's followers should be leading the quest for wisdom and knowledge, not shrinking in ignorance.

———∞∞∞———

Unfortunately, in some circles the word of wisdom and the word of knowledge have become very mystical. Too often God's wisdom and knowledge have been made trivialized. We've reduced the "word of knowledge" to nothing more than a televangelist pinpointing bodily defects in an audience or a word to sow a financial seed to receive some "miracle harvest."

Like Joseph, believers need to use the gift of wisdom, outside the church service, and in the marketplace.

The Bible teaches that God, through the gift of wisdom will give us plans, strategies, organizational designs, the ability to unravel complex equations, and other resources required for building wealth. The knowledge and wisdom essential for wealth generation doesn't come through passivity — it's given by God. We are to pursue it and seek it. As we take the initiative to petition God, He supplies the resource. God's supply of knowledge and wisdom is abundant:

> How blessed is the man who finds wisdom, and the man who gains understanding. For her profit is better than the profit of silver, and her gain better than fine gold. She is more precious than jewels; and nothing you desire compares with her. Long life is in her right hand; In her left hand are riches and honor. Her ways are pleasant ways, and all her paths are peace. She is a tree of life to those who take hold of her, and happy are all who hold her fast. The LORD by wisdom founded the earth, By understanding He established the heavens. By His knowledge the deeps were broken up, and the skies drip with dew. My son, let them not vanish from your sight; Keep sound wisdom and discretion: So they will be life to your soul, And adornment to your neck. Then you will walk in your way securely, and your foot will not stumble. When you lie down, you will not be afraid; When you lie down, your sleep will be sweet.
>
> —Proverbs 3:13-24

The knowledgeable wealth-builder gathers information. He or she studies assets and liabilities, profit margins, corporate issues, and past performance before investing in a company. However, wisdom guides in the amount and manner of investment and the use of money. Those who ignore biblical principles reap disaster.

Christ's followers should be leading the quest for wisdom and knowledge, not shrinking in ignorance. We live in that time, foreseen by Daniel, when knowledge is increasing (Daniel 12:4).

Knowledge, says management guru Peter Drucker, is the source of all competitive advantage. More than 80 percent of history's technical knowledge was acquired in the twentieth century, and scientific knowledge now doubles every ten years.[1]

In the twenty-first century, the knowledge base is expanding rapidly, and by some estimates, doubles in less than a year.[2] God, who controls all things, is releasing increasing levels of wisdom, knowledge and information for the end times. This opportunity for learning is unprecedented in history.

Throughout history, wealth has always followed social, industrial, and technological advancements. Social scientists have identified three distinct ages which serve as a brief outline of history: the agricultural age, the industrial age, and the information age. The agricultural age refers to the time period which spanned most of known history to about 1860 and was named for the main occupation of over 90 percent of all workers. The industrial age covers the time period from 1860 to about 1956, marked with the rise of industrial factories. The information age began about 1956 and continues to the present.[3]

> God wants to give you the ability to gain wealth that is relevant to your time and culture.

We are witnessing a virtual explosion of information. More information has been produced in the last thirty years than in the previous five thousand. This is seen in publications alone.

Approximately ninety-six hundred different periodicals are published in the U.S. each year, and about one thousand books are published internationally each day. Printed information doubles every eight years. A weekday edition of the New York Times contains more information than the average person was likely to come across in a lifetime in seventeenth-century England.[4]

Wealth is relevant, either to a geographical region or to a specific era. During the agricultural age, wealth was defined as farmlands. Wealth has shifted from agriculture to industry and from industry to information. Two hundred years ago, 95 percent of the U.S. work force was involved in farming. Today, less than 4 percent of the employed is farming. By 1900, 25 percent of the U.S. work force was in factories. By 1950, 65 percent of the working population was in factories. Today, only 15 percent of the current work force is in factories.[5] This chronicles the shift of wealth creation and distribution as well.

It would have been useless for God to provide Abraham with diamonds, since no market for the precious stone had been established. So God prospered him with the wealth of his day — flocks, herds, servants, and land.

Deuteronomy states that God gives us the "power to gain wealth" (Deuteronomy 8:18). This is crucial to understand since God is not going to give you wealth; rather, He will give you the power to gain wealth. This principle is true throughout history and throughout the countries of this world. Regardless of your age, ethnicity, or country, God wants to give you the ability to gain wealth that is relevant to your time and culture.

Today, we are in the age of intelligence. Intellectual property has the highest value of any asset in our society. We serve a God who desires to distribute intellectual property so we can prosper in our present-day economy. Believers should be positioned favorably in our time.

The Starting Point

History's greatest example of knowledge and wisdom joined perfectly in one person is Jesus Christ. Colossians 2:3 says, "all the treasures of wisdom and knowledge are hidden in Him." To know Christ is to have access to all He knows. Thus, the acquisition of knowledge and wisdom begins with receiving Christ as Savior and Lord.

> The fear of the Lord, is the beginning of knowledge — but fools despise wisdom and instruction.
>
> —Proverbs 1:7

> O the depth of the riches both of the wisdom and knowledge of God!
>
> —Romans 11:33a

LAW FIVE

The Law of Creative Power

Creativity is the logical product of wisdom and knowledge and manifests itself in ideas, inventions, and innovation.

The book of Proverbs states,

> I wisdom dwell with prudence, and find out knowledge of witty inventions.

> —Proverbs 8:12

Humans have the capacity to create because we are made in God's image. We meet God in the beginning of the Bible as Creator. Our creative capacities are so great they manifest early in life. My son, Joshua, for example, like all children, is surprisingly creative. When he was barely eight, he took a box I had left over from a mail order item and turned it into an airplane. He attached wings, installed a phone, contrived some controls — even had his favorite blanket. That evening when I got home, my little boy was in the box, and his mind was on a TransAtlantic flight!

Jesus says the Kingdom of Heaven is for children and adults with a childlike heart. We must be born again and enter the Kingdom as children. Imagination awakens the reflection of God's creativity in us, and the child-like heart with its huge capacity to dream and dare is essential for our ability to innovate.

Innovation takes objects around you and turns them into something else, something more, something unique. I hold my Bible, a physical object made from items in nature. A tree supplied paper. Animal skin provided the leather. Chemicals made through the combination of elements found naturally in the world supplied the ink. Then the Holy Spirit infused the natural elements that constitute the book with supernatural power and meaning. This is a picture of God's linking of the natural and spiritual. He innovates with clay and dust, produces a human body, and then He pours in His Spirit. God is both creative and innovative!

Christians SHOULD BE THE WORLD'S MOST *creative* PEOPLE.

In the early days of our country, 90% of all inventions came from Christians! They included medical breakthroughs, scientific discoveries, technological advancements, social structures, and organizational strategies.

This is precisely what history shows. On January 11, 2004 scholar Michael Novak spoke to a Sri Lankan group about the moral base of capitalism. Novak provided profound insight about the link between creativity and prosperity. He said:

" . . . God created humans in his own image, to be co-creators. Each woman and man is born with the inalienable right to personal economic initiative, the right to invent and to create. Each human being is an Imago Dei, an image of God, born to be creative and inventive. One sees this in the very opening of *Smith's Inquiry into the Nature and Cause of the Wealth of Nations*

(1776), in his example of the invention of the machine for mass-producing pins. Such invention is the chief cause of new wealth. This emphasis upon invention and creativity is the distinctive characteristic of the capitalist economy. The capitalist economy is not characterized, as Marx thought, by private ownership of the means of production, market exchange, and profit. All these were present in the pre-capitalist aristocratic age. Rather, the distinctive, defining difference of the capitalist economy is enterprise: the habit of employing human wit to invent new goods and services, and to discover new and better ways to bring them to the broadest possible public.[1]"

Professor Rodney Stark also understands well the link between the creativity arising from biblical faith and prosperity. In his book, *The Victory of Reason: How Christianity Led to Freedom, Capitalism and Western Success,* Stark writes that:

"Without Christianity's commitment to reason, progress, and moral equality, today the entire world would be about where non-European societies were in, say, 1800. This would be a world with many astrologers and alchemists but no scientists. A world of despots, lacking universities, banks, factories, eyeglasses, chimneys, and pianos. The modern world, to which globalization aspires, arose only in Christian societies. Not in Islam. Not in Asia. Not in a secular society — there having been none."[2]

Your assignment: Find a problem that needs a solution and solve it.

Stark recalls that Chinese scholars were asked,

"Look into what accounted for the success, in fact, the preeminence of the West all over the world." After considering possible military, economic, political and cultural explanations, they concluded that the answer lay in what the Chinese scholars saw as the "heart" of the West's preeminent culture: Christianity. These non-Christian and non-western scholars had "no doubt" that "the Christian moral foundation of social and cultural life was what made possible the emergence of capitalism and the successful transition to democratic politics." Apparently, many of their countrymen agree. Whereas there were approximately 2 million Christians in China when Mao came to power in 1949, today there are upwards of 100 million. What's more, Christianity is especially popular among the "best educated" and most modern Chinese.[3]

Noah constructed an ark the size of a football field, and with more rooms than the Titanic. This "state-of-the-art" vessel could never have been built without the creative hand of God.

Michael H. Hart wrote a book called *The 100: A Ranking of the Most Influential Persons in History.* Eighty-percent of the people listed were Christians. They included scientists, inventors, and others who affected humanity with their creative gifts.[4]

That creativity and innovation ought to continue today. Imagine what could happen with a round table of Christ's sharpest disciples. There would be prayer and strategizing. The Church ought to be in the forefront of pulling together business and technical people to spur product innovation. When there's a problem in culture, assemble a group of believers whose natural insight has been enhanced by the Holy Spirit, and ask them to provide an answer.

God's people are planted in the heart of a society to provide creative solutions. The truth is that everyone on the earth has the ability to solve a problem. Having access to the creativity and innovation of God should make Christians the greatest problem solvers in the world. That is your assignment. Find a problem that needs a solution and solve it. When you do, wealth and riches will follow.

Throughout Scripture, God provided individuals with innovative and creative solutions to major, complex problems. More than 6,000 years ago, Noah constructed an ark the size of a football field, and with more rooms than the Titanic. This "state-of-the-art" vessel could never have been built without the creative hand of God. Creativity is an attribute of God. He spoke to nothing and it became everything. Give God your nothings and He will help you turn them into something.

By faith we understand that the universe was formed at God's command, so that what is seen was not made out of what was visible.

—Hebrews 11:3 (NIV)

As you enter your workplace, look at how to make it better—not just how to earn a check. Find ways to improve your job and sharpen systems. Create new management processes. Be innovative by establishing new production procedures. Develop fresh marketing and sales approaches.

Rather than blaming your employer for not making the company profitable enough, provide solutions. It's not his or her issue; it's yours —if you want to get ahead. People who have employed that strategy have ended up owning companies, or at least being asked to become partners in the enterprise. Why not you?

The more we activate The Law of Creative Power in a manner that benefits our society and solves problems, the more we manifest His image. And the more we know Him and allow Him to work through us, the more creative we will be — and that includes being creative and innovative with our money.

Law Six

The Law of Divine Endowments

What we do arises from who we are. Being precedes doing. Thus, our functional activity is a product of our true identity. Ask a person, "Who are you?" and the answers will be many. "I am an accountant," one will say. "I am a parent," another might reply.

This shows our penchant for defining ourselves in terms of what we *do* rather than who we are. It's important, then, to consider the functionality that arises from our essential being and expressed as our gifts, talents and skills.

Many people miss opportunities to build wealth because they don't understand their true identity and the abilities related to it. Peter Drucker states, "Most Americans do not know what their strengths are. When you ask them, they look at you with a blank stare, or they respond in terms of subject knowledge, which is the wrong answer." The Law of Divine Endowments is the gifts, skills, and talents given by God to enhance and accomplish His purposes in our lives and in His Kingdom.

Talents come naturally through family lines, cultural milieu, and social influences. Talents, however, must be aligned with gifts. Attempt to develop a talent not consistent with who you are as an individual and not in line with your strengths, and you have a prescription for frustration.

> Most Americans do not know what their strengths are. When you ask, they look at you with a blank stare, or they respond in terms of subject knowledge, which is the wrong answer.

In their book *Now, Discover Your Strengths*, Marcus Buckingham and Donald Clifton state:

"Unfortunately, most of us have little sense of our talents and strengths, much less the ability to build our lives around them. Instead, guided by our parents, by our teachers, by our managers, and by psychology's fascination with pathology, we become experts in our weaknesses and spend our lives trying to repair these flaws, while strengths lie dormant and neglected." [1]

Skills are the practical abilities we can acquire, hone, and develop. They constitute our crafts, whether those we enjoy as hobbies, or the ones we use to earn a living and build wealth.

These practical skills, linked with our natural talents and supernatural gifts, produce works in the material world that accomplish purposes in the spiritual realm.

This is what happened when God called Moses to build the Tabernacle. The Lord, who is objectively and factually omnipresent, focused and localized His manifest presence in a particular place. The Tabernacle was known as the "tent of meeting" because it was the place where man conferred with God (Exodus 27:21).

The Tabernacle would have been considered a wonder of the world in Moses' day. So advanced was the Tabernacle that God had to visualize the completed structure to Moses and reveal the blueprint so that he could construct it. He descended from the mountain of God and was faced with the daunting task of mobilizing the workers to build this incredibly innovative structure.

The problem the Israelites faced was that the technologies, skills, crafts and talents weren't advanced enough to build what God had ordered. The color purple, the process of interweaving gold in linen, and the pottery God requested were yet to be invented or discovered. Such furniture as the Mercy Seat, the Ark of the Covenant, the Table of Shewbread, and the seven-branch candlestick posed additional difficulty for the Jewish craftsmen.

Currently, our church is in a major building project. When the general contractor showed me the mechanical plans of the facility, I thought, "I don't know what I'm looking at!" Yet, the contractor was familiar with every detail on the plans. This is exactly how the Jews must have felt looking at the Tabernacle plans. How were they going to complete this awesome task? They did it only through the intervention of God. Look at how He equipped them:

> See, I have called by name Bezaleel the son of Uri, the son of Hur, of the tribe of Judah: And I have filled him with the spirit of God, in wisdom, and in understanding, and in knowledge, *and in all manner of workmanship, To devise cunning works, to work in gold, and in silver, and in brass, And in cutting of stones, to set them, and in carving of timber, to work in all manner of workmanship.* And I, behold, I have given with him Aholiab, the son of Ahisamach, of the tribe of Dan: and in the hearts of all that are wise hearted I have put wisdom, that they may make all that I have commanded thee; The tabernacle of the congregation, and the ark of the testimony, and the mercy seat that is thereupon, and all the furniture of the tabernacle, And the table and his furniture, and the pure candlestick with all his furniture, and the altar of incense, And the altar of burnt offering with all his furniture, and the laver and his foot, And the cloths of service, and the holy garments for Aaron the priest, and the garments of his sons, to minister in the priest's office, And the anointing oil, and sweet incense for the holy place: according to all that I have commanded thee shall they do.
>
> —Exodus 31:2-11 Emphasis added

God released the spirit of wisdom for divine endowments on the camp of Israel. Everyone open to His instruction and available for His use received immediate knowledge, gifts, natural talents, and all manner of craftsmanship!

A builder, who in one moment had no clue as to where to start, and in the next, had the ability of instant craftsmanship. A seamstress couldn't conceive of the intricate curtains she's to make of animal skins for the Tabernacle, and suddenly has full understanding.

> The techniques He gave to these Jews for building His house became marketable in other products.
>
>

Perhaps the gifts of God came deep in the night. Maybe men and women who worked skillfully with their hands had dreams in which the Holy Spirit told them what to do.

It could be that a metalworker had a vision of casting the rings that would hold the magnificent veil separating the Holy Place from the rest of the Tabernacle. Or maybe the seamstress, in one great visionary panorama, saw how to make a six-inch veil that would support the weight of an elephant. Throughout the camps of Israel, God gave people crafts, gifts and talents.

The Hebrew craftsmen could look at materials they had long used and suddenly see them in a different way, with new possibilities. I am amazed at "number crunchers" — People who can see things in number-relationships that most of us miss. Mathematicians and physicists are able to depict the natural phenomena of creation with formulas that lead them to expanding discoveries about space, matter, and time. Accountants and financial experts can plot the history and future of a business based on their understanding of the numbers.

Then there are physicians and medical technicians who can look at a scan or X-Ray and see what the untrained eye cannot. Consider the computer wizards — some still in their teens — who have the ability to create electronic objects that dazzle the world.

All these examples will give you a sense of what God did with those primitive Hebrew workers assigned to build the Tabernacle. According to Exodus 35:35, the Lord gave them:

...wisdom of heart, to work all manner of work, of the engraver, and of the cunning workman, and of the embroiderer, in blue, and in purple, in scarlet, and in fine linen, and of the weaver, even of them that do any work, and of those that devise cunning work.

Not only did these God-given skills allow them to build the Tabernacle, but they also gave them a **marketable commodity**. For example, people from around the world came to the camps of Israel to buy their purple, gold-laced linens, and scarlet cloths.

God blessed His covenant people with these abilities, first to build the Tabernacle and second to gain wealth. The techniques He gave to these Jews for building His house became marketable in other products.

In the early days of the United States' space program, scientists sought huge sums of money based on the promise that there would be many spin-off benefits from the technologies they would develop. And the promise has proven true. In like manner, as Israel poured wealth, energy, and skill into building the Tabernacle, they were acquiring the power that would enable them to become the world's trading partner!

So today we must ask, "*What is it God wants to do through me that will bring resources into His Kingdom, lead to its advancement, and generate wealth?*" I love these accounts of God providing crafts and skills to Israel, because it speaks of the development of human potential. Years ago, management focused on one thing only — the product. In the 1960s, students of management tell us, the concentration shifted to people. That was during the time that large corporations began to include a human resource development wing in their planning.

> What does God want to do through me that will bring resources into His Kingdom, lead to its advancement, and generate wealth?

It's evident the construction of the Tabernacle had the additional effect of bringing spiritual gifts like wisdom, knowledge, and innovation into the area of commerce. God provided for this creativity to spill over into the market place, which was not separated from kingdom growth, but actually a crucial facet of its advancement. What God showed Moses and the Hebrews sparked the entrepreneurial spirit, which arose from God's own Spirit.

When the Indianapolis Colts and Chicago Bears vied for the 2007 Super Bowl, two committed Christian coaches faced one another. When the Colts won, everyone praised Coach Tony Dungy's team building and strategizing skills. Dungy — and his counterpart, the Bears' Lovie Smith — credited the Lord with their opportunities and abilities. They even joined to purchase a full-page ad in *USA Today* declaring that, though divided on the gridiron, they were together in their commitment to Christ.

George Washington Carver was another African-American — like Dungy and Smith — filled by God with skills and a talent for innovation. Carver became fascinated with the peanut from which he created 300 products, including soap and ink. Carver developed another 118 products from the sweet potato, and 75 from pecans.

Carver's intent was to benefit poor southern farmers who were trying to eke out their survival from the soil. He, by his own admission, was always aware of the source of his gifts, skills, and talents. He gave God the glory for the inventions that resulted in prosperity for many. Carver sought no patents because he believed food plants were a gift from God. He told people, without apology, that he knew his ability to understand plant life came directly from God.[2]

People like Dungy, Smith, and Carver understand that God's divine endowments are for more than just the Church. They have unlimited potential when used in every facet of society.

For this reason, our ministry assists individuals in discovering their gifts and talents. We provide tests and assessments that help individuals discover their "gift mix" and establish their areas of strength. I encourage you to make every effort to hone in on your strengths and talents that God has given you and activate The Law of Divine Endowments.

Law Seven

The Law of the Brand

This law is the foundation upon which every other wealth creation law described in this book is built. No other law can function correctly if this one is not practiced. Our name or "brand" should be looked at as something placed in our will as a legacy left for generations after us. Not only is this law the foundation, but it transcends our natural life. Who will forget the name of John Hancock, whose signature on the Declaration of Independence was big enough that not only were the English able to read it, but every generation since? Because Hancock was the first to sign, his name became synonymous with the freedom upon which America was built.

Your name is much more than a label distinguishing you from other people. Today, young couples considering names for their babies search name books, looking for first names that rhyme with their last, or for

> A name has value.
> It represents
> the essential
> character,
> integrity, and
> accomplishments
> of an individual.

the most popular names. In previous times, a name was descriptive of the person to whom it was given. Each name was given with a prophetic nature and transferred intention for the life it was given. In the Bible, names were so important that the intervention of angels in human affairs was often characterized by name changes.

When Jacob wrestled with the Angel of the Lord in Genesis, his blessing contained a name change. So profound was this change, that it altered the very course of his destiny. The name carried with it a change of status, both socially and spiritually. The changing of Paul's name from Saul signified the new life he was given and the monumental call God placed on his life.

A person's name has value. It represents the essential character, integrity, and accomplishments of an individual. There is genuine currency in a good name. It opens doors, brings opportunity, and allows you acceptance in circles you otherwise would not be able to penetrate. The book of Proverbs says:

> A good name is rather to be chosen than great riches, and loving favor rather than silver and gold.
>
> —Proverbs 22:1 Emphasis added

Most acquaintances will never get the opportunity to know us intimately, so our character is only known by the name and reputation that precedes us. Socrates said, "Regard your good name as the richest jewel you could possibly be possessed of . . ." [1]

A bad name cannot be concealed. Someone who intends to enter into a serious negotiation or business partnership will be diligent to get under the surface and find out what you are really made of. That is why a "good name" is so important, and why it is one of the laws of wealth creation.

If your name is associated with lying, cheating, or a lack of trust, it's unlikely you're going to find many business partners.

In the corporate world, a company's name is known as their brand. Branding has become a major focus for those on the cutting edge of marketing. Corporations spend millions of dollars defining themselves through their names, symbols, and identities. Their brands are tested through focus groups, trial campaigns, selected targeted research, and only then do they build their strategy around that well-defined brand. Then they spend even more money keeping that brand name in front of the public.

According to one study, American children develop brand loyalty as early as age five. On the other end of life, by age sixty-five, the average person has watched some two million commercials. Advertisers have spent in excess of $50 billion and more to get their name in front of TV audiences.[2]

Your name is *your* brand. If companies spend hundreds of millions to make their name known through positive brand association and millions more on lawyers to protect that brand name, surely we should give priority to establishing a "good name" for ourselves!

This is exactly what was chronicled in the life of Jesus. Jesus "increased in wisdom and stature, and in *favor* with God and man"(Luke 2:52 (KJV) EMPHASIS ADDED). Even in His youth, Jesus had a good name before many. Ultimately, the religious and political establishments would despise that name as many do today. However, to the hurting, sick, and needy people, His name is matchless in its ability to bring comfort and hope.

When our names no longer symbolize integrity and justice, it's quite unlikely that others will trust us with their resources. I have walked away from business relationships — even some that had the potential to be lucrative — because individuals involved carried names that couldn't be trusted.

> Your name is your brand. If companies spend hundreds of millions to build and protect their brand, surely we should give priority to establishing a "good name" for ourselves!

On the other hand, I'm willing to enter into an agreement with someone who has a good name based on a handshake rather than a signed contract. President Theodore Roosevelt had it right when he said, *"It is better to be faithful than famous."*[3]

Over the years, I've lost thousands of dollars due to ventures that went sour. Rather than looking for ways to escape the situation, I sought to find out how to fulfill my obligations to ensure my name would not be tarnished. This is more important than the pursuit of riches. After all, I will pass my name down to my sons as a major facet of my legacy. I want it to be an asset that can aid them in the future, not a liability they have to drag around. In turn, my sons must understand that our name needs to be guarded and its use governed. What they do is a reflection on our name.

It's vital to bring back to society the stability, value, and wealth of a good name. When you make a promise or commit to something, make sure you fulfill it.

This is especially important in relationships. Countless children are continually disappointed by parents who regularly break their promises — like pledges to spend time together, attend a sporting event, watch their baseball or soccer game, or maybe just hang out.

Like the words of Harry Chapin's song, "Cat's in the Cradle," one day our children will grow up to be just like us.

> *"My son turned ten just the other day.*
> *He said, "Thanks for the ball, dad, come on let's play.*
> *Can you teach me to throw?" I said, "Not today,*
> *I got a lot to do." He said, "That's ok."*
> *And he walked away, but his smile never dimmed,*
> *Said, "I'm gonna be like him, yeah.*
> *You know I'm gonna be like him."* [4]

To break a vow is to dishonor and devalue one's name. Solomon reminds us that God holds us to our word.

> When thou vowest a vow unto God, defer not to pay it; for he hath no pleasure in fools: pay that which thou hast vowed. Better is it that thou shouldest not vow, than that thou shouldest vow and not pay.
>
> —Ecclesiastes 5:4-5

A good name is marketable. This applies not only to products, but also to people. I want to be known as a man of such high integrity that I can call my banker, tell him I need a loan to buy property, and have his response be, "John, I will make it happen!"

Some people value a highly respected name in corporate circles above being highly respected in the personal realm. You probably can think of very successful corporate people who have exceptionally poor reputations as human beings. For the Christian, there should always be a vital link between the two.

I'll never forget an experience I had a few years back with a certain Christian businessman. He was not pleased with the speed of service from one of the companies I oversee, which led to an ungodly verbal assault on my employees. When I confronted him, he stated that his "business sense" was different from his "spiritual sense." He made a clear distinction between his business life and his spiritual life.

My employees, who looked at this man as an example, lost a great deal of respect for him. His bad business affected his spiritual leadership. As I travel the country, I find people worshipping God on Sunday, yet being ungodly in business on Monday, and it is a real problem within the Body of Christ. Clearly, the Bible teaches we are to be an example in all things. In mentoring young Timothy, Paul instructed him that his selection of future leaders must meet the requirement of having a good name outside the church as well as inside the church.

A more notable example played out in national headlines was Ken Lay. For many years his name was associated with very positive endeavors in Houston, Texas. He was noted for his charitable contributions to the community. A big, shiny new building on a major thoroughfare bore the name, "Ken Lay YMCA." He had given very generously to provide the institution for the community. However, when Enron — the company he led — collapsed because of financial scandals, so did Ken Lay's good name. Now it has almost become synonymous with deception and dishonesty.

It's sad, because there were many positive elements to Ken Lay. However, to neglect the connection between what labels us personally and what marks us in our work is to shatter the reputation of both our personal name and the corporate entity to which we're linked.

I get upset when a payment is not made on time in the businesses, ministries, and companies for which I have leadership and stewardship responsibilities. Bills should be paid not only "on time," but early. Late payments affect your credit score and good name in the marketplace.

Attempting to build wealth without a good name is like trying to erect a building on quicksand! Ultimately, even the strongest edifice will be sucked downward.

I mentor many young men in their twenties who are on the way to becoming millionaires. They have the intellect, energy and drive to reach the heights of financial success. They don't have to wait until they are as old as I am to achieve financial, corporate and personal success.

This is an area where God seems to place me constantly within the emerging generation. I'm committed to helping them move forward at a faster pace, guided by the combination of these power principles of wealth creation and godly priorities.

One of these young men is a mortgage broker. He teaches clients how to rebuild their credit so they can qualify to own a home or refinance an existing loan at a better interest rate. The first thing he does is assess their existing credit, and strategize with them to improve their credit standing. This is a simple thing, but he understands how a good credit score or "good name" can save the individual thousands of dollars over time.

In 2005, the number of bankruptcies in the United States totaled over 2 million. Many people signed their names to a financial obligation and then took the easy way out by declaring bankruptcy. Only when we esteem a good name higher than riches will this trend be reversed.

It's vital to build the value of your name. If you apply yourself, you could see dramatic changes in the marketability of your name within a year. Attempting to build wealth without a good name is like trying to erect a building on quicksand! Ultimately, even the strongest edifice will be sucked downward. If you practice The Law of the Brand, people will line up to associate with you. You will be amazed at how quickly success is achieved and how many doors are opened in the business community.

LAW EIGHT

The Law of Synergy

Synergy occurs when there are two or more people or agents acting together to create an effect greater than that predicted by knowing only the separate effects of the individual agents. It is the powerful outcome of relationship.

Right relationship is the very core of salvation. Think about this: it's not *what* you know that gets you to Heaven, but *who* you know. Relationship is important to God's heart, and vital for humans made in His image. Take away relationship, and we wither. For example, many babies were abandoned in the grim communist world. They were taken to orphanages where their lives were minimally sustained. Those who had no human interaction through affectionate contact, tender words, and expressions of love, were the first to get sick and die.

Dr. Bernie Siegel found that:

> Single men are jailed more often, earn less, have more illnesses and die at a younger age than married men. Married men with cancer live 20 percent longer than single men with the same cancer. Women, who often have more close friendships than men, survive longer with the same cancers. Married or not, relationships keep us alive.[1]

The Carnegie Technological Institute reported that 90 percent of people who fail in their vocation do so because they can't get along with others.

The quality of our relationships directly impacts the quality of our lives. Sadly, many people have drifted into a mentality of isolation. The modern trinity has become "me, myself, and I."

The importance of interaction is seen in how much focus our adversary gives to destroying relationships in the Body of Christ.

A man once told his pastor, "It seems like there's been some kind of fight in every church I've ever attended." "Why should that surprise you?" the pastor replied, "We're engaged in warfare, and the Church is at the forefront of kingdom advancement. The enemy of our soul will try everything possible to destroy us."

Sadly, much "church growth" in America is from people transferring from one church to another. They get wounded in one congregation and switch to another to escape the hurt.

The Apostle Paul challenged the Galatians on the matter of relational conflict.

> But if ye bite and devour one another, take heed that ye be not consumed one of another.

> —Galatians 5:15

It's not just the Church that comes under this attack, but families, businesses, and whole communities. Jesus founded His earthly ministry on relationships. Mark writes that the Lord "appointed twelve, so that they would be *with Him*"(Mark 3:14, Emphasis added). Then the passage describes the works Jesus authorized His followers to perform. Yet, the fundamental call was to be "with Him," to be linked with Jesus in relationship. Networking is the linking of various gifts, talents, and skills to bring their respective strengths into unity around a common goal. This is the thrust of the Spirit's revelation through Paul regarding the Church. He writes:

> Now there are diversities of gifts, but the same Spirit. And there are differences of administrations, but the same Lord. And there are diversities of operations, but it is the same God which worketh all in all. But the manifestation of the Spirit is given to every man to profit withal.
>
> —1 Corinthians 12:4-7

What is true in the spiritual domain is applicable and valid in the material world. My leadership responsibilities include the oversight of ministries, businesses, and people. Over the years, I have learned the valuable asset of having diverse consultants. One of the most important relational networks I have is made up of my banker, lawyer, and accountant. They provide vital counsel regarding what resources I have available and how best to use them.

> Where no counsel is, the people fall: but in the multitude of counselors there is safety.
>
> —Proverbs 11:14

I have been able to acquire properties, structure companies, sustain wealth, and properly manage assets because of the valuable counsel provided through these relationships. Without the synergy created by those strategic relationships, I would not be where I am today.

Paul stated in his ministry that he had a window of opportunity open to him, but that opportunity brought many new adversaries.

> For a great door and effectual is opened unto me, and there are many adversaries.
>
> —1 Corinthians 16:9

If new levels bring new devils, then as we progress, we should be diligent to increase the multitude of counselors who walk with us to contend with these new adversaries. David was one who surrounded himself with a team of strategists as a part of his "Mighty Men." These men had profound understanding and insight into the natural, economic, political, spiritual, and prophetic times of that age.

> And of the children of Issachar, which were men that had understanding of the times, to know what Israel ought to do; the heads of them were two hundred; and all their brethren were at their commandment.
>
> —1 Chronicles 12:32

Pride hinders us from asking for guidance. Many are reluctant to receive instruction and hold back from seeking wise counsel. They will pillage an inheritance, or crash and burn financially, and *then* decide to seek advice. We can be saved from disaster if we recognize the wisdom in others, and seek it.

> When we stray from God's principles we set ourselves up for failure.

The Church needs to be able, once again, to give spiritual oversight to the business community, as well receive instruction and insight from those in the marketplace. When we stray from God's principles, relating to investments, we set ourselves up for failure. Enterprises built on shady deals, half-truths, and lies are sustained only by more lies. Spiritual oversight will ensure that you do not build wealth upon wrong principles. Spiritual advisors hold us to eternal truth, just as lawyers help us stay in the boundaries of civil law, accountants within the framework of good financial practices, and honest bankers within a positive debt structure.

America's founders understood this and provided a system of checks and balances through the establishment of a government consisting of three branches — Executive, Legislative, and Judiciary. Within the Executive Branch, the president is surrounded by his cabinet members. Through this broad-ranging network of relationships, the president benefits from critical information on national defense, agriculture, commerce, and other vital activities of the nation.

> Without counsel purposes are disappointed: but in the multitude of counselors they are established.
>
> —Proverbs 15:22

Every coach has a coaching staff, and every manager has a management team including King David.

Prospering businesses operate through relational networks, where the contributions of all the partners, associates, and employees are combined to create the synergy to produce positive results.

This was even true for first century fishermen:

> When He had finished speaking, He said to Simon, "Put out into the deep water and let down your nets for a catch." Simon answered and said, "Master, we worked hard all night and caught nothing, but I will do as You say and let down the nets." When they had done this, they enclosed a great quantity of fish, and their nets began to break; so they signaled to their partners in the other boat for them to come and help them. And they came and filled both of the boats, so that they began to sink.
>
> —Luke 5:4-7 Emphasis added

This is a Kingdom principle. Churches that operate independently of each other limit kingdom advancement. When you labor independently, you are really just working with a fishing pole. No matter how good you are, you'll still only catch one fish at a time. The "net" for these men represented the power of networking that led to a huge harvest of fish.

Peter had a business partnership with the Zebedees. Possibly, this partnership was so strong that Jesus allowed it to function, even within His ministry. Jesus pulled these three associates into a closer relationship with Him. Peter, James, and John became His "cabinet." They had first learned to work together in the marketplace, then Jesus brought this combined strength into His inner circle.

The Scriptures give insight to the synergy that is created with multiple committed people pulling together.

> Five of you will chase a hundred, and a hundred of you will chase ten thousand, and your enemies will fall before you by the sword.
>
> —Leviticus 26:8

Solomon understood the importance of relational networks and wrote:

> **Two are better than one**; because they have a good reward
> for their labor. For if they fall, the one will lift up his fellow:
> but woe to him that is alone when he falleth; for he hath not
> another to help him up. Again, if two lie together, then they
> have heat: but how can one be warm alone? And if one prevail
> against him, two shall withstand him; and a threefold cord is
> not quickly broken.
>
> —Ecclesiastes 4:9-12 Emphasis added

Solomon is indicating that the rewards for networking far surpass our individual efforts. In this portion of Scripture, we discover four specific benefits that can be gained from successful partnerships:

1. Their rewards are greater.

2. There is accountability and support.

3. They produce and maintain passion.

4. They are better equipped for battle.

Jesus taught there's an enhancement in the power of prayer through unified relationships:

> Again I say to you, that if **two of you agree** on earth about
> anything that they may ask, it shall be done for them by My
> Father who is in heaven. For where two or three have gathered
> together in My name, I am there in their midst.
>
> —Matthew 18:19-20 (NASB) Emphasis added

If networking relationships are vital for the business of God's Kingdom, then they are critical for generating wealth!

Immigrants traditionally have understood this. In the late nineteenth and early twentieth century, waves of Irish and Italian immigrants arrived in the United States. The large families and neighborhoods pulled together to work out a prosperous life. Likewise, today's immigrants bring networking to new levels. Irene, a real estate agent, was amazed the first time she sold a home to a Chinese man. He had come to America with his immediate family, and then extended family members arrived. They all got jobs and lived in a cramped apartment while they saved money. What amazed Irene was that they pooled their resources and paid cash for a large house.

This same concept is used to purchase businesses and many capture the American dream of opportunity and wealth by networking.

And when these relationship-based networks are broken, so is prosperity. I'm from an Italian background, as you might guess by my name. We know how to argue over eggplant, pasta, and sauce. I have uncles who haven't spoken for years because of disagreements over meatballs. The result is the dissipation of energy and the wasting of the great resource of relationship that is the backbone of networks.

Jesus put His Church together through relationship-building. He didn't call us "Christians" — that label came from the pagan society at Antioch. They used it to identify the Christlikeness they saw in the followers of Christ. Jesus came to make *disciples* — learners, apprentices, and followers. He came to enter into relationships with those willing to enter an abiding bond with Him and His ways.

Sadly, some people find it difficult to network with Christians. Harvey, an older man with a limited pension, decided to supplement his meager income by going into business with Stan, a "solid Christian." Stan didn't tell Harvey he had floated from job to job, had a mountain of debt, and loved pyramid schemes. Stan ripped off Harvey's computer, depleted the old man's remaining savings, and stonewalled him, refusing to honor the terms of their verbal agreements.

> The fact is that not everyone who bears the name "Christian" is a true disciple.

The fact is that not everyone who bears the name "Christian" is a true disciple. Gandhi reportedly said, "Oh, I don't reject your Christ. I love your Christ. It's just that so many of you Christians are so unlike your Christ."[3]

I am leery of doing business with brand name "Christians," but eager to network with genuine disciples. So, get beyond the label "Christian" to the essence "disciple" as you build business relationships.

The best of these relationships are established through agreement. The language of business includes "contract" and "covenant." It takes both, but the most effective enterprises begin with covenant. A contract is based on and enforced by law, but a covenant rests on commitment. You *comply* with the terms of a contract, but you *commit* to the agreements established in covenant.

I find that whenever you have a believer not willing to enter into a contract, it speaks volumes about his covenant commitment. Business partnerships in the Kingdom should have contracts. My marriage to my wife is a covenant agreement that is also backed up by a marriage license or "contract."

> If two of you agree on earth about anything that they may
> ask, it shall be done for them by My Father who is in heaven.
>
> —Matthew 18:19 (NASB)

My prayer is that you apply The Law of Synergy and begin to network and build a cabinet of counselors who can assist you on your journey of wealth creation.

Law Nine

The Law of Communication

Communication is the flow and exchange of life. It dictates the quality of community and holds treasures for those who master it.

Through communication we cross-pollinate; we create life and death. Your words and the Words of Christ spoken through you have the power to shape your life and the lives of others. Communication is the thermostat that sets the quality of life.

Communication is the building block of civilizations. With words we enchant, entice, enthrall, entertain, and educate. In the book of Revelation, John sees a new image of the Savior and writes, "out of his mouth went a sharp two-edged sword" (Revelation 1:16).

To speak is power. With words, wars have started and ceased. It was the weapon of communication that stopped world wars and saved the lives of countless soldiers. History records it was communication that ignited social change, cultural progress, and injustice.

Martin Luther King Jr.'s, "I Have a Dream" speech sparked a movement, which marked the end of segregation in America. Nelson Mandela was imprisoned for his words against the horrors of the apartheid government of South Africa. His words were so powerful that upon his release from twenty-seven years of imprisonment, he was elected president of South Africa. Winston Churchill's passionate words ignited a country to stand and fight against the unrelenting military of the evil Nazis.

> On the path of success, there will be some obstacles that cannot be handled through conventional means.

It was sermons that sparked spiritual renewal and revivals of the past. The Wesley brothers, Jonathan Edwards, D.L. Moody, George Whitfield, and Charles Finney all used the spoken word to ignite a significant change in our culture.

To speak is power, and the devil is petrified by those who know how to communicate.

Out of our mouths can proceed arrows, life, and impregnation. It is important to understand that some things in life are "caught" and not taught. They are caught through communication.

> Death and life are in the power of the tongue, and those who love it will eat its fruit.
>
> —Proverbs 18:21

This verse tells us that we need to develop an appetite for life. I find many individuals who desire success and prosperity, but do not take control over the way they communicate. They fail to coordinate their speech with their desires. Paul instructed the Ephesian Church of the dangers of "corrupt communication."

Let no corrupt communication proceed out of your mouth, but that, which is good to the use of edifying, that it may minister grace unto the hearers.

—Ephesians 4:29

The disciples turned cities upside down, set captives free, healed the sick, raised the dead, and delivered demoniacs all through the power of the spoken Word. Jesus revealed that there are some issues in life that have to be spoken to.

For verily I say unto you, That whosoever shall say unto this mountain, Be thou removed, and be thou cast into the sea; and shall not doubt in his heart, but shall believe that those things which he saith shall come to pass; he shall have whatsoever he saith. Therefore I say unto you, what things so ever ye desire, when ye pray, believe that ye receive them, and ye shall have them.

—Mark 11:23-24

On the path of success, there will be some obstacles that cannot be handled through conventional means.

Communicating is like a fine diamond having many facets. There are countless works detailing characteristics of communication, but when it comes to wealth creation, there are three characteristics that are vital: anger management, conflict resolution, and the power of negotiation.

1. Anger Management

In his book, *"The 21 Irrefutable Laws of Leadership,"* John Maxwell tells the story of automotive innovator, Henry Ford.

"Henry was so in love with his Model-T that he never wanted to change or improve it, nor did he want anyone else to tinker with it. One day when a group of his designers surprised him by presenting him with the prototype of an improved model, Ford ripped its doors off the hinges and proceeded to destroy the car with his bare hands." [1]

This angry streak in Ford contributed to Ford Motor Co.'s plummet from having 50 percent of the market in 1914 to a 28 percent market share in 1931.

The Bible reveals a great deal about uncontrolled anger. Proverbs 25:28 says, "He that hath no rule over his own spirit is like a city that is broken down, and without walls."

Anger produces an unpredictable atmosphere not conducive to productive business. I prefer not to enter into business relationships with individuals who have a streak of anger.

Being able to control your emotions and exhibit self-control regardless of your circumstances is a key to success. The Bible also states that a man who rules his spirit is better off than the man who conquers a city. Being self-controlled can have a positive impact on the whole of your life. Many marital problems are the result of unreleased emotions verbalized with an angry undercurrent.

Paul instructs us in Ephesians 4:26, "Be ye angry, and sin not: let not the sun go down upon your wrath." This means it is possible to be very upset, yet still maintain control.

2. Conflict Resolution

When it comes to conflict, there are two types of people. There are those who show up with a bucket of gas in hand. When they are finished, the conflict has escalated. The other comes with a bucket of water, and they have a knack for putting out fires and resolving problems.

Good communicators carefully frame their message. Proverbs 15:1, for example, tells us that "A soft answer turneth away wrath: but grievous words stir up anger." The human tongue will ignite either a living hell or a living heaven on earth. James tells us that the tongue is a world of iniquity and that it determines the natural course of life. Our tongue is the rudder that steers us through life.

A soothing tongue is a tree of life, but perversion in it crushes the spirit.

—Proverbs 15:4

Conflict within a business can prove costly. It results in low production, low efficiency, high employee turnover, and red ink. But a successful communication's strategy that considers style as well as content is a wealth builder. I have learned that it's not what you say, but how you say it that determines a positive outcome.

Most people live in such a way that they seek to avoid conflict at all costs. I learned many years ago that life without conflict is impossible. Embracing this idea caused me to learn the tools and techniques necessary to engage and resolve problems as they arise.

Understanding that conflict was inevitable, Jesus left instruction for His Church to resolve the issues that arise between two or more people. He said if a conflict occurred between you and someone else, to confront that individual in an attempt at resolution. If the issue was not resolved, bring in a third party. If it persisted, take it to church leadership.

> Most people live in such a way that they seek to avoid conflict at all costs. I learned many years ago that life without conflict is impossible.

Additional wisdom regarding communications is also revealed in Proverbs 21:23: "He who guards his mouth and his tongue, Guards his soul from troubles." There are people who blurt out whatever comes to their mind at the moment, fulfilling the old adage, "loose lips, sink ships." The person who throws words around indiscriminately and thoughtlessly brings much trouble on himself and fails to nurture the partnerships that build wealth.

3. Power of Negotiation

Negotiation is a skill that can bring you tremendous success in all aspects of life. Everybody negotiates. Whether at home with your family, at work with your boss or employees, or at the store purchasing an item, we are all in a state of constant negotiation.

Even the success of a marriage is achieved through negotiation. The skill of family life rests on the realization that things may not always be exactly as I want them, as my wife prefers, or meet the kids' desires. Negotiation has to go on continually in a home.

Amazingly, there are CEOs, presidents, and chief operating officers of big companies who don't know the art of negotiation. They seek to lead large numbers of employees, but can't resolve conflict. Or, these managers don't understand the power of praise and recognition as incentive devices. Rather than framing propositions on a win-win basis, they try to operate from a win-lose, meaning, "I win, you lose."

> Negotiation has to go on continually, even in a home.

In fact, people who fail as communicators often don't care what happens to the other person. Negotiation plays a key role in the multitude of decisions that must be made in the day-to-day interactions with my wife and children. Since everybody may not get what they want all the time, it's necessary that mutual agreements be made so that we can live in harmony.

When negotiating in business, I don't look at just a single transaction, but future transactions as well. I'm looking to develop a relationship through negotiation that will create long-term prosperity.

Roger Dawson, in "*Secrets of Power Negotiating*," defines three distinct levels of successful negotiation. They are:

※ 1. Establish criteria,

※ 2. Get information about the other side.

※ 3. Reach for compromise and find a common ground: a win-win situation.[2]

I find that when you can create a win-win situation, both parties will walk away feeling like winners, satisfied by the outcome, and willing to deal with each other again.

Many people expect to get everything for nothing, and that's the exact reason why they have nothing. The Apostle Paul employed the art of negotiation in his evangelistic endeavors.

> Though I am free and belong to no man, I make myself a slave to everyone, to win as many as possible. To the weak I became weak, to win the weak. I have become all things to all men so that by all possible means I might save some.
>
> —1 Corinthians 9:19, 22 (NIV)

Why do we so often drop the ball when it comes to communicating?

Often, the problem is we become information-disseminators rather than communicators, and the two are *not* the same. People concerned only with the delivery of data are focused on the information, not the people who comprise the target audience. What they care about is the data, not the individuals. Once they have delivered the information, they believe their job to be done. Skilled communicators start with their audience.

> Skilled communicators start with their audience.

They are concerned about how people receive information and what they do with it.

The difference between teachers and communicators is that teachers take simple things and make them complex, while communicators take complex things and simplify them. I always strive to be the latter.

Communicators give heed to the way they deliver or package their message. This is because the human mind can only absorb so much information.

Daily we are inundated with demands, requests, and challenges — all of which contain information that must be digested and acted upon. Our psyche erects a screen to filter out what we don't regard as relevant. The first thing to go will be information that is presented in such a way as to "turn us off."

Communicators are sensitive to the impact of their style and message. Effective communicators prosper because they get across information in such a way it can be easily processed, persuaded, and acted upon.

So, the communicator — as opposed to the data-scatterer — is a considerate thinker. This is what the book of Proverbs informs us:

> The preparations of the heart in man, and the answer of the tongue, is from the LORD.
>
> —Proverbs 16:1

If you want to be successful in any field, you must adhere to the Law of Communication.

Law Ten

The Law of Discipline

You cannot build nor sustain wealth without practicing The Law of Discipline. Much in the way of wealth, inheritance, and advancement has been squandered through undisciplined lives.

Discipline is about training your mind and building your character for the purpose of producing self-control. It's knowing when to say "yes" or "no," and acting accordingly! Contrast, for example, Mike Tyson and George Foreman. For some, Tyson was known as "The Baddest Man on the Planet." One source notes: "During his prime Tyson was considered unbeatable, but his once-dominant career was undermined by personal problems, lack of preparation, and periods of imprisonment."[1] "My whole life has been a waste," he told USA Today on June 3, 2005. "I've been a failure."

> More money is not the answer. The answer is more discipline, and a lack of discipline often leads to a lack of money.

At one point, Tyson was getting as much as $30 million per fight, but in September 2006, he was forced to launch a humbling tour attempting to raise money for "spiraling debt."[2]

George Foreman, who also wore the heavyweight-boxing crown, became noted for his charitable works. Like Tyson, Foreman earned millions in the boxing ring. However, he also worked as a pastor and established ministries that touched young people and taught them the spiritual values, discipline, and enterprise by which he himself lived. Often, the programs were fully funded by Foreman himself.

Many people think, "If I only had more money, I can do 'this' or 'that.'" Yet, more often than not, more money is not the answer. The answer is more discipline, and a lack of discipline often leads to a lack of money. Hardly anything shows this more than the state of public education in America. The approach Congress takes is to increase spending. Yet, all the wealth of Fort Knox can't solve the problems that burrow deep within our public schools.

The Bible places a high value on discipline. For example, Paul compares life and its enterprises to running a race:

> Do you not know that those who run in a race all run, but only one receives the prize? Run in such a way that you may win. Everyone who competes in the games exercises self-control in all things. They then do it to receive a perishable wreath, but we an imperishable. Therefore I run in such a way, as not without aim; I box in such a way, as not beating the air; but I discipline my body and make it my slave, so that, after I have preached to others, I myself will not be disqualified.

> —1 Corinthians 9:24-27 (NIV)

Athletes understand that success is determined by self-discipline. Paul uses the analogy of athletics to state that his spiritual life needs to be as disciplined as that of a competitive athlete.

Once while having lunch with Qadry Ismail, former NFL wide receiver and member of the 2000 Super Bowl Champion Baltimore Ravens, we began to discuss the perplexing short careers of some of the brightest NFL stars. He told me stories of athletes who possessed much raw talent, yet entered training camp overweight, out of shape, and throughout the season lacked discipline and commitment. Qadry, whose career spanned more than ten years, credited his longevity and success with a great off-season work ethic and a disciplined lifestyle.

Economic scholar Max Weber shocked people in the twentieth-century with his book, *The Protestant Ethic and the Spirit of Capitalism.*[3] Weber suggested that the biblical values embraced by evangelical Christians stirred them with an ethic characterized by discipline and a willingness to work hard. Many have sought to refute Weber's conclusions, but the record shows it's true. Studies of the relationship between beliefs and prosperity have supported this as well.

> Hard work is tied closely to the value of self-discipline in the biblical worldview.

Hard work is tied closely to the value of self-discipline in the biblical worldview. The bible puts it this way:

> I went by the field of the slothful, and by the vineyard of the man void of understanding; And, lo, it was all grown over with thorns, and nettles had covered the face thereof, and the stone wall thereof was broken down. Then I saw, and considered it well: I looked upon it, and received instruction. Yet a little sleep, a little slumber, a little folding of the hands to sleep: So shall thy poverty come as one that travelleth; and thy want as an armed man.
>
> — Proverbs 24:30-34

Socialism and communism are two of the world's failed belief systems. One tragic example was America's Jamestown Colony. Early settlers found it hard to raise crops. So, some of the colonists at Jamestown decided to build a storehouse right in the middle of the village green. Everyone was to bring some of their harvest to the storehouse, and those with need could take what they wanted. Soon, production declined. So many were taking from the storehouse that there were fewer and fewer working hard in the fields. The project collapsed as human nature took over.

The Bible also sees through people who try for fast wealth. Proverbs 13:11 says:

> Wealth gotten by vanity shall be diminished: but he that gathereth by labor shall increase.

The Law of Discipline needs to be infused into the hearts of our young people. It concerns me that many of the next generation of American workers who will compete in the global marketplace of the future, lack the self-discipline and work ethic to excel at a simple part-time job.

We are qualified for wealth building when we are willing to exercise self-discipline.

Undisciplined lifestyles always result in squandered wealth. Consider, for example, the crushing debt brought on by compulsive buying. Compulsive shoppers have a "baseline preoccupation with shopping," says Professor Donald Black. Tension mounts until it must be satisfied. The person shops and finds the stress relieved, "at least for the time being," finds Dr. Black.[4] That is, there is no aim behind the shopping except to shop.

The undisciplined and lazy person somehow thinks the harvest will "just happen." Much of the Church is still waiting for a check in the mail. Others see wealth as something to be snatched. They may play a state lottery, hoping to become an instant millionaire, or chase pyramid schemes. However, real wealth is the result of a building process. It requires the solid footing of The Law of Discipline and a commitment to hard work.

Engaging in such practices as prayer, fasting, devotion, and scriptural memorization help us in developing Godly disciplines. It's also true that we are qualified for wealth building when we are willing to exercise self-discipline.

LAW ELEVEN

The Law of Management

Management in its simplistic form is the art of coordinating and harmonizing our lives.

How many of us are still waiting for our dreams and goals to come to fruition? Unfortunately, many people have dreams and aspirations, but they fail to develop a management system for their life. The structure of their life brings them in the opposite direction of their goals, plans, and pursuits.

To experience long-term success in our lives, we need to be able to effectively manage our relationships, investments, families, assets, and liabilities.

Take cities for instance. The management of a city is crucial to its safety and productivity. Police and sanitation departments are ways a city government will manage hundreds of thousands of inhabitants. If a simple thing like sanitation is not overseen correctly, things can really begin to stink. Just imagine the depth of issues that could emerge.

God won't bless a mess. Growth, success, and prosperity that happens instantly will in many cases overload a person because they haven't been able to raise the level of their management skills.

Proverbs 11:1 says, "A false balance is an abomination to the Lord. But a just weight is His delight." God expects our lives to be balanced. To maintain balance, you must have the ability to correctly manage all your endeavors.

When life isn't managed properly, it can cause co-dependency, conflict, confusion, abuse, or addictions. Usually, if an individual is poorly managing one area of life, that issue is spilling over into other areas.

Companies spend millions on management systems, especially during mergers and acquisitions. A simplistic view of management can be seen in the example of a cook at a restaurant. If he cannot manage his grill, then dinners will come out late, half-cooked, and not in the proper order. There is nothing worse than a restaurant that is not efficient in the kitchen. At that point, the ambience, atmosphere, and decor no longer matter, only the delay of the dinner.

> When life isn't managed properly, it can cause co-dependency, conflict, confusion, abuse, or addictions.

A successful management system synchronizes five specific elements: planning, organization, leadership, motivation, and supervision.

The plan determines what needs to happen in the future (next week, next month, next year, over the next five years, etc.) and develops an action strategy. Organization gathers all available resources required to successfully execute our plan. Leadership and motivation employs the skills to get others to accept your plan and play an effective role in accomplishing it. Supervision monitors the implementation, checks progress against plans, and modifies the plan as it is needed.

How much can God give us? The better question is: "How much can we manage?" What is our capacity for caring for what God releases to us? He will give in proportion to our ability and willingness to manage His resources.

The parable of the talents informs us in Matthew 25:15 that God distributed talents according to the servants' ability to handle them:

> And unto one he gave five talents, to another two, and to another one; to every man according to his several ability; and straightway took his journey.
>
> —Matthew 25:15

In this Scripture, a "talent" refers to an increment of money. Therefore, their ability to manage money was the basis upon which they would receive.

I know men and women of God who have tremendous anointing. God has empowered them generously. Yet, they have not been able to succeed because they have not practiced the Law of Management. This is true of businesses, organizations, and churches as well.

> How much can God give us? The better question is: "How much can we manage?"
>
> ——❦——

Moses, who was one of the greatest prophets and writers in history, hit a brick wall in his life. The book of Exodus records this dangerous time:

> And it came to pass on the morrow, that Moses sat to judge the people: and the people stood by Moses from the morning unto the evening.
>
> —Exodus 18:13

When his father-in-law, Jethro, arrived to the camp of Israel and witnessed what was happening, he warned Moses of the severity of the situation.

> And Moses' father in law said unto him, the thing that thou doest is not good. Thou wilt surely wear away, both thou, and this people that is with thee...
>
> —Exodus 18:17-18

It is worthy to reiterate that Moses did not lack anointing. Rather, he lacked a proper management system to accompany his leadership. Moses had to both lead and manage the children of Israel.

Jethro understood that burnout, exhaustion, frustration and confusion in many cases are the fruit of a poorly managed life.

This point marked a major transition in Moses' life. Once he received and accepted the counsel of Jethro, it created a paradigm shift that enabled him to implement The Law of Management.

In verse 19, Jethro says to Moses:

> Hearken now unto my voice, I will give thee counsel, and God shall be with thee: Be thou for the people to God-ward, that thou mayest bring the causes unto God.
>
> —Exodus 18:19

God desires to be in the details of a highly managed life.

God was already with Moses, but desired to bring him to a new dimension.

When God made the decision to allow Israel to wander in the desert for forty years until a stronger generation could come forth, the mission and calling of Moses changed. The responsibility now fell to Moses to guide Israel through a metamorphosis. He needed to transform Israel from despairing ex-slaves into a powerful nation unified by its faith in God. The Law of Management plays a critical role. Together with God, Moses established 613 commandments (Mizvots) that covered every aspect of civilized life, including how to worship and work together, how to eat right and stay healthy, how to resolve conflict and live with one another justly, and how to celebrate God and never forget His blessings.

God desires to be in the details of a highly managed life. I realize in my own life that God wants to work with me and provide me the ability to manage my life so I can achieve His goals.

Today, people are called to both lead and manage just as Moses did. The entrepreneur, business owner, CEO, and manager must all learn to lead and manage their day-to-day operations. In the book, *Moses on Management*, author David Baron states part of Moses' genius was that he was able to grow into both of these roles:

"While he possessed certain innate characteristics of leadership such as commitment, tenacity, and passion for justice, he had to learn many elements of leadership and management on the job. Analyzing how he did it — how he resolved conflicts, created rules and rituals, dealt with his people's complaints and lack of skills, and kept everyone inspired for forty years — provides a wealth of practical information."[1]

Out of all the books I read, the management category is at the top of the list. I am consistently adding books on management because I want to handle everything God desires to bestow upon me. The truth is, you cannot build, create, or maintain wealth without The Law of Management in motion. King Solomon said it is the little foxes that spoil the vine.

> Take us the foxes, the little foxes, that spoil the vines: for our vines have tender grapes.
>
> —Song of Solomon 2:15

A poorly managed life often gives way to "little foxes" that steal the fruit God desires to give us.

LAW TWELVE

The Law of Diversification

The Law of Diversification is very broad and applicable to many aspects of life. It is used by our education system to create more culturally diverse student populations in our schools. Corporations and businesses also use this law to expand their sphere of business activity. In an attempt at diversification, a company will engage in opportunities outside the scope of its normal business model or begin to do business in a new geographical region.

Diversification is also a familiar investment method used by financial planners for their clients. It is a strategy that creates portfolio income for an investor. Diversification, in the investment application states that when you invest, you should ensure that your portfolio is dispersed across the various asset classes so you can balance your risk exposure and yield a specific return on your investments. This will cause you to look at stocks, bonds, mutual funds, real estate, annuities, cash, and life insurance vehicles as separate asset classes that need to be considered in diversifying your investment portfolio.

Diversification has been the key to my personal and corporate financial success. In 2005, I was asked by the Department of Mental Health and Addiction Services (DHMAS) and the Access To Recovery Program to speak on the topic of entrepreneurial ventures in the non-profit sector. At the meeting, I challenged organizations to step "outside the box" of normal fund creation and begin to allocate resources specifically for wealth creation. I laid out a basic strategy for non-profits to implement the Law of Diversification that would generate multiple streams of income for the organization.

In terms of creating wealth, the Law of Diversification must be applied to income which can be separated into three specific categories:

◆ Earned Income

Earned income consists of salaries, commission, hourly wages, bonuses, profit Sharing, etc. Earned income is simply the monies earned from the direct result of your labor.

◆ Passive Income

Passive income represents money generated from investments and assets. Passive income consists of portfolio income (dividends, distributions, interest received) and investment property income, etc. Intellectual property, published works, patents, and similar sources are all examples of passive income.

◆ Unearned Income

Unearned income includes gifted money or inherited money. It is income received with no action being taken to earn it.

Most Americans focus all their efforts on earned income. All their time and energy is poured into a job or profession. Our government and the wealthy class encourage this because the wealthy and the government both need the middle class to pay the taxes since our government allows the creation of tax shelters so wealthy individuals can reduce their tax exposure. When that happens, it becomes crucial for the government to receive its funding from a large, taxpaying, middle class.

It doesn't matter how high taxes are raised on the wealthy, because they only represent 3 percent of our country's population. The middle class consists of a larger pool of people and thus is targeted as the income-generator for the government.

> It doesn't matter how high taxes are raised on the wealthy, because they only represent 3 percent of our country's population.

The truth is you will never generate wealth through just your earned income unless a strategy is used to transfer some of your earned income to create passive income. If the focus of your financial progress is through raises, promotions, or bonuses, you may be successful at improving your lifestyle, but you will not be able to create real wealth.

Charles Givens, in his book "*Wealth Without Risk*" had a great way of describing wealth creation and diversification. He said, "*If you don't expect to win the lottery, and you don't have the option of inheriting large sums of money, you only have five ways to increase your wealth:*

1. Putting yourself to work—Employment
2. Putting other people to work—Business
3. Putting your ideas to work—Inventing, marketing and consulting
4. Putting your money to work—Investing
5. Putting other people's money to work—Leverage" [1]

Diversification is a result of an observant worldview. Rather than focusing on a single way to achieve income, diversifiers look for worth in anything and everything.

As we become observant of all things around us and all the divine opportunities that abound in our varied world, we begin to grasp the potential for developing multiple income streams. Wise investors place their money in

> The outpouring of God is sufficient to fill every pot that you present to Him.

a variety of investment vehicles. The diversified investor observes opportunities in every market including real estate, commodities, and equities.

Diversification was at the heart of an Old Testament miracle. The Scriptures tell the story of the prophet Elisha:

> Now there cried a certain woman of the wives of the sons of the prophets unto Elisha, saying, Thy servant my husband is dead; and thou knowest that thy servant did fear the LORD: and the creditor is come to take unto him my two sons to be bondmen. And Elisha said unto her, what shall I do for thee? Tell me, what hast thou in the house? And she said, Thine handmaid hath not any thing in the house, save a pot of oil. Then he said, Go, borrow thee vessels abroad of all thy neighbors, even empty vessels; borrow not a few.

> And when thou art come in, thou shalt shut the door upon thee and upon thy sons, and shalt pour out into all those vessels, and thou shalt set aside that which is full. So she went from him, and shut the door upon her and upon her sons, who brought the vessels to her; and she poured out.

> And it came to pass, when the vessels were full, that she said unto her son, Bring me yet a vessel. And he said unto her, there is not a vessel more. And the oil stayed. Then she came and told the man of God. And he said, Go, sell the oil, and pay thy debt, and live thou and thy children of the rest.

> —2 Kings 4:1-7

The crucial element of this story is the Law of Diversification. Elisha instructed the women to have multiple pots available to be filled. This miracle could have been produced with the filling of just one pot. But there is a principle in these verses that we must catch. The outpouring of God is sufficient to fill every pot that you present to Him. God's supply is unlimited. Therefore, the only thing that limits this flow is a lack of "multiple pots." This principle is echoed at the wedding feast in Cana, where Jesus filled six pots of wine instead of just refilling one.

This story also reveals the financial wisdom of God. God knows the markets better than any analyst. God filled the pots with a commodity for which there was a high demand. He could have filled it with anything, but He knew the market for oil and provided the women with a valuable asset on which they could capitalize.

God knows what the future holds for the stock market, oil, and gold. Our God desires to steer us towards the right opportunities and guide us to the most profitable investments.

Unfortunately, when it comes to income streams, most believers present God with only one pot for Him to pour resources into, and that is their earned income. Rather than gathering additional pots, they rely on one avenue of wealth.

This is a principle in life that the wealthy firmly understand. In the process of creating wealth, these individuals use their earned income to accumulate assets that will generate passive income.

Wealthy people understand that they need to own assets that will pay for their liabilities.

Wealth is not the abundance of possessions you own. To simplify this, I have created my own definition of wealth as opposed to riches. Riches are everything that a person acquires with their money — cars, boats, houses, jewelry, and other expensive items. Since some of these things also come with a degree of liability, I do not classify them as "wealth."

To measure how rich you are, evaluate what would happen if you stopped working today. The extent of how long you could survive on your savings and current assets until all is exhausted is how rich you are.

Wealth is a perpetual source of resources that is functioning without my labor. For example, my house is not connected to city water, but to a well. For fifteen years, our well has provided a wealth of water to take showers, wash clothes, wash cars, clean, and fill the pool. That's true wealth, money working for me rather than me working for money. And in order to achieve that, you must diversify your income streams.

When a person owns an asset that pays for their liabilities, he or she is poised to create significant wealth. If it costs a person $40,000 a year to live, and

> Most believers present God with only one pot for Him to pour resources into—their earned income.

287

he or she is able to find investment properties that yield $40,000 a year, that individual has become wealthy, because financial livelihood is no longer contingent on "earned income." Wealth begets wealth, which is why we often hear the phrase, "the rich get richer." Wealthy people buy assets, which increase their income, while poor people buy liabilities that increase their expenses.

The popular board game "Monopoly" has been a great way for me to teach my children this principle. Who can forget trying to jockey for the opportunity to buy "Broadway" or "Park Place," all while trying to stay out of jail. Through this game, my sons have learned the value of purchasing board property and that money can be earned by having people land on their houses or hotels. The player who accumulated the most income would be able to survive the roll of the dice and be best positioned to win the game.

A person is defined as "wealthy" when their passive income pays for their expenses. At that point, they have achieved a level of financial independence and can add to their wealth.

Let's expand on the story of the pots of Elisha to help illustrate the Law of Diversification. One pot represents your financial livelihood. Resources or income flow into this pot, while expenses and liabilities (like car payments and mortgage notes) poke holes in the pot, draining its resources. If you make too many holes, you'll have more money draining out than flowing in. Before you poke too many holes in your pot, you'd better make sure you have the flow to sustain it. If you cannot sustain the amount of holes you create, you'll be "swimming in debt."

This is exactly where many Americans are today. They are becoming tired because of the consistent energy needed to stay afloat in managing debt and expenses. At this point, many start charging their lifestyle on credit cards. Some will blame their boss for lack of pay, complain that they are paying too many taxes, or cast blame upon the wealthy.

The key is to get out of the single pot approach to wealth. The strategy to accomplish this is to minimize your leakage by plugging up all unnecessary drainage (liabilities). By doing this, you can begin to free up some of your *earned income* which now can be allocated towards creating additional pots.

These additional pots can flow resources or *passive income* into your financial livelihood. When this happens, you are no longer treading water, but have reached solid financial ground. You are now free to use your time and energy to pursue numerous endeavors and begin creating substantial wealth while fulfilling God's purposes for your life. (See diagram.)

The Law of Diversification, when applied to wealth and economics presents a powerful paradigm shift.

Having passive income is so important in creating a lifestyle of wealth creation. In his best selling book, *"Multiple Streams of Income,"* Robert G. Allen explains that:

> "Not all streams of income are created equal. Some streams are linear, and some are residual . . . Income streams from a salary are linear. You get paid only once for your effort. And

when you don't show up for work, neither does your paycheck. With residual income, you work hard once and it unleashes a steady flow of income for months and even years. You get paid over and over again for the same effort." [2]

Investment properties, published works, inventions, and patents have the ability to produce this "residual" or passive income. Most people are just one good idea away from becoming millionaires.

I recently read a story about a young college student seeking to fund his college education. One night while brainstorming, he developed an idea to sell advertising space on a Web site. He figured he could make $1 million if he started selling ads or "virtual real estate" to businesses for a dollar a pixel. Today, "The Million Dollar Homepage" is sold out, and the young man has made his million.

There is no limit to the Law of Diversification. We serve a diverse and creative God who eagerly desires to help us on the journey of wealth creation. With the mind-set of diversification, you will begin to see opportunities you've never noticed before and be poised for financial independence.

Assets and Passive Income

Investment Property (Multi-Family House, Strip Mall, Etc.)

Portfolio Income (Stocks, Bonds, Mutual Funds, Etc.)

Intellectual Property [Patents, Copyrights, Published Works (Songs,Books, Etc.)]

CONCLUSION

This is the hour for the Church to arise and position itself during the greatest wealth transference in history. Wealth in the hands of the godly has incredible potential to do good and to raise a righteous standard.

Each of the Twelve Biblical Laws of Wealth Creation is an individual area of study. Many people have committed themselves to a lifelong quest of mastering just one of these laws.

How long does it take God to prepare a man for success? That depends on the man! It may take God a lifetime to prepare a man for what He can give him in a moment. The Bible tells us that God elevates kings and He removes them.

Blessed be the name of God for ever and ever: for wisdom and might are his: And he changeth the times and the seasons: he removeth kings, and setteth up kings: he giveth wisdom unto the wise, and knowledge to them that know understanding:

— Daniel 2: 20-21

These twelve laws are your life's preparation for many moments of success.

The greatest question concerning wealth is not how much God can give you, but rather; "How much can you handle?"

Too much of the modern prosperity message is associated with formulas or mysticism, rather than stewardship. Stewardship invokes the foundational element of trust. As we need to trust in the Lord with our lives, so He desires that we are trustworthy stewards with what He gives us.

Jeremiah noted:

Blessed is the man that trusteth in the LORD, and whose hope the LORD is. For he shall be as a tree planted by the waters, and that spreadeth out her roots by the river, and shall not see when heat cometh, but her leaf shall be green; and shall not be careful in the year of drought, neither shall cease from yielding fruit.

—Jeremiah 17: 7-8

The Lord desires to develop and maximize our lives in every area so we can be as that tree planted by the water. Applying these principles will be at times difficult or frustrating, but the fruit is bountiful and immeasurable! A life characterized by these laws will abound in excellence in every endeavor.

There is nothing more threatening to the kingdom of hell than a well-planted, fruitful believer.

My passion in writing this book is to empower believers everywhere to run with God's vision for their lives. It is also to provide direction for the Church in creating wealth to change our culture.

The Rich Church message needs to sweep through our churches. I long to see a powerful, poverty-free, Church reclaiming the gates of influence for the Kingdom of God.

I challenge you to not allow this book to sit idly on your bookshelf, but to use it as a tool for civic and spiritual success. I encourage you to share this book with your family, friends, and church community. Apply the biblical truths of this book, and God will use you in new spheres of influence to accomplish His agenda as He blesses you and builds His Kingdom on this earth.

WANT *more*?

ORDER THE *12-Week Multi-Media Curriculum*
for your church or organization today!

www.MoneyByDesign.tv

Achieve FINANCIAL INDEPENDENCE

Create LONG LASTING WEALTH

Become DEBT FREE

Enjoy THE FRUIT OF GIVING GENEROUSLY

Empower yourself to be financially secure and live a more prosperous and fruitful life with Money By Design.

Find out more about being an instructor of this multi-media curriculum.

This is the only curriculum on the market that integrates debt management and wealth creation from a Biblical perspective.

Church running this curriculum are experiencing financial freedom.

Money By Design positions your organization to reach your community.

In this time of financial uncertainty, Money By Design empowers churches to educate and equip their congregants with a solid financial foundation.

BIBLIOGRAPHY

Rich Church, Poor Church is the culmination of over twenty years of reading, study, and life experience. In addition, much research in related and unrelated fields has contributed to the end product you are holding in your hands. To acknowledge every resource consulted for this work would be exhaustive, wearisome, and for all practical purposes — impossible. Instead, the following is a list of works that are most influential to the author or that would provide the reader with additional information on specific related topics.

1. **Torah Rediscovered**
    by Ariel Berkowitz, D'vorah Berkowitz
    Paperback: 173 pages
    Publisher: Shoreshim Publishing Inc; 4th edition (2004)
    Language: English
    ISBN-10: 0975291408
    ISBN-13: 978-0975291405

2. **According to God's Heart**
   A Biblical Case for a Torah Lifestyle (Paperback)
   by Ariel Berkowtiz
   Publisher: Shoreshim Publishing, Inc (2003)
   Language: English
   ISBN-10: 0975291475
   ISBN-13: 978-0975291474

3. **Jews, God, and History**
   2nd Edition
   by Max I. Dimont
   Paperback: 592 pages
   Publisher: Signet Classics; 2nd edition (June 1, 2004)
   Language: English
   ISBN-10: 0451529405
   ISBN-13: 978-0451529404

4. **Indestructible Jews**
   by Max I. Dimont
   Publisher: Signet (December 4, 1973)
   ISBN-10: 045105895X
   ISBN-13: 978-0451058959

5. **Essential Talmud**
   Thirtieth-anniversary Edition (Paperback)
   by Adin Steinsaltz
   Publisher: Basic Books; 30Anniversary Ed edition (September 30, 2006)
   Language: English
   ISBN-10: 0465082734
   ISBN-13: 978-0465082735

6. **Everyman's Talmud**
   The Major Teachings of the Rabbinic Sages (Paperback)
   by Abraham Cohen
   Publisher: Schocken
   Language: English
   ISBN-10: 0805210326
   ISBN-13: 978-0805210323

7. **The Fight for Jerusalem:**
   Radical Islam, the West, and the Future of the Holy City (Hardcover)
   by Dore Gold
   Publisher: Regnery Publishing, Inc.
   Language: English
   ISBN-10: 159698029X
   ISBN-13: 978-1596980297

8. **The Path**
   by Laurie Beth Jones
   Paperback: 224 pages
   Publisher: Hyperion (August 19, 1998)
   Language: English
   ISBN-10: 0786882417
   ISBN-13: 978-0786882410

9. **The Greatest Generation**
   by Tom Brokaw
   Hardcover: 464 pages
   Publisher: Random House
   Language: English
   ISBN-10: 1400063140
   ISBN-13: 978-1400063147

10. **The 21 Irrefutable Laws of Leadership**
    by John C. Maxwell
    Hardcover: 256 pages
    Publisher: Thomas Nelson (September 18, 1998)
    Language: English
    ISBN-10: 0785274316
    ISBN-13: 978-0785274315

11. **Multiple Streams of Internet Income**
    by Robert G. Allen
    Paperback: 288 pages
    Publisher: Wiley; 1 edition (April 5, 2002)
    Language: English
    ISBN-10: 047121888X
    ISBN-13: 978-0471218883

12. **Cracking the Millionaire Code**
    Your Key to Enlightened Wealth
    by Mark Victor Hansen and Robert Allen
    Hardcover: 320 pages
    Publisher: Harmony (May 31, 2005)
    Language: English
    ISBN-10: 1400082943

13. **Conversations with Millionaires**
    What Millionaires Do to Get Rich,
    That You Never Learned About in School!
    by Mike Litman and Jason Oman
    Paperback: 238 pages
    Publisher: Conversations with Millionaires LLC (October 30, 2001)
    Language: English
    ISBN-10: 1931866007
    ISBN-13: 978-1931866002

14. Rich Dad, Poor Dad
What the Rich Teach Their Kids about Money,
That the Poor and Middle Class Do Not!
by Robert T. Kiyosaki, and Sharon L. Lechter
Paperback: 207 pages
Publisher: Business Plus (April 1, 2000)
Language: English
ISBN-10: 0446677450
ISBN-13: 978-0446677455

15. The Millionaire Next Door
The Surprising Secrets of America's Wealthy
by Thomas J. Stanley, and William D. Danko
Hardcover: 258 pages
Publisher: MJF Books (September 2003)
Language: English
ISBN-10: 1567315682
ISBN-13: 978-1567315684

16. The Millionaire Mind
by Thomas J. Stanley
Paperback: 416 pages
Publisher: Andrews McMeel Publishing (August 2, 2001)
Language: English
ISBN-10: 0740718584
ISBN-13: 978-0740718588

17. God @ Work
by Rich Marshall
Discovering the Anointing for Business
Paperback: 160 pages
Publisher: Destiny Image Publishers (June 20, 2000)
Language: English
ISBN-10: 0768421012
ISBN-13: 978-0768421019

18. Power of Positive Prophecy
Finding the Hidden Potential in Everyday Life
by Laurie Beth Jones
Hardcover: 288 pages
Publisher: Hyperion (October 6, 1999)
Language: English
ISBN-10: 0786863501
ISBN-13: 978-0786863501

19. Moses on Management
50 Leadership Lessons from the Greatest Manager of All Time
by David Baron, Lynette Padwa
Paperback: 320 pages
Publisher: Pocket (October 3, 2000)
Language: English
ISBN-10: 0671032607
ISBN-13: 978-0671032609

20. The Issachar Factor
by Glen Martin, Gary McIntosh
Paperback: 208 pages
Publisher: B&H Publishing Group (January 1999)
Language: English
ISBN-10: 0805420177
ISBN-13: 978-0805420173

21. Finding Favor With the King
by Tommy Tenney
Paperback: 224 pages
Publisher: Bethany House (December 1, 2004)
Language: English
ISBN-10: 0764200178
ISBN-13: 978-0764200175

22. Secrets of Power Negotiating
by Roger Dawson
Publisher: Career Press; 2nd edition (November 15, 2000)
Language: English
ISBN-10: 1564144984
ISBN-13: 978-1564144980

ENDNOTES

Section I

CHAPTER 5

1. While we are not completely certain of the actual author of this Psalm, it is strongly believed to be David. The writing style is extremely consistent with his early Psalms and his complaint about the ungodly prospering. This question is alluded to throughout his biography and other writings.

CHAPTER 6

1. The Barna Research Group, Ltd. is an independent marketing research company located in Southern California. Since 1984, it has been studying cultural trends related to values, beliefs, attitudes, and behaviors.

CHAPTER 7

1. Edmund Burke, Irish orator, philosopher, and politician (1729 - 1797)

2. www.brainyquote.com

3. G. Craige Lewis, "The Truth Behind Hip Hop" EX Ministries

CHAPTER 9

1. Midrash is a Hebrew word referring to a method of exegesis of a biblical text. The term "midrash" also can refer to a compilation of Midrashic teachings, in the form of legal, exegetical, or homiletical commentaries on the Tanakh (Jewish Bible). http://en.wikipedia.org/wiki/Midrash

2. Ghetto — During medieval days, the word "ghetto" defined small areas which served as living quarters for up to one thousand people situated outside large cities. The entire ghetto was walled with a gate, which served as an entrance and exit. Ghettos could easily turn into slums.

3. Adapted from Jews, God and History, Max I. Dimont. Signet Classic Series, 2004, pp 211, 212

4. Talmud: the collection of ancient Jewish writings that make up the basis of Jewish religious law, consisting of the early scriptural interpretations —Mishnah—and the later commentaries on them—Gemara.

5. Ibid, p 111

6. Ibid, p 119

7. Author's suggested reading books listed in bibliograghy.

8. Judeo-Christian (or Judaeo-Christian) is a term used to describe the body of concepts and values which are thought to be held in common by Judaism and Christianity, and typically considered (sometimes along with classical Greco-Roman civilization) a fundamental basis for Western legal codes and moral values. In particular, the term refers to the common Old Testament/Tanakh (which is a basis of both moral traditions, including particularly the Ten Commandments); and implies a common set of values present in the modern Western World.

CHAPTER 10

1. http://www.consumercredit.com/docsCOLLEGEDEBTGUIDELINES.pdf

2. http://entrepreneurs.about.com/od/famousentrepreneurs/p/michaeldell.htm

3. Capitalism - An economic system based on the private ownership of the means of production and distribution of goods, characterized by a free competitive market and motivation by profit.

4. Jews, God, and History, Max I. Dimont. Signet Classic Series, page 266

CHAPTER 11

1. Warren Buffet Quote - http://www.usatoday.com/news/nation/2006-0625-buffett-charity_x.htm

CHAPTER 13

1. http://www.marriagedebate.com/pdf/MothersFathersMatter.pdf

CHAPTER 14

1. Duncan C. Manzies -- As quoted in Bob Phillips, Phillips' Book of Great Thoughts & Funny Sayings, (Wheaton, IL: Tyndale House Publishers, Inc, 1993), p. 255.

CHAPTER 15

1. Modern economics was defined by the title of Adam Smith's famous book, An Inquiry Into the Nature and Causes of the Wealth of Nations. Since its publication in 1776, economists have been studying the institutions that produce and distribute goods and services within our society—households, businesses, non-profit organizations, markets, and governments.

2. http://en.wikipedia.org/wiki/Inheritance

3. http://www.radiancefranchise.com/the_market.php

4. http://findarticles.com/p/articles/mi_m4021/is_4_25/ai_100751507/pg_3 Sociologist Paul Schervish, director of the Institute for Social Welfare Research at Boston College and his colleagues calculated the sum of all American inheritances to be distributed over the next half-century to be $41 trillion. A staggering pile of cash by any measure, Schervish deemed the estimate conservative, based on a modest growth rate in wealth of 2 percent annually. The high estimate came in at an eye-popping $136 trillion.

5. Tom Brokaw, The Greatest Generation, - Published by Random House Trade Paperbacks, 2001.

6. Martin Luther King, Jr. http://en.wikipedia.org/wiki/Martin_luther_king

7. Young Protestant Pastors - http://www.crosswalk.com/1247552/

8. Japan's new leadership - CNN Money - http://money.cnn.com/1996/10/31/economy/generational_changes_pkg/

9. Bill O'Reilly, Cultural Warrior,-Published by Broadway, 2006

Section II

THE MIDAS TOUCH

1. 'Economists want to know: Do Europeans work less because they believe less in God?' By Joshua S. Burek, Christian Science Monitor, February 22, 2005, page 12

2. Ibid.

3. See, for example, David Aikman, Jesus In Beijing: How Christianity Is Transforming China and Changing the Global Balance of Power, Washington: Regnery Publishing, 2003.

LAW 1.

1. Retrieved from http://www.amanet.org/resources/time-management. htm?CMP=KAC-G3102&pcode=XAR7&gclid=CL3Q3Iv6jYoCFSTWgAodoxvWew.

2. Stephen R. Covey, The 7 Habits of Highly Effective People, New York: The Free Press, 1989.

3. Will Rogers, Leadership, Vol. 2, no. 1.

4. "To Verify," Leadership. -- Reported in American Demographics, July, 1990

LAW 2.

1. "Knowledge Management," By Brian T. Wright, May 24, 1999, page 5. Retrieved from www.eng.iastate.edu/iugreee

2. Retrieved from www.emory.edu/TEACHING/Report/AppendixD.html

3. Learning Network Magazine, Minneapolis: Performax Learning Network, October, 1988, 2.

4. George Shultz, quoted by Wurman, 34-35. Also see Alvin Toffler, Future Shock, 30-31.

5. Ibid

LAW 3.

1. Michael Novak, "Wealth and Virtue: The Moral Case for Capitalism," delivered before the Mont Pelerin Society, Sri Lanka, January 11, 2004. See www.michaelnovak.net.

2. Rodney Stark, The Victory of Reason: How Christianity Led to Freedom, Capitalism and Western Success, New York: Random House, 2005.

3. Ibid

4. Michael H. Hart, The 100: A Ranking of the Most Influential Persons in History, New York: Citadel Press, 1992.

LAW 4.

1. Marcus Buckingham and Donald O. Clifton Ph.d., Now, Discover Your Strengths (Free Press, 2001)

2. Retrieved from http://en.wikipedia.org/wiki/George_Washington_Carver

LAW 5.

1. Socrates, retrieved from http://www.quotationspage.com/quotes/Socrates

2. "Facts and Figures About Our TV Habit," Real Vision, retrieved from http://64.233.167.104/search?q=cache:DLPq8npObnkJ:www.tvturnoff.org/images/facts%26figs/factsheets/FactsFigs.pdf+amount+money+spent+develop+brand+name&hl=en&gl=us&ct=clnk&cd=7.

3. Theodore Roosevelt-- As quoted in Bob Phillips, Phillips' Book of Great Thoughts & Funny Sayings, (Wheaton, IL: Tyndale House Publishers, Inc, 1993), p. 127.

4. Harry Chapin, "Cat's in the Cradle" retreived from http://www.digitaldreamdoor.com/pages/lyrics/cats_in_cradle.html

LAW 6.

1. "Mike Tyson," Wikipedia, retrieved from http://en.wikipedia.org/wiki/Mike_Tyson.

2. "Debt-ridden Tyson Returns to Ring," BBC Sport Boxing, September 29, 2006, retrieved from http://news.bbc.co.uk/sport2/hi/boxing/5393536.stm

3. Max Weber, "The Protestant Ethic and the Spirit of Capitalism" - Published by Routledge, 2001.

4. "You Might Be a Shopaholic," By Bankrate.com. Retrieved from MSN.money, http://moneycentral.msn.com/content/SavingandDebt/P58684.asp.

LAW 7.

1. Bill Beckham, The Second Reformation: Reshaping the Church for the 21st Century, Houston: Touch Publications, 1995.

2. Mark DeVries, Family-Based Youth Ministry, Downers Grove, IL: InterVarsity Press, 1994, pp. 40-41.

3. Andrée Aelion Brooks, Children of Fast-Track Parents, - Published by Penguin, 1990

4. Elton Trueblood, Your Other Vocation, New York: Harper, 1952.

5. Richard Leider and David Shapiro, Repacking Your Bags, - Berrett-Koehler Publishers, 2002

6. Laurie Beth Jones, The Path,- Published by Hyperion, 1996.

7. Frankl's findings and conclusions are discussed in his book, Man's Search for Meaning (Boston: Beacon Press).

LAW 8.

1. Dr. Bernie Siegel, Homemade, May, 1989. Retrieved from http://www.bible.org/illus.php?topic_id=1242.

2. Lloyd Perry, Getting the Church on Target, Chicago: Moody Press, 1977.

3. "Mahatma Gandhi," wikipedia, retreived from http://en.wikiquote.org/wiki/Mohandas_Gandhi#On_religion

LAW 9.

1. David Baron, Moses on Management- Published by Pocket Books a division of Simon & Schuster, Inc. 1999 p.xiv

LAW 10.

1. John C. Maxwell, 21 Irrefutable Laws of Leadership - Published by Thomas Nelson, 1998 p.121

2. Roger Dawson, The Secrets of Power Negotiating - Published by Nightingale-Conant.

LAW 11.

1. Retrieved from http://www.newmansown.com/faqs.cfm#q2.

2. "Philanthropy Expert: Conservatives Are More Generous," By Frank Brieaddy, Religion News Service,. Retrieved from http://www.beliefnet.com/story/204/story_20419_1.html.

3. Ken Davis and Tom Taylor, Kids and Cash - Published by Oaktree Publications. 1979,

4. James S. Hewett, Illustrations Unlimited (Wheaton: Tyndale House Publishers, Inc, 1988), p. 462.

LAW 12.

1. Charles J. Givens, Wealth Without Risk - Published by Simon & Schuster, 1988, pp. 262-263.

2. Robert G. Allen, Multiple Steams of Income, Published by John Wiley & Sons, Inc., 2000, pp. 31

ABOUT THE AUTHOR

John Louis Muratori is a sought-after speaker with a unique message that crosses denominational and cultural barriers.

He is a recognized authority in organizational management and strategic planning, advising numerous agencies including the Department of Homeland Security and the Department of Mental Health. John has served as a consultant for many national ministries and mentors CEOs, millionaires, and ministers across the nation.

John is the founder and president of multiple companies and non-profit corporations. He is also the executive director of Turning Point Christian Center, a nationally acclaimed faith-based substance abuse rehabilitation program.

John has authored several books including Seven Women Shall Take Hold of One Man. He resides with his wife, Carmela, and two boys in Connecticut.

We are looking for fresh, cutting-edge manuscripts that have a relevant message for this hour.

To submit your manuscript, visit

www.gatekeeperpublishing.com

You can download a manuscript submission form on the "Publishing" page.

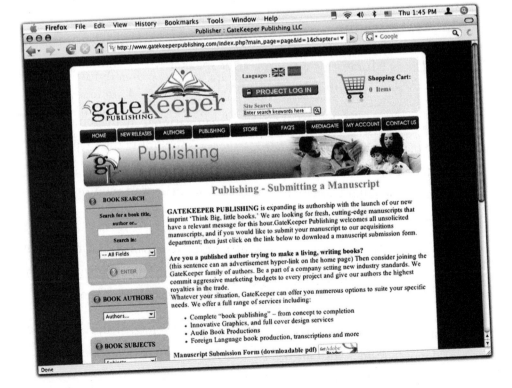

Are you a published author trying to make a living writing books?

Consider joining the GateKeeper family of authors. Be a part of a company setting new industry standards. We commit aggressive marketing budgets to every project and give our authors the highest royalties in the trade.

Whatever your situation, GateKeeper can offer you numerous options to suit your specific needs. We offer a full range of services including:

Complete "book publishing" – from concept to completion

Innovative graphics and full cover design services

Audio book productions

Foreign Language book production, transcriptions and more

To see our full range of services or for information on submitting your manuscript, visit our Web site. You can find our downloadable "Manuscript Submission Form" on the "Publishing" page.

Resources for Your Walk.

Our Resource Center offers dynamic messages on a variety of topics to enrich your personal devotional time or to share with someone who needs a lift.

- **FIRST FRUITS:** *This powerful and challenging message will give you strategies for a successful life.*

- **THE LIFE OF ENOCH (HOW TO HAVE A WALK THAT PLEASES THE LORD):** *Hidden truths about Enoch's relationship with God that we can use to ensure our life is also pleasing to God.*

- **THREE SIGNS YOU ARE APPROACHING HOLY GROUND:** *The heart of God is to lead every believer to a place of Holy Ground.*

- **THE HOUR OF VISITATION:**

Are there certain times that are more conducive to seek God? In this message, John Muratori reveals from the Scriptures a specific "Time of Visitation" from the Lord.

FIND A

fresh WORD

for EVERY DAY!

JOHN MURATORI
MINISTRIES

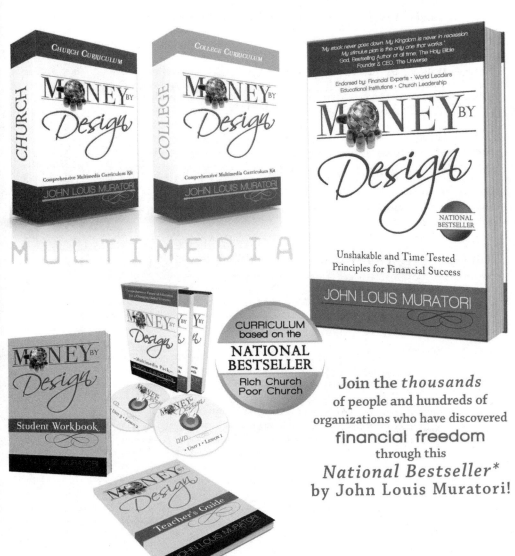

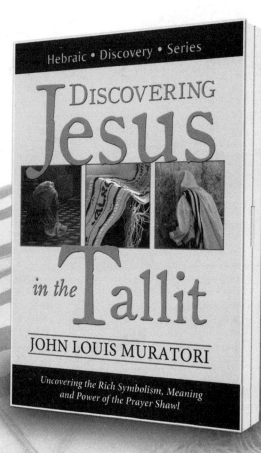

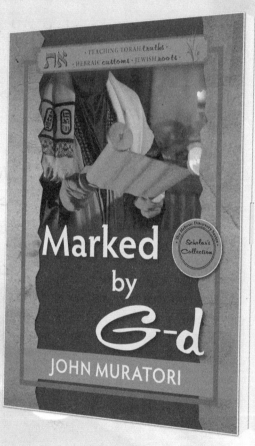

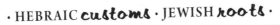

Phil!

Change is inevitable but transformation is intentional

Money By Design

12 week curriculum

(Comprehensive strategy to affectively get your life in order)

Pushing the Envelope

4 key Attributes of M.B.D.

① Convenient to use - D.V.D. Proctor

② Flexible

② Provides Additional Benefits

③ Inspires Trust

④ Un-matched - Nothing Available for Believers

___

The Goal of Money by design is to go beyond (Debt Management)

P.J.

5 Outcomes of Money B.D.

① Spark creativity, entrepenurship

② Create an atmosphere of generosity

③ Increase your influence in the business community.

④ Creates a platform for kingdom vision

Different Ways & Venues that M.B.D. can be taught.

---

① Church - Purchas Curriculum ① Purchase

{ 1 Inst.
  student
  MBD - discs
  legal right

Poster
w/ Questions

② Review

③ Sign-Up

④ Course designed for 12 weeks
(Hours/day?)

Suggestion: Church
Purchase kits
for students

⑤ Purchase Student kits
student kit
└ Workbook
  └ Code for Audio download

⑥ Run the Class

---

② College - Correspondence
        └ No teacher

Podcasts

③ Personal Curriculum -
DVD's
workbook (student)
textbook
downloads

Ladder Effect

P.S.
Content in all the material is Not the same.